RODALE'S
SUCCESSFUL ORGANIC GARDENING®
LAWNS, GRASSES
AND GROUNDCOVERS

RODALE'S
SUCCESSFUL ORGANIC GARDENING®
LAWNS, GRASSES AND GROUNDCOVERS

LEWIS AND NANCY HILL

Rodale Press, Emmaus, Pennsylvania

Our Mission

We publish books that empower people's lives.

RODALE BOOKS

If you have any questions or comments concerning this book, please write to:

Rodale Press
Book Readers' Service
33 East Minor Street
Emmaus, PA 18098

Library of Congress Cataloging-in-Publication Data

Hill, Lewis.
    Lawns, grasses and groundcovers / Lewis and Nancy Hill.
       p.   cm. — (Rodale's successful organic gardening)
    Includes index.
    ISBN 0–87596–665–9 hardcover — ISBN 0–87596–666–7 paperback
    1. Lawns. 2. Ornamental grasses. 3. Ground cover plants
4. Organic Gardening. I. Hill, Nancy. II. Title. III. Series.
SB433.H56 1995
635.9'64—dc20   94–44856
                                     CIP

Rodale Press Staff:
    Executive Editor, Home and Garden Books: Margaret Lydic Balitas
    Editor: Nancy J. Ondra
    Copy Editor: Carolyn R. Mandarano
    Editor-in-Chief: William Gottlieb

Produced for Rodale Press by Weldon Russell Pty Ltd
107 Union Street, North Sydney NSW 2060, Australia
a member of the Weldon International Group of Companies

    Chief Executive: Elaine Russell
    General Manager: Karen Hammial
    Managing Editor: Ariana Klepac
    Editor: Libby Frederico
    Editorial Assistant: Cassandra Sheridan
    Horticultural Consultant: Cheryl Maddocks
    Copy Editor: Yani Silvana
    Designer: Honor Morton
    Picture Researcher: Elizabeth Connolly
    Illustrators: Tony Britt-Lewis, Mike Gorman, Barbara Rodanska, Jan Smith
    Indexer: Michael Wyatt
    Production Manager: Dianne Leddy

A KEVIN WELDON PRODUCTION

Distributed in the book trade by St. Martin's Press

    4 6 8 10 9 7 5 3   hardcover
    4 6 8 10 9 7 5 3   paperback

Opposite: *Hosta sieboldiana* 'Elegans'
Half title: *Pulmonaria saccharata*
Title page: *Elymus hispidus* and *Hosta* 'Halcyon'
Opposite contents: *Viola odorata*
Contents: *Geranium sanguineum*
Back cover: *Cortaderia selloana* (center), *Geranium himalayense* (bottom)

CONTENTS

INTRODUCTION

A home surrounded by a spacious lawn is often part of the American dream. A tidy, well-kept lawn invites you to picnic, entertain friends, play badminton, walk around barefoot, or just doze in a lawn chair. With all these pleasant associations, it's no wonder lawns are popular! A beautiful lawn also provides an elegant setting for your home and makes a smooth background for trees, shrubs, flowers, and other landscaping. The open space provides little cover for snakes, rodents, and other creepy creatures and more security from thieves and muggers who might approach behind trees and shrubs.

But despite all of these and other benefits, it's easy to have a love-hate relationship with your lawn. You may adore the green carpet but despise the required noisy mowing, meticulous trimming, routine fertilizing, and other chores necessary to make it look so neat and lush. Conscientious landowners also worry about the air pollution created by gas mowers and the soil and groundwater pollution caused by highly advertised chemical fertilizers and pesticides—products that poison the soil and endanger children, pets, and birds.

Fortunately, you can have your lawn and enjoy it, too. Modern, low-maintenance lawns are not second class in any way, and they look healthy and well-cared-for without so many demands on your time. Best of all, they are safe to enjoy, and there's no need for a "Keep off the Grass" sign. Many developments have made lawns easier to care for. New mowers and trimmers make the job safer and easier. Organic fertilizers keep the soil healthy; better techniques help to discourage disease, minimize weeds, and reduce the necessity of watering. There are grasses that are ideal for your soil type and climate, those that are more pest-resistant, and others that are slower growing so they need less frequent mowing.

If you stop to think about your lawn, you may realize that there are some parts you never really use, although you still have to maintain them. Or maybe you're tired of just looking at a monotonous expanse of green in your yard. If you're bored of looking at or maintaining your lawn, consider planting part or all of the open area with groundcovers and ornamental grasses instead of lawn grasses. Both come in an enormous range of heights, sizes, shapes, and foliage colors and textures; many also have colorful, attractive flowers. They need no mowing or dethatching and little, if any, fertilizer; plus, they are usually pest-free. Ornamental grasses and groundcovers contain such a wide diversity of plants that you're sure to find at least one that's perfect for your needs and growing conditions.

Rodale's Successful Organic Gardening: Lawns, Grasses and Groundcovers is your guide to beautifying and maintaining your home landscape with all of these attractive, easy-care plants. You'll learn how to create a new low-maintenance lawn from scratch and how to reduce the work on an established one. You'll find out about the many exciting and beautiful ornamental grasses you can use to replace part of your lawn or to accent shrub plantings and flower beds. And you'll discover the diverse group of great groundcovers that can protect your soil, unify your landscape, and look wonderful at the same time. So say goodbye to your boring, bedraggled lawn and hello to your lush, new, low-maintenance landscape!

Make your yard a showplace with practical lawn areas, beautiful ornamental grasses, and easy-care groundcovers. A well-planned yard looks beautiful year-round without demanding all of your time for maintenance.

How to Use This Book

Lawn grasses, ornamental grasses, and groundcovers play a key role in creating a practical and attractive landscape around your home. These adaptable plants protect your soil, provide areas for recreation and relaxation, and accent taller plants like perennials, shrubs, and trees. *Rodale's Successful Organic Gardening: Lawns, Grasses and Groundcovers* will guide you through all of the steps of choosing the right plants to beautify your yard and caring for them to keep them looking good.

The lawn is the most obvious feature in many landscapes. "Creating a Low-maintenance Lawn," starting on page 12, will help you to keep it attractive without dedicating all of your time to its care. You'll discover how to plan and install a new low-maintenance lawn and how to spruce up and reduce work on an established one. You'll also find tips on choosing the right turf grasses for your climate and your needs.

Once your lawn is started and growing well, you'll want to maintain it to keep it looking its best. In "Caring for Your Lawn," starting on page 36, you'll find helpful hints on knowing when and how to mow, fertilize, and water for healthy growth. You'll also learn how to aerate your lawn to provide ideal conditions for vigorous root growth and how to deal with thatch, that buildup of undecayed material at the soil surface that can lead to weak, spotty turf.

While there is something to be said for the smooth, uniform look of turf grasses, don't overlook the fact that grasses can be exciting and colorful as well. Ornamental grasses come in a dizzying array of heights, habits, bloom times, and colors, so there's sure to be at least one for any site you want to accent. You can use mass plantings of ornamental grasses to replace unnecessary lawn areas, or grow them as accents in flower borders or as screens to block ugly views. Many of the smaller grasses are perfect along paths or mixed with foundation plantings. "Growing Ornamental Grasses," starting on page 54, covers the basics of selecting the right grasses for your garden, planting them properly, and caring for them for year-round beauty.

If you're searching for those finishing touches that can make your landscape look complete, don't forget to look down to (not down on!) groundcovers. Underplanting trees and shrubs with these low growers is a great way to add extra interest and reduce trimming chores at the same time. Groundcovers are also a super solution for problem sites—like slopes, dry shade, or wet spots—that are hard to keep up. You may even enjoy the beautiful flowers and striking foliage enough to plant groundcovers in place of part or all of your lawn! "Gardening with Groundcovers," starting on page 90, will give you ideas for using these versatile plants in all parts of your yard. You'll also find out how to choose the best groundcovers for your needs and how to plant them properly for years of lovely, low-maintenance growth.

Plant-by-Plant Guides

Actually deciding which plants you want to grow is one of the most fun parts of planning any landscape. It can also be one of the most frustrating, if you don't have the information you need to make a good choice. The encyclopedic guides in this book show you many of the best plants that are available and tell you exactly what sort of growing conditions and maintenance each plant needs.

Lawn grasses are divided into two sections: "Cool-season Lawn Grasses," starting on page 26, and "Warm-season Lawn Grasses," starting on page 31. Cool-season grasses are best adapted to more Northern climates, and warm-season grasses are best suited to Southern gardens. Flip to the section that applies to your climate, then read through the entries to find out which grasses are ideal for your conditions and needs.

The "Guide to Ornamental Grasses," starting on page 70, and "Guide to Groundcovers," starting on page 106, are arranged alphabetically by each plant's botanical name. Only know the common name? Look it up in the index, and you'll find a cross-reference to the plant in question. If you don't know which plants you want to grow, just browse through the photos and look for plants that will fit your needs and your site. For each plant, you'll find information on the preferred site and climate, growing tips, and suggested landscape uses. Each entry has a color photograph to help you choose new plants you'd like to try or to help you identify those that may already exist on your property.

Below is a diagram of a sample page from one of the plant-by-plant guides, showing what to look for on these informative pages.

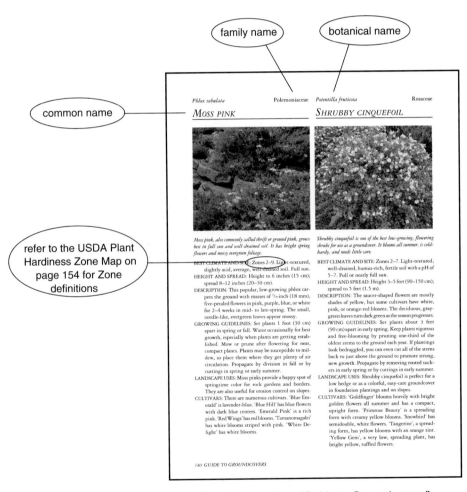

Sample page from "Guide to Groundcovers"

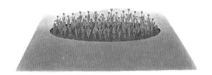

CREATING A
LOW-MAINTENANCE LAWN

A lush, velvety green lawn can be a great addition to your home, but it can also become an obsession that dominates your summer weekends and empties your pocketbook. Compared to gardeners around the world, Americans are particularly hung up on keeping impeccable lawns. Taking into account the cost of mowers, trimmers, waterers, aerators, dethatchers, spreaders, grass seed and plants, fertilizer, lime, weed killers, pest controls, and labor, Americans spend more money on lawns each year than the gross national product of many countries.

Fortunately, you can have a healthy, attractive lawn without going through lots of money or devoting weekends to tedious work. Understanding the conditions your property has to offer and deciding what you want from your yard will help you plan and maintain an easy-care lawn that you can enjoy and admire.

Smart lawn layout goes a long way toward achieving a care-free lawn. This includes simple things like planning gentle curves and replacing struggling grass with groundcovers. In "Planning an Easy-care Lawn" on page 14, you'll learn more about these and other tips to help you create an easy-care lawn from scratch.

A key part of planning for low maintenance is selecting the right grasses for your site. Lawn grasses—or turf grasses, as they are technically called—are extremely sensitive to their environment. Your climate, light and shade conditions, and soil type all affect which grasses will thrive there and which will need a great deal of maintenance to survive. Certain grasses are naturally vigorous; other types are weaker and more vulnerable to insects and diseases.

Once you decide where you really need to have lawn, "Choosing the Right Grass" on page 16 will help you figure out which kind of grass is best for your needs. By choosing those that suit your climate, light, and soil conditions, you can create a vigorous, attractive lawn that resists diseases, insects, and weeds without relying on chemicals and a shed full of equipment. Best of all, children and pets can play on your environmentally friendly lawn without danger of exposure to toxic insecticides and herbicides.

Starting a new lawn is like planting a garden—you need to prepare the soil well, plant at the right time, and care for the area properly to get the grass off to a healthy start. You'll find all the basics you need to know in "Starting a New Lawn" on page 18.

What if you already have a lawn that you're tired of caring for? "Reducing Lawn Maintenance" on page 22 is full of helpful hints for cutting down on yard work while still keeping your lawn looking attractive.

If you have an existing lawn that's weedy or sickly looking, don't be too eager to rip the whole thing up. "Renovating an Existing Lawn" on page 24 will help you decide if the lawn is worth saving or not. You'll also find lots of hints on how to repair a salvageable lawn to bring it back to peak condition without the expense and hassle of starting over.

You don't need to sacrifice all of your free time to have a great-looking lawn. Limit your lawn to areas where you really *need* grass, then use low-maintenance techniques to make the work easy.

Planning an Easy-care Lawn

If you're starting with a bare lot, don't be in a hurry to get the lawn going right away. By planning your site for low maintenance before you plant a seed or install the first piece of sod, you'll drastically reduce the amount of work you'll need to do in the years to come.

Here's a handy checklist of things you'll want to consider when planning a low-maintenance lawn.

- **Start small.** The old adage "Admire large gardens but plant a small one" applies equally well to lawns. Even the smallest lawn takes a certain amount of time to keep it mowed, fed, and reasonably weed-free. If your time or energy is limited, it makes sense to plant lawn grass only on the amount of land you can easily maintain.

- **Plant grass where it will grow best.** Lawn grasses thrive with lots of sun, ample moisture, and fertile soil. In shady spots and areas with wet, dry, or infertile soil, it will take extra effort to keep the grass looking even halfway decent. Groundcovers and ornamental grasses are great choices for spots that are too shady, dry, or wet for lawn grasses to grow well.

- **Keep your lawn on the level.** Smooth, level sites make for easiest mowing. Lawns on a gentle slope are fine, but steep grades can make mowing exhausting and hazardous. Sturdy groundcovers like daylilies (*Hemerocallis* spp.) and creeping juniper (*Juniperus horizontalis*) are well suited for holding slopes without much maintenance. Mowing is also difficult around exposed tree roots and in rocky or rough areas; go for groundcovers here, too.

- **Plan for pathways.** Constant foot traffic can wear out even the most durable grasses, so install gravel or paved paths where you want people to walk. Also make pathways between garden areas wide enough to push a mower through; otherwise, you'll have to lift the mower to get it through without damaging the plants on either side of the path.

- **Keep clutter to a minimum.** Anything in the middle of the lawn demands more time and effort for careful mowing and additional trimming. If possible, keep swings, benches, birdbaths, and other features around the outside of the lawn area.

When laying out your low-maintenance lawn, try to avoid grassy slopes. They make mowing a real hassle.

Small lawns are usually easy to care for, but tiny spaces with many curves and narrow paths are very difficult to mow.

A plastic or metal edging strip isn't very noticeable, and it will reduce the amount of trimming you need to do.

- **Cluster plants for easy care.** Group trees and shrubs into planting beds with groundcovers beneath them. That way, you'll avoid having to mow and trim around individual plants.
- **Avoid fancy curves and tight angles.** Keep lawn edges straight or gently rounded, avoiding sharp curves and narrow spots that are difficult to trim.
- **Plan for easy edge maintenance.** Installing edging strips along fences, flower beds, and walkways will eliminate almost all of those boring trimming chores. You'll find more details on different edging treatments in "Minimize Tedious Trimming" on page 23.

Grouping trees, shrubs, and flowers into planting areas looks attractive and makes maintenance a breeze.

Moss Lawns—A Turf Alternative

A mossy carpet can be an attractive substitute for a lawn of turf grass wherever grasses have a hard time surviving—in damp, shaded, acidic spots with poor soil. Moss needs no mowing, weeding, fertilizing, dethatching, or aerating, and if it dries out during a drought, it quickly revives and greens up after the first rain. Most mosses are tough, attractive plants that can stand as much foot traffic as many grasses.

David Benner, an expert on moss lawns, has succeeded in covering his Pennsylvania property with 25 species of moss without planting a single one. He simply acidified the soil to between a pH of 5 and 5.5. The pH was so low that it killed the grass and weeds, but it was inviting to mosses.

To create your own moss lawn, start with a small area first. Check the pH with a soil test kit from your local garden center. If needed, add sulfur according to the package directions to lower the pH to between 5 and 5.5. Within 6 to 8 weeks, most of the grass and weeds will have died, and the bare topsoil should be ready to encourage moss.

Moss spores are fine as dust and can blow through the air for hundreds of miles before they settle and start to grow in your yard. If you already have a moss patch that you want to expand, dig small patches, along with a bit of soil to hold them together, in early spring. Plant the moss where you want it to grow, firming it into the soil so you leave no air space. Then keep it moist for a few weeks until it becomes established. It will take about 1 year for most mosses to form a dense carpet.

The only maintenance necessary for a moss lawn is to remove leaves in the fall so they don't smother it. Use a leaf blower or flexible plastic rake after the ground freezes. Or lay garden netting over the moss in late summer, and then lift it in fall to gather up the dropped leaves. As long as conditions are right, you can have one of the oldest plants on earth as your lawn—a soft, handsome, unconventional, and low-maintenance alternative to grass.

Choosing the Right Grass

Out of the thousands of grass species that grow all over the world, only a dozen or so are well suited for lawn use. The best produce narrow, rich green or blue-green leaves, grow in low dense mats, and have deep, sturdy roots that support vigorous growth. If you want to create a beautiful, low-care lawn, you need to select one or more of the grasses that will thrive in your particular climate and site conditions.

Cool- and Warm-season Grasses

Depending on where you live, your grass choices will be limited by your average summer and winter temperatures.

Cool-season grasses, those commonly used in Northern lawns, grow well in the mild temperatures of spring and fall. In the summer, their growth slows; they may even go dormant (stop growing) during periods of hot weather. Extended heat and drought can kill cool-season grasses.

Warm-season grasses are best adapted to Southern gardens. These species grow best in late spring and summer; they slow down in fall and go dormant in winter. Warm-season grasses can be weakened or killed by cold winter temperatures.

To keep a warm-season lawn green all winter in the South, some people overseed with a cool-season grass such as fescue or rye in the fall. The cool-season grass will grow throughout the winter, then die in spring when hot weather arrives and the warm season grass begins to grow again.

Cool-season Grasses
Annual ryegrass
Bent grass
Bluegrass
Perennial ryegrass
Red Fescue
Tall Fescue

Warm-season Grasses
Bahia grass
Bermuda grass
Buffalo grass
Centipede grass
St. Augustine grass
Zoysia grass

Consider Your Climate

Lawn grasses are described as either cool season or warm season, depending on their temperature requirements. The cool-season grasses grow best in the North, in temperatures from 60° to 75°F (15° to 24°C). That's why a lawn of bluegrass (which prefers cool climates) seldom grows well in the heat of a Florida summer. Likewise, if you live in the North, don't expect great

Perennial ryegrass is a durable cool-season grass.

success with the zoysia grass you admired on a trip to Atlanta: Zoysia and other warm-season grasses thrive when temperatures are between 80° and 95°F (27° and 36°C). For more information on selecting the right grass for your area, see "Cool- and Warm-season Grasses."

Think about Your Site Conditions

Once you know which grasses will thrive in your climate, you can narrow your choices even further by considering two other factors: your growing conditions and your plans for using the lawn.

Like many other garden plants, most turf grasses thrive in bright, sunny areas with balanced, well-drained but evenly moist soil. If your site can't provide these ideal conditions, rethink your plans to have a lawn in that spot. Grasses struggling along in too much shade tend to be weak and spindly; seeds sown in soggy spots may rot before they even sprout.

Nursing weak, sickly looking turf takes a lot of work, and a poor patch of lawn won't add anything to the appearance of your yard. In many cases, you'll have much better luck planting groundcovers that are adapted to the growing conditions your property has to offer. (You'll learn more about choosing and growing suitable groundcovers in "Gardening with Groundcovers," starting on page 90.)

 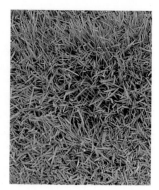

St. Augustine grass (*left*) and zoysia grass (*right*) are good warm-season turf grasses for Southern lawns.

For lawns in shady spots, try creeping red fescue (in the North) or St. Augustine grass (in the South).

Choosing a turf grass to match your site and soil conditions will help you create a lush, healthy lawn.

Bent grass prefers cool climates.

If you really want to have a lawn in less-than-ideal conditions, you'll have to tailor your grass choices to match the available sunlight, soil, and moisture. Here are some of the most common challenges to lawn growing, along with suggestions of appropriate cool- and warm-season grasses.

• **Drought-prone areas** In hot-summer areas, try bermuda grass or buffalo grass. Cool-season tall fescue and wheat grass are better in more temperate zones.

• **Shady sites** No grass thrives in deep shade, but a few types grow well in spots that get only a few hours of direct light or a full day of bright but filtered light. If you really want to grow a lawn under trees, try Chewings fescue or 'Pennlawn' red fescue in Northern areas. Tall fescue will take some shade in cool Southern gardens; St. Augustine grass grows well throughout the South.

• **Very acid or alkaline soil** If your soil has a pH that's very high (alkaline) or low (acid), you'll get the best results if you choose a lawn grass that is adapted to that condition. Cool-season Canada bluegrass, Chewings fescue, and

hard fescue can adapt well to acid soil. In alkaline areas, try cool-season perennial ryegrass or wheat grass or warm-season bermuda grass.

• **Salty soil** Salt, carried by coastal winds or runoff from melting snow on roads and sidewalks, can damage or kill tender lawn grasses. No lawn grass is completely salt-proof, but cool-season fescues and warm-season St. Augustine grass are quite tolerant.

• **High-traffic areas** Turf grasses vary widely in their ability to withstand wear and tear. If you need a grass that can stand up to heavy use, consider cool-season perennial ryegrass or tall fescue or warm-season bahia grass, bermuda grass, or zoysia grass.

Play areas need heavy-duty lawn grasses.

If you want an instant effect and can afford the extra expense, consider starting your new lawn with sod.

Starting a New Lawn

A newly graded and tilled lawn, like a freshly dug flower bed, is filled with potential. There are no mistakes to correct, and you are free to create a space that is environmentally sound and easy to maintain.

Seed, Sod, or Sprigs?

You have three main options for starting a new lawn: sowing seed, laying sod, or planting plugs or sprigs. The one you'll choose depends on how much you're willing to spend and how fast you want to get the lawn started.

Seed-grown Lawns Seed is the least expensive way to establish a lawn, making it the method of choice for many homeowners. Seed is also the only way to start many of the desirable new turf grass cultivars. On the down side, it can take several months before a new seed-grown lawn is ready for regular use, giving weeds a chance to spring up. Seeds are also prone to being eaten by birds or washed away by rain, especially on sloping sites.

Starting with Sod Sod is basically just strips of turf that have been cut from one area to be installed in another, creating an instant lawn. A landscaper or turf farm operator will deliver precisely the amount of lawn you need, ready to lay out on your yard like carpet.

A sod lawn is more expensive than seeds, and you may not be able to get precisely the grasses you want. However, sod does have its advantages. In addition to having a lawn you can use quickly, it eliminates the work of seeding and enduring several weeks of the dust and mud that bare earth can produce. The sod is usually free of insects, diseases, and weeds, and it won't be ruined by heavy rains. You can install it at times of the year that seed won't germinate.

Plugs and Sprigs If you're starting a lawn of zoysia grass, bermuda grass, centipede grass, or St. Augustine grass and can't face the expense of sod, plugs or sprigs are a good choice for you.

Plugs are like small strips or cubes of sod, usually grown in trays of 12 or 24 plugs. The number of plugs you'll need for a given area depends on the size of the plugs, the size of the area, and how fast you want the grass to fill in.

Sprigs are individual grass plants or runners that have been dug from the soil and pulled apart. They are usually sold in pieces by the bushel, which amounts to 1 square yard (1 sq m) of sod. Most lawns need 4 or 5 bushels per 1,000 square feet (93 sq m).

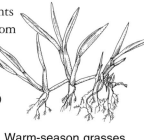

Warm-season grasses may be sold as sprigs.

When to Plant

The best planting time depends on which grass you are growing and how you plan to start it.

When to Sow Seed Plant seed of warm-season grasses in late spring or early summer. The best temperatures for germination are between 70° and 90°F (21° and 33°C). If you sow seed after midsummer, the warm-season grasses may struggle to survive the winter.

From late August to mid-September, when the temperature is between 60° and 85°F (15° and 30°C), is the best time to seed a new lawn with cool-season turf grasses. The seeds sprout and grow much better during cooler weather, when weed growth slows and fall rains keep the seedlings moist. In Northern climates, early- to mid-spring planting can also be successful if you keep the seedlings watered until they are well established. However, spring plantings are more prone to weeds, and summer heat can damage the roots of tender plants, leading to sparse growth.

Plan on 4 weeks from the time you plant until the grass looks like a lawn and at least 3 months of growth before you can use it heavily.

When to Lay Sod or Plant Sprigs or Plugs You can install sod, sprigs, and plugs pretty much any time they are available, as long as you keep them well watered for several weeks after planting. The best time, however, is when the grass is actively growing. Early summer is ideal for warm-season grasses, spring or fall for cool-season types. Don't try to install sod, plugs, or sprigs on frozen ground.

Preparing the Site

No matter how you plan to plant your lawn, good soil preparation is the key to getting it off to a healthy start.

Check the Soil Depth First, dig down to determine the depth of the topsoil in the lawn area, especially if you have a new home site. If the darker topsoil layer measures less than 4 inches (10 cm) deep over the lighter subsoil, spread enough new soil to reach that depth.

Take a Soil Test The best insurance you can get for a healthy lawn is taking a soil test before you plant. Once you know the pH and nutrient content of your soil, you'll know what—if any—fertilizers and amendments you need to add. You can buy a simple home test kit at your local garden center, or have your soil tested by a lab. Lab tests (done by a private lab or your state Cooperative Extension Service) are usually more accurate and provide detailed reports of the results.

Follow the instructions on the package for collecting a sample. If you're getting a lab test, be sure to

If you prepare the site well before planting, your lawn will get a good start and look great for years to come.

ask for recommendations for organic fertilizers and amendments. Allow at least 6 weeks to get your results.

If you don't want to bother with a soil test, you may be able to guess at your soil's fertility by how well other plants in your area are growing. Remember, though, that it's much easier to prevent problems than to fix them later! You could end up struggling with a weak, sickly looking lawn for years, blaming pest or disease problems and not realizing that the soil nutrients or pH are out of balance. Even if you do identify

---

Grass Seed Buying Tips

Choose grass seed from a garden store or catalog according to your climate, site (soil type and light conditions), and the use it will receive. You can buy seed as straight, mixtures, or blends. Straight grass seed consists of only one species or one cultivar. A mixture contains two or more species, such as fescue, perennial ryegrass, and bluegrass in various proportions. A blend is a mixture of two or more cultivars of the same species of grass, such as 'America', 'Manhattan', and 'Princeton' Kentucky bluegrass.

Straight warm-season grasses produce the best lawns in the South, but in cool climates, mixtures or blends are better choices. A typical cool-season lawn mixture consists of one-half bluegrass for beauty, one-quarter to one-third endophyte-enhanced fescues for toughness and pest-resistance, and the remainder perennial

ryegrass for quick effect and durability. Mixtures may also include white clover, for drought resistance, and annual rye, which germinates quickly and stabilizes the soil until the other grasses begin to grow. Avoid bargain mixes: they often are based on less-desirable grasses like annual ryegrass.

To calculate the amount of seed you'll need, first measure the area of your lawn to get the square feet; then follow the rate of seeding recommended on the package. When in doubt, buy a little more seed than you think you'll need so you won't run out; weeds will quickly fill any bare spaces left in a sparsely sown lawn. Always try to use fresh seeds, too, rather than leftovers, which may be dead. If you must use old seed, plant twice as much as you would if it were fresh.

the problem correctly, it could take a year or two for the soil amendments you add to take effect and provide improved growing conditions.

Add Needed Amendments Unless your soil is high in nutrients and organic matter, you'll probably need to amend the soil to provide good growing conditions for the new lawn. To add organic matter, spread a 1-inch (2.5 cm) layer of organic material (aged manure or compost) over the area. Also add a natural fertilizer, such as a 4-3-3 blend of nitrogen, phosphorus, and potassium, following the directions on the package. Till in the material to a depth of about 6 inches (15 cm).

If a soil test showed that the pH is below 6.5, add enough garden lime (not hydrated lime or quicklime) to raise the pH to that level. Ten pounds of garden lime per 100 square feet (4.5 kg per 9.3 sq m) raises the pH of most soils about one point. Scatter the lime over the soil, or use a spreader for more even coverage. Till the lime into the soil. (If possible, allow a bit of time—about a week, or ideally one heavy rain—between fertilizer and lime applications to minimize any reaction between them.)

Smooth the Soil Before planting, level the tilled earth to eliminate bumps and depressions. You can smooth out a small lawn with a metal garden rake, but a commercial grading rake that you rent is much easier and more effective for large areas. Be sure that

When planting small lawn areas, it's easiest to scatter the seed by hand. Spread it as evenly as you can.

the lawn slopes away from buildings so hard rains or melting snows won't drain into your basement. Also have it slope downward slightly toward a road or driveway, so water won't accumulate on the grass.

After getting the slope you want, rake the area to smooth it and to remove any rocks and weed roots. Soak the ground thoroughly if it doesn't rain, and let it settle for 3 or 4 days or more before planting. When the soil has settled, resmooth it, if necessary, before planting.

Planting Grass Seed

On a day that's not breezy, you can fling grass seed off the tips of your fingers and get fairly even coverage in a small area. In most cases, though, you'll get better results with either a two-wheeled, drop-type seeder or a rotary broadcast seeder that throws out the seeds over a wide area. Both are often available for rent at hardware or garden-supply stores. The drop type is better for precise seeding, especially if you are working near gardens or other areas where you don't want seed to fall. Overlap the strips slightly to ensure good coverage. The wheel tracks left by the spreader will mark where you have already applied seed.

Rake the seeds lightly into the topsoil, about ¼ inch (6 mm) deep, so that most of them are no longer visible on the surface. They must have good contact with the soil for germination, so it is helpful—but not essential—to firm the surface and eliminate air pockets by

Preparing a smooth surface before planting will encourage seed germination and make later mowing much easier.

Laying Sod

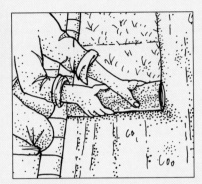

Start laying sod along a straight edge, like a walk.

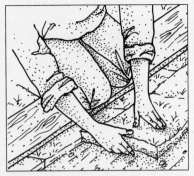

Protect the first row with a board as you lay the next one.

Use the head of a rake to press the sod pieces into the soil.

going over the site once with a light lawn roller.

Surround the area with a string fence and install "Keep off the Grass" signs. To keep birds from snacking on the seeds, cover the area with cheesecloth or a floating row cover until seedlings appear, or mulch it lightly with salt hay or other weed-free hay.

If it doesn't rain, water the soil daily to keep it moist (but not wet) until the seeds have sprouted and started growing. Different grass species germinate at different speeds—from less than a week to as long as 30 days—so if you're planting a mixture, keep in mind that they won't all sprout at once.

Establishing Sod

Install the sod as soon as it arrives, if at all possible; otherwise keep it damp and shaded until you're ready for it. Ask your supplier for instructions on handling and laying the sod strips. After installation, press the sod into the soil by tamping with the back of a rake or by rolling with a light roller; then water thoroughly.

Planting Plugs and Sprigs

Plant plugs or sprigs 6 to 12 inches (15 to 30 cm) apart in each direction in thoroughly tilled soil. (The exact spacing will vary on the type of grass you're growing; ask your supplier for the recommended spacing for the kind you purchase.) An easy method to keep the spacing right is to mark straight, shallow furrows across the lawn about 12 inches (30 cm) apart, then set the sprigs or plugs in these furrows from 6 to 8 inches (15 to 20 cm) apart. Roll the surface lightly after installation, and water it well.

Some grasses are sold as plugs in trays.

After Planting

Whether you have seeded the lawn, installed sod, or planted plugs or sprigs, never let it dry out until the grass is well rooted (generally after 3 to 4 weeks). If the weather is mild and not windy, a good rule of thumb is to water every 2 or 3 days for 3 weeks. In hot, dry weather, your new lawn may need water several times a day to keep the soil moist and allow good growth.

Don't walk on the lawn any more than necessary until the grasses are growing vigorously, and hold off on mowing until they are at least 3 to 4 inches (15 to 20 cm) tall. Set the mower about 3 inches (7.5 cm) high for the first few mowings; then reduce it to the optimum height for the grass you are growing (as given in "Cool-season Lawn Grasses," starting on page 26, and "Warm-season Lawn Grasses," starting on page 31).

If rainfall is lacking, use sprinklers to keep the soil evenly moist until your new lawn is established.

Reducing Lawn Maintenance

Planning a lawn for low maintenance right from the start makes sense, but it isn't always a realistic option. Maybe you moved into a new house and lacked the time, energy, or budget to buy groundcovers and plan paths; you just scattered some grass seed around to cover up the bare soil. Or perhaps you live in a house that already has a high-maintenance lawn. When you're ready to cut down on yard-care chores, follow the tips below to reduce the work while still having a good-looking lawn you can use and enjoy.

Reduce Lawn Area

The first step to consider if you have a large lawn is shrinking its size. Steep slopes, shady bowers, and soggy areas that are difficult to mow are ideal spots for low-maintenance groundcovers, ornamental grasses, ferns, or perennials that spread or form large clumps.

Transform any lawn space that you don't really need into something more useful or less work. If you hate mowing but enjoy growing showier plants, consider converting some or all of your unused lawn to flower beds or shrub plantings. Or transform excess lawn space into a semi-wild or meadow area, where the grass will need mowing only about once a month. Wildflowers, spring bulbs, ornamental grasses, ferns, and low-growing shrubs look great in such a spot.

Improve your yard's appearance by replacing compacted, worn-out grass paths with gravel or paving.

Provide Good Basic Care

After you've scaled your lawn down to the size you need, follow these simple guidelines to reduce the time you spend caring for it.

Mowing Avoid mowing on a set once-a-week schedule—mow your lawn only when it really needs it. Cut your grass at the recommended height or slightly higher to keep weeds under control. If you reseed new lawn areas, look for slow-growing turf grass cultivars that need mowing less frequently. For more mowing tips, see "Mowing—A Manicure for Your Lawn" on page 38.

Minimize trimming by linking individual trees and shrubs into larger beds underplanted with groundcovers.

Limiting your lawn area will give you more time to maintain the turf that's left and keep it looking top-notch.

A well-planned mowing strip will keep your garden looking neat without hours of hand-trimming.

If you don't want to install a permanent mowing strip, dig a small ditch barrier to keep grass out of flower beds.

Watering Avoid watering your lawn if it isn't absolutely necessary: It not only wastes water but irrigated grass also needs mowing more often. Unless the grass is very delicate (such as in a newly planted area) or the drought is prolonged, your lawn will revive as soon as the rains return. For more tips on reducing watering chores, see "Watering: Why, When, and How Much?" on page 42.

Fertilizing When you mow, leave the grass clippings on the lawn to fertilize it and eliminate raking at the same time! Apply organic fertilizers, which tend to release nutrients more gradually and over a longer period than chemical fertilizers, so you'll make fewer applications. You'll also avoid dramatic growth spurts that demand more frequent mowing and the lush growth that's more prone to pests and diseases. For more details on buying and applying organic fertilizers, see "Fertilizing for Good Growth" on page 46.

Controlling Pests If a particular pest or disease causes a problem every year, overseed your existing lawn with the tough new problem-resistant turf grass cultivars. "Handling Turf Troubles" on page 48 covers many more tips for keeping your lawn healthy and naturally less prone to pests and diseases.

Make a sturdy mowing strip with paving slabs, bricks, or boards. Set the surface of the strip at ground level.

Minimize Tedious Trimming

In many cases, maintaining the edges of your lawn is more of a hassle than mowing the whole middle part. To minimize trimming, install edgings that allow you to mow close to flower beds, trees, benches, and other garden objects. Edgings also keep lawn grasses from creeping into gardens and help to prevent weeds and groundcovers from spreading out into the lawn.

A simple ditch barrier cut in the soil, 2 to 5 inches (5 to 12.5 cm) wide and 4 to 6 inches (10 to 15 cm) deep, is one possible edging treatment. Sunken solid edgings are generally better because they are less obvious and longer lasting. Install plastic or metal edging strips buried vertically in the soil, with the top edge below the lawn surface. For a sturdy edging that you can run the mower wheels over, install landscape timbers, bricks set on edge, or railroad ties with the surface of the edging at ground level.

Set birdbaths, benches, and sundials on stone or paving blocks set flush with the ground so you can mow close to them with no hand trimming. Replace lawn growing along structures with flower gardens or groundcovers so you won't have to trim there, either.

Eliminate trimming around individual trees and shrubs by encircling the bases with weed-suppressing landscape fabric topped with bark mulch. If several trees and shrubs are growing near each other, link them into one larger planting area; replace the grass between the plants with mulch or groundcovers.

Renovating an Existing Lawn

Lawns often begin to look worn out as the years go by, either from neglect or because they weren't given a good start at planting time. If your lawn needs help, you must decide whether to install a completely new lawn or simply give your existing lawn a facelift. You should strongly consider starting over if:

- The ground under the lawn is so rough and bumpy that it is hard to mow evenly.
- It has large bare spots or worn compacted areas.
- More than 50 percent of the surface of the lawn is covered with weeds.

In such cases, the best prescription is to remove the existing turf and weeds and replant with easy-care grasses that thrive in your climate. Strip off the existing grass with a spade or a rented sod-cutting machine; pile the removed turf in an out-of-the-way spot to decompose. Then follow the guidelines covered in "Starting a New Lawn" on page 18 to recondition the soil and plant the area with seed, sod, or sprigs.

If at least half of the area is grass, if the surface is fairly level, and if the weeds aren't overpowering, improving the lawn is an easier and better alternative. The area will be less disturbed, so you'll have less dust and mud, and you can continue to use most of the lawn as you recondition the threadbare areas. Patching up a lawn is also cheaper and easier than starting from scratch.

If you only have a small patch of lawn, it's worth a little effort to make it look its best.

If you enjoy growing flowers and dislike lawn care, consider turning some of the lawn into flower beds.

Begin with Spot Treatments

Renovating a ragged lawn will take a little time, but it can be worth the effort. Mending the worn and torn spots is the first step in lawn renovation. If foot traffic has worn paths in the grass, build gravel, stone, brick, or paved paths where you want people to walk; if necessary, plant shrubs or install low fences to discourage shortcuts. Sometimes snowplows or traffic disturbs the perimeter of the lawn; repair the edges with a shovel and some new topsoil. If vigorous grasses have crept over the sidewalk or into the garden or street, some judicious edging may be necessary.

In late summer or early fall, fill in any cavities and depressions in the lawn with sifted topsoil and level off the humps. Loosen trampled, compacted areas by digging or tilling. Till or spade up any bare spots and areas of the lawn where weeds dominate (dig out the weeds by hand as thoroughly as possible first). Firm the soil with a roller, sprinkle organic lawn fertilizer over the area (following the application directions on the bag), and rake it in lightly.

Now it's time to sow the seed. You'll find grass seed mixtures formulated especially to fill in bare spots; try to find a mix that will match the rest of your turf grass. Scatter the seed over the area and rake it into the soil, leaving it smooth.

Rake or dig to loosen up bare spots; then reseed them.

Raising the height of your mower blade for the first few trimmings will help a newly seeded lawn get established.

To spruce up areas where the grass is thin, use a technique called overseeding: Rake the area thoroughly to loosen the soil surface, scatter seed over the existing grass, and rake again lightly. Spread a thin layer of sifted topsoil over the seed.

Keep newly seeded lawn areas watered until the grass is established. After a few weeks, if any spots of new grass aren't growing well, sprinkle a liquid fertilizer such as liquid seaweed or fish emulsion over them. The grasses on newly seeded plots are fragile for most of their first season, so avoid walking on them any more than necessary.

Set the mower at 3 inches (7.5 cm) for the first two or three mowings; the taller grass will be more vigorous and shade out weed seeds. After that, move the blade to the optimum height setting for the kind of grass you are mowing. For more mowing tips, see "Mowing—A Manicure for Your Lawn" on page 38.

Revitalize the Whole Lawn

Once you've spot-treated problem areas, let them grow for a few months until they match the rest of the lawn. The following spring is the time to give the whole lawn a thorough reconditioning.

The soil in old or worn-out lawns is often compacted and will benefit from aeration. Use an aerator over all but the newly planted areas to encourage grasses to thrive and compete better with weeds. (For complete information on this technique, see "Aerating a Hard-packed Lawn" on page 44.)

Worn-out lawns are likely to lack humus, too, so spread a thin layer of aged manure or compost over the entire surface. Add a nutrient boost by applying a complete organic fertilizer at the rate prescribed on the bag. If a soil test shows that the pH is too low (acidic) or high (alkaline), wait until a rain has washed in the fertilizer, then apply lime to raise the pH or sulfur to lower it. (Your soil test results will tell you how much of either material to apply.)

The little extra attention you spend on renovating your lawn will pay off when you can admire the lush, green results. Keep it that way with the maintenance techniques discussed in "Caring for Your Lawn," starting on page 36, and your renewed lawn should remain healthy indefinitely with little other effort.

To loosen the soil in small compacted areas, push the tines of a garden fork into the soil and wiggle the handle.

Prepare old or worn-out lawn areas for reseeding by loosening the soil surface with vigorous raking.

Agrostis tenuis   Gramineae

BENT GRASS, COLONIAL

Think carefully before sowing bent grass in a home lawn. Pure bent grass turf demands lots of maintenance to look respectable, and it's prone to drought and diseases.

BEST CLIMATE AND SITE: Zones 3–8. Light-textured, well-drained soil that contains an average amount of humus and nutrients and has a pH of 6–7. Can tolerate acid soil. Full sun, but tolerates light shade.

CHARACTERISTICS: This creeping grass has fine leaves and a pale green color. Bent grass has good salt tolerance and withstands close mowing, but it can't stand heavy foot traffic, it needs regular watering and fertilizing, and it is prone to many pests and diseases. When mixed with other species, bent grass can crowd them out, leading to patchy turf. For this reason, bent grass is sometimes considered a weed in home lawns.

GETTING STARTED: If you are willing to put the time and effort into putting green–quality turf, sow bent grass seed in the spring at the rate of 2 pounds per 1,000 square feet (900 g per 93 sq m). Seed germinates in 12–26 days.

MOWING HEIGHT: $1/2$–1 inch (6–25 mm).

SPECIAL MAINTENANCE: Bent grass needs close mowing as often as twice a week and preferably with a reel-type mower. Because of its shallow roots, frequent watering and frequent light applications of fertilizer are necessary. Due to its weak growth, it is prone to winter injury, drought, snow mold, and other diseases.

Festuca arundinacea Gramineae	*Festuca rubra* var. *rubra* Gramineae

FESCUE, TALL

FESCUE, CREEPING RED

Thanks to its deep roots, tall fescue is heat-tolerant and among the most drought-resistant of all cool-season grasses. It is also excellent for erosion control.

The soft, fine-textured blades of creeping red fescue are pleasant to walk on, but they can't take heavy wear. This grass isn't a good choice for play areas.

BEST CLIMATE AND SITE: Zones 2–7. Grows well in most soil types. Full sun or light shade.

CHARACTERISTICS: Sometimes called meadow fescue, tall fescue is a wide-bladed, sharp-edged, clump-forming grass that takes a great deal of wear and tear. It grows so strong that it can crowd out weeds as well as less vigorous, fine-textured turf grasses. Tall fescue is a good choice for play areas, roadsides, and low-maintenance areas. The only place you'd probably want to avoid it is in a highly manicured lawn, where its broader blades and clumping habit would give the turf a coarse look.

GETTING STARTED: Plant in either spring or fall, sowing 8 pounds per 1,000 square feet (3.2 kg per 93 sq m). Seed germinates in 12–22 days.

MOWING HEIGHT: 2–3 inches (5–7.5 cm).

SPECIAL MAINTENANCE: Tall fescue doesn't need much special care. You may need to overseed bare spots in spring or fall. Mow fairly high so the grass stays vigorous and looks more even.

CULTIVARS: Look for improved tall fescue cultivars; these are more attractive, tolerate harder use, and are more resistant to insects and disease. 'Colchise', 'Falcon', 'Guardian', 'Olympic', 'Mustang', 'Pacer', and 'Titan' are only a few of many cultivars. They have narrower leaves and tend to be less clumping than the species but are equally drought-resistant.

BEST CLIMATE AND SITE: Zones 2–8. Adapts to most soil types, even dry soil. Full sun or light shade.

CHARACTERISTICS: Creeping red fescue spreads slowly by rhizomes, survives in difficult locations, and looks nice when cut high. Its thin, fine blades are deep green, but the base of the plant is red. Creeping red fescue is not rugged enough for heavy foot traffic, but it *is* one of the best grasses for shady spots in the North. It is often mixed with perennial rye grass to overseed warm-season grasses when they become dormant in fall.

GETTING STARTED: For an all-fescue lawn, plant at the rate of 4 pounds per 1,000 square feet (1.8 kg per 93 sq m) in spring or early fall. You may also find creeping red fescue mixed with bluegrass or perennial ryegrass; apply according to the rate suggested on the label. Seed germinates in 12–22 days.

MOWING HEIGHT: 2 inches (5 cm).

SPECIAL MAINTENANCE: Fertilize only when growth is poor; creeping red fescue is actually less competitive when it gets lots of fertilizer. It is quite drought-tolerant, so you'll seldom need to water. Overwatering may encourage fungal diseases, which are also prevalent in hot, humid seasons.

CULTIVARS: Some of the best include 'Agram', 'Illahee', 'Koket', 'Longfellow', 'Pennlawn', 'Rainier', 'Reliant', and 'Scaldis'.

FESCUE, CREEPING RED—Continued   RYEGRASS, ANNUAL

Creeping red fescue is an excellent cool-season lawn grass for shady areas. It is relatively drought-tolerant and seldom needs fertilizer to look its best.

RELATED SPECIES:

F. longifolia, hard fescue, is similar in most characteristics to *F. rubra* but grows more slowly and is more disease-resistant.

F. rubra var. *commutata,* Chewings fescue, is a fine-bladed, dark green variety that is more upright and clump-forming rather than spreading; otherwise it resembles red creeping fescue. Its cultivars include 'Centers', 'Highlight', 'Jamestown', 'Long-fellow', 'Mary', 'Shadow', and 'Tamara'.

Annual ryegrass is mainly used for quick cover while perennial grasses are getting established. It grows rapidly, so it needs frequent mowing.

BEST CLIMATE AND SITE: Zones 3–7. Grows on a wide range of soil types. Full sun or light shade.

CHARACTERISTICS: Annual ryegrass is a rather coarse grass with light green leaves. It is rugged enough to stand moderate use, it holds its color well, and it is drought-resistant. It will set seed and die after one season, so it is not meant for permanent lawns. It is used primarily in mixes with perennial grasses as a quick cover to hold the soil until the higher-quality grasses sprout and take hold. However, beware of cheap lawn mixes that are more than 20 percent annual rye. Straight annual rye is sometimes used to overseed warm-season lawns to provide green during the winter months.

GETTING STARTED: Plant annual rye in the spring in the North at the rate of 2–3 pounds per 1,000 square feet (0.9–1.35 kg per 93 sq m) for an all-rye lawn. If sowing a mix, follow the rate suggested on the label. In the South, overseed existing warm-season lawns in fall at 3–5 pounds per 1,000 square feet (1.35–2.25 kg per 93 sq m). Seed germinates in 7–12 days.

MOWING HEIGHT: 2 inches (5 cm).

SPECIAL MAINTENANCE: If annual rye is mixed with other grasses as a "nurse crop," water the planting in dry weather to help the less vigorous grasses get established and survive competition from the rye. Annual rye is disease- and insect-resistant.

Lolium perenne　　　　　Gramineae

RYEGRASS, PERENNIAL

Perennial ryegrass is one of the most popular cool-season lawn grasses. It looks great alone or mixed with bluegrass, and it's relatively pest- and disease-resistant.

In the North, grow perennial ryegrass as a multipurpose lawn. In the South, it's a good choice for overseeding warm-season lawns for winter color.

BEST CLIMATE AND SITE: Zones 3–7. Grows on a wide range of soil types. Full sun but tolerates light shade.

CHARACTERISTICS: Perennial ryegrass sprouts quickly for a fast lawn effect. Its light green color and wide leaves make it appear rather coarse, but the newer cultivars are more attractive. Perennial ryegrass is tolerant of foot traffic and is more insect- and disease-resistant than other lawn grasses, especially when it's enhanced with endophytes (fungi that live within the grass plants and discourage insect pest feeding). Perennial ryegrass is one of the most popular choices for all-purpose home lawns. It is also useful for overseeding warm-season grasses for winter color.

GETTING STARTED: Choose the cultivars recommended for your area for the best results. Plant either in spring or late summer in the North. For an all-perennial-ryegrass lawn, plant 2–3 pounds per 1,000 per square feet (0.9–1.35 kg per 93 sq m). For a finer-quality lawn, choose a perennial ryegrass/bluegrass mix; seed at the rate suggested on the package. If oversowing an existing warm-season lawn, sow in fall at 3–5 pounds per 1,000 square feet (1.35–2.25 kg per 93 sq m). Perennial ryegrass seed germinates in 7–12 days.

MOWING HEIGHT: Cut at 3 inches (7.5 cm) for the first three mowings of the season and 2 inches (5 cm) for later mowings.

SPECIAL MAINTENANCE: If your lawn contains a strain of perennial ryegrass that has coarse, pale green leaves, mow it closer than the recommended height a few times to hold back its rapid growth and to encourage growth of the better grasses in the mixture. Perennial ryegrass needs little fertilizer once it's well established.

CULTIVARS: 'Aquarius', 'Commander', 'Derby', 'Fiesta', 'Manhattan II', 'Pennant', 'Pennfine', 'Regal', 'Repel', 'Sunrise', and 'Tara' are some of the many cultivars with better color and narrower leaves. They combine well with other cool-weather grasses and are good for winter color on Southern lawns. 'Affinity' is recommended for shady lawns.

Poa pratensis   Gramineae

BLUEGRASS

Fine-bladed bluegrass forms a beautiful smooth turf in full sun. To stay in peak condition, it needs annual fertilizing and regular watering in dry weather.

Start bluegrass from seed or sod. For added wear tolerance and pest and disease resistance, mix it with endophyte-enhanced perennial ryegrass and fescues.

BEST CLIMATE AND SITE: Zones 4–7. Light-textured, well-drained soil that contains an average amount of organic matter and nutrients and has a pH of 6.5–7. Full sun.

CHARACTERISTICS: Bluegrass is one of the highest-quality, fine-bladed grasses for Northern lawns that receive plenty of sunlight and moisture. Its narrow, upright-growing, blue-green blades have a smooth look when mown. Bluegrass can't tolerate a lot of traffic, so don't plant it alone for a heavily used lawn. Some recent cultivars are superior in color and disease resistance to the species and can stand shorter mowing, but some also lack the vigor of the original.

GETTING STARTED: For an attractive lawn, plant blends of several compatible bluegrass cultivars at 1¹/₂–2 pounds per 1,000 square feet (675–900 g per 93 sq m). Seed germinates in 12–30 days. For a more rugged lawn, use a mix of bluegrass, perennial rye, and fescues, especially those that are endophyte-enhanced. Bluegrass is one of the most popular grasses grown on sod farms; bluegrass sod is often available in blends and mixtures.

MOWING HEIGHT: Mow species at 2–2¹/₂ inches (5–6 cm). Some cultivars tolerate lower mowing at 1¹/₂–2 inches (3–5 cm).

SPECIAL MAINTENANCE: Bluegrass spreads by shallow, underground rhizomes and requires frequent watering during dry periods. It also benefits greatly from an annual light feeding in late summer or early fall. It is likely to need dethatching from time to time. The species is more disease-prone than the cultivars.

CULTIVARS: Bluegrass cultivars come true from seed, so it isn't necessary to start them from expensive plugs or sprigs. Check with your garden center to see which cultivars are recommended for your area. 'Merion', an old strain, is susceptible to rust, develops thatch easily, and needs frequent fertilizing to look its best. 'Adelphi', 'America', 'Bristol', 'Eclipse', 'Gnome', 'Kenblue', 'Manhattan II', 'Merit', 'Newport', 'Park', 'Pennsar', 'Princeton', 'Vantage', 'Victa', 'Viva', and 'Windsor' are better grasses, but they are only a few of the many favored by landscapers and homeowners. 'Canadian Bluegrass', though a coarser, more rugged grass than the species, tolerates shade better and is often planted on athletic fields.

Axonopus affinis   Gramineae

CARPET GRASS

Carpet grass isn't especially attractive, but it can be used in Southern lawns where other grasses grow poorly. Overseed with a cool-season grass for winter color.

BEST CLIMATE AND SITE: Zones 8–9. Moist, sandy, somewhat acid soil. Full sun.

CHARACTERISTICS: Carpet grass is a light green, creeping, coarse grass that spreads by stolons. Like other warm-season grasses, it turns brown for the winter. Carpet grass is pest- and disease-resistant and needs little fertilizer. But it is very cold-sensitive, doesn't withstand heavy wear, and grows poorly in areas with seasonal dry spells. Carpet grass is recommended only for lawns in the Deep South, where nothing better will grow.

GETTING STARTED: Plant $2^1/2$ pounds of seed per 1,000 square feet (1.125 kg per 93 sq m) in spring or late summer. Or, if available, plant sprigs or plugs 6–12 inches (15–30 cm) apart in well-prepared soil.

MOWING HEIGHT: $1^1/2$ inches (4 cm).

SPECIAL MAINTENANCE: Overseed with a cool-season grass, such as annual or perennial ryegrass, in fall if you want a green winter lawn. Don't let carpet grass get too tall, or the coarseness of the grass and the ugly seed heads will be more obvious.

Bouteloua gracilis Gramineae

GRAMMAGRASS, BLUE

Blue grammagrass is tough and usually trouble-free. It's a good choice for low-maintenance lawn and unmowed areas; the summer flowers and seed heads are quite attractive.

BEST CLIMATE AND SITE: Zones 3–10. Good in dry soil. Full sun or light shade.

CHARACTERISTICS: Blue grammagrass grows in dense clusters, with narrow, blue-green leaves. Although it is a warm-season grass and is frequently included in mixes for lawns in the Southwest, blue grammagrass also has good cold tolerance. It can take foot traffic and is drought-resistant, although it will go dormant and turn brown during prolonged dry spells. Blue grammagrass is good for either low-maintenance lawn areas or for unmowed meadows, where it grows 10–24 inches (25–60 cm) high. It is even grown as an ornamental flowering grass throughout North America. It is often called mosquito grass because of the unique shape of the flowers, which resemble mosquito larvae.

GETTING STARTED: Sow 1–1½ pounds of seed per 1,000 square feet (450–675 g per 93 sq m) in spring.

MOWING HEIGHT: 1½–2 inches (37–50 mm).

SPECIAL MAINTENANCE: Blue grammagrass grows slowly, so it needs little care and infrequent mowing. Most insects and diseases don't bother it.

Buchloe dactyloides Gramineae

BUFFALO GRASS

If you live in a hot, dry climate and really want to have a lawn, consider growing buffalo grass. It seldom needs fertilizing or watering, and it resists pests and diseases.

BEST CLIMATE AND SITE: Zones 3–9. Tolerates any soil, but prefers an alkaline pH. Full sun.

CHARACTERISTICS: This clump-forming, native prairie grass is one of the best choices for dry, hot climates because it tolerates drought. Its fine-textured, blue-green blades make a dense, gray-green lawn, and it can stand being mown at a low height. Its ultimate height is only 4–6 inches (10–15 cm) if unmowed, and it grows well and looks nice on roadsides, even when unmowed and completely neglected. It is often used for erosion control. Buffalo grass tolerates cold, heat, and foot traffic, and it seldom needs fertilizer.

GETTING STARTED: Plant 5 pounds per 1,000 square feet (2.25 kg per 93 sq m) in late summer or early fall. Seed can germinate in as little as 20–30 days, although it may take up to 2 years to fill in. For faster results, look for buffalo grass plugs (plant them 12 inches [30 cm] apart) or sod.

MOWING HEIGHT: 1½–2 inches (37–50 mm).

SPECIAL MAINTENANCE: This slow-growing, low-maintenance grass may need mowing only once a month. It also needs very little water or fertilizer and is resistant to diseases and insects.

CULTIVARS: 'Bison' and 'Prairier' are improvements over the wild species. 'D.D.B-1' grows to a height of only 3 inches (7.5 cm).

| *Cynodon dactylon* | Gramineae | *Eremochloa ophiuroides* | Gramineae |

Bermuda Grass

Centipede Grass

Bermuda grass is a vigorous, fast-spreading turf grass. It can also creep into flower beds and over paving, so contain it with barrier strips and trim the edges often.

Although its pale green color and coarse texture keep it from being recommended for a first-class lawn, centipede grass does form a dense, vigorous, low-maintenance turf.

BEST CLIMATE AND SITE: Zones 7–9. Prefers light-textured, well-drained, fertile soil. Full sun.

CHARACTERISTICS: Bermuda grass is a vigorous, spreading Southern grass with a medium to fine texture. It spreads by both stolons (aboveground runners) and rhizomes (underground runners). Bermuda grass tolerates heat and drought well because of its deep roots. It is disease-resistant and tolerant of salt and foot traffic. Bermuda grass turns brown after the first frost and stays brown until spring. Scatter some cool-season grass seed, such as ryegrass or fescue, over the lawn in the fall if you want a green lawn all winter.

GETTING STARTED: Plant seed in either spring or early fall at the rate of 1–2 pounds per 1,000 square feet (450–900 g per 93 sq m). Seed germinates in 7–25 days. Cultivars are usually available as plugs or sprigs; plant them 4–12 inches (10–30 cm) apart in a well-prepared bed.

MOWING HEIGHT: Mow species at $1^1/_2$–2 inches (37–50 mm). Mow cultivars at $^1/_4$–1 inch (6–25 mm).

SPECIAL MAINTENANCE: Bermuda grass grows best when lightly fertilized twice a year with a complete lawn fertilizer; follow the application rate suggested on the package.

CULTIVARS: 'Texturf 10' has a low growing habit that produces dense, high-quality turf. 'Cheyenne' has good cold tolerance and drought resistance.

BEST CLIMATE AND SITE: Zones 7–9. Grows well in a wide range of soil types, even those that are moderately acid. Full sun to light shade.

CHARACTERISTICS: Centipede grass is insect-resistant and needs only infrequent feeding, but it can stand only light use. It spreads by stolons (aboveground runners).

GETTING STARTED: Plant seed at the rate of $^1/_2$ pound per 1,000 square feet (225 g per 93 sq m) in late summer. Seed germinates in 15–20 days. Or plant sprigs or plugs 6–12 inches (15–30 cm) apart in well-prepared soil. Sod may also be available; plant it in late spring or early summer.

MOWING HEIGHT: $1^1/_2$–2 inches (37–50 mm). Needs mowing only once every 2–3 weeks and usually grows only to 4 inches (10 cm) if unmowed.

SPECIAL MAINTENANCE: Although it requires little maintenance, centipede grass isn't extremely drought-tolerant, so you may need to water deeply once every few weeks during hot, dry spells. It can also turn yellow if iron is lacking in the soil. Prevent this by making sure the soil is adequately supplied with organic matter. To correct an iron deficiency, apply iron chelate in leaf spray or granular form. Remember that the grass's normal color is yellow-green; applying extra fertilizer won't make it greener and can inhibit good growth.

CULTIVARS: 'Centennial', 'Centiseed', 'Oklawn'.

Paspalum notatum   Gramineae

BAHIA GRASS

Bahia grass is adaptable and easy to grow, and it holds its green color well. The leaf blades of this coarse grass are tough, so be sure your mower is sharp!

BEST CLIMATE AND SITE: Zones 7–9. Grows in a wide range of soil types, including sandy and infertile soils. Sun to moderate shade.

CHARACTERISTICS: This glossy, green, easy-to-grow grass keeps its color better than other warm-season grasses. It tolerates shade and foot traffic fairly well and spreads quickly by underground runners (rhizomes). Its deep roots make it a good choice for controlling erosion. However, it is coarse and needs mowing frequently, so use it where a high-quality lawn is not essential.

GETTING STARTED: Plant seed in spring or early fall at the rate of 4 pounds per 1,000 square feet (1.8 kg per 93 sq m). Seed sprouts in 7–12 days.

MOWING HEIGHT: 2–2$^{1}/_{2}$ inches (5–7.5 cm).

SPECIAL MAINTENANCE: Bahia grass can stand more neglect than most grasses and is quite drought-tolerant. Light applications of a complete organic fertilizer in both spring and fall will encourage healthy growth; follow the recommendations on the fertilizer package. Bahia grass is likely to develop thatch and is susceptible to dollar spot, chlorosis, and sometimes mole crickets.

CULTIVARS: 'Argentine' is one of the best cultivars for Southern lawns. 'Paraguay', 'Pensacola', and 'Saurae' have good cold tolerance; they are grown as far north as New Jersey.

Stenotaphrum secundatum   Gramineae

ST. AUGUSTINE GRASS

St. Augustine grass is one of the best turf grasses for shady Southern gardens. It doesn't tolerate heavy wear but usually recovers well from damage.

BEST CLIMATE AND SITE: Zones 8–9. Prefers moist, sandy soil, but grows in a range of soil conditions as long as it has enough moisture. Full sun to light shade (takes full shade once established).

CHARACTERISTICS: The coarse, thick blades of St. Augustine grass grow quickly into a dense, attractive turf in spots where finer grasses grow poorly. It is remarkably resistant to salt spray and wind and is good along Southern coastal areas. However, St. Augustine grass needs frequent watering in hot areas, and it is susceptible to chinch bugs and diseases such as brown patch, dollar spot rust, and St. Augustine grass decline (SAD) virus.

GETTING STARTED: Seed is not available. In spring or early summer, either plant plugs or sprigs 6–12 inches (15–30 cm) apart in prepared soil or lay sod.

MOWING HEIGHT: 2–3 inches (5–7.5 cm). Use a sharp mower blade to get a clean cut; otherwise, leaf tips may turn brown.

SPECIAL MAINTENANCE: St. Augustine grass spreads vigorously by aboveground runners (stolons), which can lead to a buildup of thatch. Help control this problem by raking the lawn occasionally and by mowing the grass high. Fertilize lightly once or twice during the growing season.

CULTIVARS: Cultivars such as 'Bitter Blue', 'Floratine', 'Seville', and 'Sunclipse' have a finer leaf texture than the species.

Zoysia japonica   Gramineae

ZOYSIA GRASS

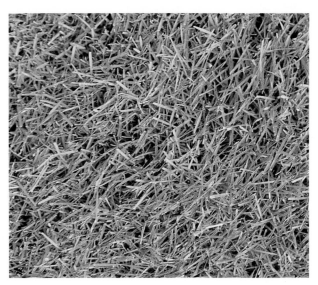

Zoysia is tough and drought-resistant, making it a good choice for most Southern lawns. Yearly fertilization will help it to keep its deep green color.

Zoysia grass is sometimes available from seed, but most cultivars are sold as sprigs, plugs, or sod. Seeded, sprigged, or plugged zoysia lawns can be slow to establish.

BEST CLIMATE AND SITE: Zones 6–9. Light-textured, well-drained soil that contains an average amount of humus and nutrients and has a pH of 5.5–6.5. Full sun to light shade.

CHARACTERISTICS: Few lawn grasses are as highly advertised as zoysia, and some ads make it sound like a miracle plant. Zoysia is certainly among the best lawn grasses for most of the South. It is drought-resistant and, once established, produces a rich, thick turf that competes beautifully with weeds and other grasses. It spreads by both stolons (aboveground runners) and rhizomes (underground runners).

Zoysia grass forms thatch easily, but this doesn't inhibit its growth as much as with many other grasses. A slow grower, it needs less frequent mowing than most other warm-season grasses. And because it is deep-rooted, it doesn't need frequent watering either. It is resistant to pests and tolerates foot traffic well. Although it may survive cool Northern temperatures, the grass turns brown at the first frost, which means that you must live with a dead-looking lawn for over half of the year. (Unlike many other warm-season grasses, zoysia can't be overseeded with cool-season grasses for winter color.)

GETTING STARTED: Zoysia seed is sometimes available; sow 4–5 pounds per 1,000 square feet (1.8–2.5 kg per 93 sq m). Mixing in seeds of cool-season grasses can help cover the soil and discourage weeds while the zoysia seedlings are getting established.

Most zoysia cultivars are available only as sod, sprigs, or plugs. Lay sod or plant sprigs or plugs 6–12 inches (15–30 cm) apart in thoroughly prepared soil in spring or early summer. It may take 2 years for sprigs or plugs to fill in completely.

MOWING HEIGHT: 1–2 inches (2.5–5 cm). Use a sharp mower blade to get a clean, even cut.

SPECIAL MAINTENANCE: Since zoysia grass lawns can be slow to establish, the bare soil can provide an open invitation to weeds. Setting out plugs or sprigs at closer spacings at planting time can minimize problems; otherwise, you may need to control weeds by hand. Feed lightly once a year, and remove thatch as needed.

CULTIVARS: Many cultivars are superior to the species, so choose those recommended for your climate. Good ones include 'Bel Air', 'El Toro', 'Emerald', 'Meyer', and 'Sunburst'.

CARING FOR YOUR LAWN

Although there are many tricks you can use to reduce your yard work, any lawn will need some basic maintenance to stay in good condition. Most grasses need occasional doses of fertilizer to look their best; in periods of dry weather, watering may be necessary to keep them green and growing well. When weeds, insects, and diseases appear, you must cope with them as soon as possible. If the soil becomes compacted or if thatch develops, you'll need to fix those problems, too.

Some lawns obviously demand more maintenance than others. The size and layout of your lawn are two factors that influence how much time you'll need to spend on it. The quality of lawn that you want also has a major effect on your maintenance time.

High-quality lawns are primarily for show: They're designed to be looked at and seldom used. The grass is soft, velvety, and handsome, without a weed in sight. Though these perfect lawns are beautiful, they demand careful mowing, regular feeding, and painstaking protection from weeds and other pests to look great all the time.

Kids doing cartwheels, dogs chasing around in circles, and family reunions at the backyard picnic table demand a more utilitarian lawn and a rugged grass mix that can withstand plenty of foot traffic. A few weeds don't matter on this type of turf, and it needs a minimum of care beyond regular mowing and fertilizing.

Lawns that double as backyard athletic fields get the hardest use. The wear and tear of football, baseball, and other running games puts pressure on the turf and compacts the soil, damaging grass roots. This type of lawn needs frequent aeration and plenty of fertilizer to keep it looking good.

Grassy spots in out-of-the-way, limited-use areas such as orchards and semiwild fields are the least fussy and need only minimum attention to be satisfactory. Monthly mowing with a sickle bar, string mower, or hand scythe is all you need to keep the space looking respectable.

No one kind of lawn is best for every home. It depends on what sort of look you want, what you'll use the lawn for, and how much time you have to maintain it. In this chapter, you'll learn the basics of caring for any kind of lawn: mowing, watering, aerating, dethatching, fertilizing, and controlling weeds, pests, and diseases. The handy calendar in "Lawn Care through the Year" on page 52 takes the guesswork out of timing lawn maintenance chores, so you'll know just what you need to do and when you should do it.

Once you know the basics of good lawn care—including proper mowing, watering, and aerating—you can create and maintain a beautiful, healthy lawn without relying on synthetic chemicals.

Mowing—A Manicure for Your Lawn

There's something special about the crisp look and fresh smell of a lush, newly mown lawn. To keep your lawn looking its best, it's important to mow it at the right height, at the proper time, and with the right equipment.

How High to Mow

Whenever you mow grass, you are forcing plants that would naturally grow much taller to survive at a lower height. A tightly clipped lawn may be attractive, but close mowing is a sure way to weaken even the healthiest lawn. If you've ever wanted a reason to put off mowing the lawn, here's a rundown of some of the advantages of letting the grass grow taller:

- Mowing at a moderate height leaves the grass with ample leaf surface, encouraging a strong root system that can support the plants during drought or extreme cold.

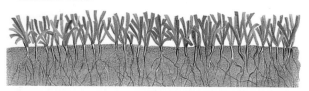

Mowing Pointers

Here are a few handy tips to help you mow your lawn safely and efficiently.

- Before each mowing, always examine the lawn for sticks, toys, ant hills, or other objects that might damage your mower.
- If your mower has a side discharge and you want to grind the clippings finer, aim the discharge so the clippings fall on the area you haven't mowed yet.
- Overlap each pass slightly to eliminate ridges in the grass.
- Mow only when the grass is dry, since the blades stand straighter and you can cut them more evenly. Wet grass clogs a mower and leaves outlines of wheel marks in the grass.
- Remember that a power mower is a serious piece of equipment that can cause severe injuries to careless users. Keep your feet, hands, and other parts of your body away from the blade when the mower is running.

As you mow, overlap the previous pass slightly to eliminate ridges and get a smooth, even surface.

- Taller grass has extra leaf area for photosynthesis, so it is more vigorous and, in turn, more disease-resistant.
- Longer grass blades protect the crown of the plants from injury and insulate it from heat.
- Taller grasses shade the seeds of weeds like crabgrass, purslane, and chickweed, blocking out the light they need for germination.
- Contrary to popular belief, you can wait longer between mowings when you set the blade higher. When you mow it short, the grass tries to replace its lost blades as quickly as possible, so it requires more frequent mowing.

Different grasses have different optimum heights for best growth; you'll find this information in the individual entries in "Cool-season Lawn Grasses," starting on page 26, and "Warm-season Lawn Grasses,"

Make mowing easier and avoid damaging plants by trimming back stems and leaves that are leaning into the lawn.

starting on page 31. In the South, most lawns contain only one kind of grass—all zoysia or all bahia grass, for example—so it's easy to follow the height recommendation for that grass.

In the North, lawns generally contain mixtures of several different cool-season grass species, and those species may grow best at different heights. In this case, it's most efficient to compromise on the mowing height and follow these general guidelines:

During the summer, setting your mower blade 2 inches (5 cm) high will keep cool-season grasses looking good. Raise the mowing height slightly in spring and fall.

- Set the mower blade at $2^1/_2$ to 3 inches (6 to 8 cm) for the first two or three mowings each spring to deter the sprouting of annual weeds.
- During the summer, lower the mower blade to about 2 inches (5 cm). During long dry spells, either avoid mowing entirely or set the mower blade $^1/_4$ to $^1/_2$ inch (6 to 12 mm) higher; the taller grass will help shade the crowns of the plants and keep them cooler.
- In the fall, many people raise the cutting height back to $2^1/_2$ to 3 inches (6 to 8 cm) to check the sprouting of weed seeds blown in during the summer and early fall. The longer grass blades also provide extra protection for the turf over the winter.

How Often to Mow

It can be tempting to start a once-a-week mowing routine—you just point the mower in the right direction

If your grass is fairly tall when you mow, you may want to collect the clippings and use them as mulch.

and plod along mindlessly behind it every Saturday afternoon. The lawn gets mowed whether it really needed it or not, and you've done your duty.

If the weekends are your only free time, a set mowing routine may be your only option. But if you really want your lawn to look its best, plan your mowing schedule around how fast your grass is actually growing. Ideally, you should mow often enough so you don't remove more than the top $^1/_3$ of the blade. Removing more of the leaf surface than that can shock the grass plants, and they may become thin and weak. If your soil is fertile and the grass is healthy, you may need to mow every 4 or 5 days in early spring and during rainy periods to keep up with the lush growth.

The "one-third off" rule may be difficult to follow, especially when 2 weeks of steady rains result in fast-growing grass. If the lawn has grown too tall, gently rake any leaning grass the opposite way to get it standing straight enough to cut. Then set the mower higher than usual for the first cut, and a few days later, mow it again at the proper height. When cutting tall grass, it's sometimes helpful to raise the front of the mower one notch higher than the rear.

If the clippings clump up on the lawn, rake them up for the compost pile, or use them as a weed-suppressing mulch around your vegetables, shrubs, or perennials. Otherwise, leave the grass clippings on the lawn where they'll decompose, add nutrients to the soil, and act as a mulch for the grass crowns. Many mowers have mulching attachments that grind the clippings into fine pieces, helping them to break down faster.

Choosing Mowing Tools

There is no one type of mower that's best for every yard. The kind you pick depends on how large your yard is and how much time and effort you want to put into mowing.

Reel Mowers In the days before engine-powered mowers, heavy reel mowers were the only option for homeowners who wanted a well-clipped lawn. Today's lighter, easier-to-push models do a good job, burn no unrenewable resources, don't pollute, and are quiet. Golf course caretakers use gas-powered reel-type machines for the smooth, close mowing necessary for bent grasses, but the blades can't be set high enough for the best care of most home lawns, leading to more frequent mowing if you use them.

Gas-powered Mowers The gas-powered rotary mower is probably the most commonly used piece of yard-care equipment. It cuts tall grass and weeds better than reel types, and it's easier to adjust and sharpen. Various push and self-propelled walk-behind models, as well as riding models, are available in a wide range of sizes and horsepowers for any size lawn. Some are equipped with grass baggers to collect the mown grass or with mulchers that finely chop the clippings. Some have electric starters, and all have numerous safety features. These power mowers need regular care to keep them running right; see "Basic Mower Maintenance" for tips.

Electric Mowers Electric mowers have many advantages

Push mowers are easy to handle in small spaces.

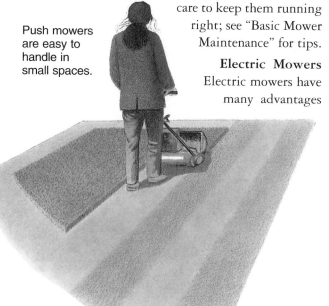

A reel mower is a good option if you have a small yard. Reel mowers are quiet and make a sharp, clean cut.

and are ideal for small lawns. They are quiet, nearly maintenance-free, and they don't pollute the air with noxious fumes. Some electric mowers operate with long cords (make sure you always know where the cord is, so you don't accidentally mow over it!); others use rechargeable batteries and can cut for up to an hour or more on a single charge.

Whatever kind of mower you decide on, choose a model from a reliable, well-known manufacturer, and avoid cheap bargain tools. Also, don't buy a wide-model mower—one with a cutting area of 30 inches (75 cm) or more—unless it has a "floating" base or you have a very smooth lawn. Wide mowers with a set base can scalp the lawn's surface as they mow over the higher bumps, leaving bare patches.

If you have a medium- to large-sized yard to maintain, you may choose a gas-powered rotary mower.

Run the wheels on one side of your mower along the mowing strip to keep the lawn edge neat and trimmed.

Trimming the Edges

Trimming is an essential step if you want your mown lawn to look "finished." Trimming is also time-consuming and can create painful blisters when you use hand shears or clippers. A portable gasoline or electric string trimmer can save you a great deal of work when you're clipping around gardens, buildings, or other objects. These tools are also handy for cutting tall grasses and weeds. Be careful when using them near the base of trees and shrubs, however; the spinning nylon string can easily damage tender bark.

To greatly reduce all trimming chores, install edging strips and groundcovers so you can cut all of the grass edges as you mow. For more tips, see "Minimize Tedious Trimming" on page 23.

Before putting your mower away, it's a good idea to brush off any grass clippings clinging to the blades.

Basic Mower Maintenance

The number one rule for getting a good-looking cut is to keep your mower blade sharp. Dull blades tear off grass tops instead of slicing them clean, leaving tattered tips that turn brown in a day or two. Dull blades also make the mower hard to push.

Sharpen the blade after every 24 hours of mowing at least; more frequent sharpening is better. Either have your dealer sharpen it or do it yourself with a file or sharpening stone; you may also need a grinding wheel to remove nicks in the blade. Some people invest in two blades so they can use the spare while the dull one is being sharpened.

The mower itself will stay in good shape for a long time if you follow the manufacturer's maintenance directions. Periodically lubricate the wheels and keep the underside of the mower clean. Consider spraying the blade with a nonstick coating to lessen grass build-up there (even cooking-oil sprays work for this purpose). Check the grass discharge area to be sure it stays open so clippings won't bunch up on the lawn. If you have a gasoline model, use only clean gasoline and oil, and maintain the air filter.

After the last mowing in the fall, sharpen the blade so you won't have that chore in the busy spring. Drain the crankcase of a gas mower, and replace it with fresh oil according to the directions that came with the machine. Or take it to a professional for sharpening and cleaning. (Fall and winter are excellent times, since the pros are usually less busy then.) Store your mower over the winter according to the manufacturer's recommendations. With a new spark plug and fresh tank of gas in the spring, your mower should be ready to go.

When rainfall is lacking, you'll need to water newly seeded areas regularly until the seedlings are established.

If you irrigate established lawn areas, be sure to water until the soil in the root zone is thoroughly moist.

Watering—Why, When, and How Much?

If your geraniums or tomato plants are wilted, it's obvious that you need to get out there with a watering can right away. But how do you know if your lawn needs water? Do you really need to water it at all? The answers to these questions depend on what kind of grass you have and how perfect you want your lawn to look.

A general rule of thumb is that established grasses require at least 1 inch (2.5 cm) of water every week during the growing season to grow well. In reality, though, water needs vary widely. Heavy, clayey soils hold more water, so they can go longer between waterings than fast-draining sandy soils. Hot, windy weather can dry out an area in a few days; during spells of cool, cloudy weather, lawns may not need water for weeks.

Lawn grasses themselves vary in their need for moisture. Some are drought-tolerant enough to survive for a long time without watering. Cool-season grasses often become dormant and somewhat brown during the hottest months, but they recover quickly after a few days of soaking rain. Warm-season grasses keep growing through the summer, so they need more careful watering to stay alive.

Watering is time-consuming, unless you have automatic sprinklers, and expensive

rotary sprinkler

if you are on metered water or using an electric pump. It also wastes water. To encourage a green turf without watering:

- Include deep-rooting, drought-resistant turf species such as fescues and clover when you start a new lawn or overseed an existing lawn. Scatter the seeds over the existing grasses just before a hard rain in early spring or late summer, and cover them lightly with topsoil or sifted compost.
- Add compost to your lawn if the soil is dry or sandy. Compost supplies organic matter, which breaks down to add humus to the soil. Humus stores water, so the soil will need watering less often.
- Cut the grass at least 2 inches (5 cm) high, and raise the height to 2¹/₂ to 3 inches (6 to 7.5 cm) as you approach a dry season. The additional foliage height encourages deeper roots that can reach moisture farther down in the soil.
- Stop watering if possible, or water as deeply but less frequently, if you know a drought is imminent. The grass will then become dormant and be able to survive with very little moisture.

If you try all of these water-saving techniques and still don't have luck with your low-water lawn, consider reducing or eliminating the turf in favor of drought-tolerant species of ornamental grasses and groundcovers. By choosing plants that are better adapted to your natural rainfall (or lack thereof), you can have a yard that looks good all summer without wasting time and money on watering.

When to Water

If you live in an area where summer rainfall is scarce or unpredictable, watering may be the only way to keep your lawn looking good (or simply keep it alive). But before you grab the hose, take a minute to look below the soil surface; then you'll see whether the grass roots are really dry or not.

Use a spade to remove a block of turf from a not-too-obvious spot of lawn. Set the turf aside, and dig down 6 to 12 inches (15 to 30 cm) deep. If the soil is still moist, wait several days and test again before watering.

stationary sprinkler

If the soil is hard or powdery, it's time to water. (Replace the soil and turf piece after each test.)

Most lawn experts agree it is wasteful to water in the middle of a hot day; much of the moisture will evaporate before penetrating to the root zone of the plants. If your lawn has had disease problems in the past, morning watering is probably the best time; otherwise, watering in the evening is a good choice.

How to Water

A hand-held hose works well to irrigate a tiny lawn, but if you water often or have a large lawn, automatic sprinklers that are rotary, oscillating, or stationary are more practical. The most expensive but least obvious and least troublesome are automatic systems with supply pipes buried in the lawn and concealed sprinkler heads. You can program them to come on and go off at preselected times, and they are ideal for watering late at night. For best results, it's worthwhile to employ a professional to install an automatic system.

Using a sprinkler to irrigate your lawn during the day is wasteful, since much of the water is lost to evaporation.

Choosing the right grass for your climate and mowing at the right height will give you a more drought-resistant lawn.

How Much to Water

Each time you water, moisten the soil around the roots, at least 4 to 6 inches (10 to 15 cm) deep. The amount you need to apply depends somewhat on your type of soil, but make sure you provide at least ³/4 to 1 inch (2 to 2.5 cm) total each time. Lesser amounts will linger near the surface, encouraging shallow roots and weak plants. Light rains—even downpours—that last only a few minutes have the same effect.

Measure the amount of water reaching each area of your lawn from watering or rainfall by using rain gauges. Or set empty coffee cans around the area covered by the sprinklers.

Be aware that different types of soil absorb water at different speeds. Sandy soils absorb water quickly, sometimes as fast as you can pour it on; 1 hour of steady watering can provide all the lawn needs. Clayey soils, on the other hand, absorb only about ¹/10 inch (2.5 mm) of water per hour. If you apply the water faster than that, the excess will run off and be wasted.

If you notice runoff when you're watering, turn off the sprinklers, give the surface water a chance to soak in, then start watering again. A 10-minutes-on, 50-minutes-off watering cycle may be the only way to thoroughly water sloping or heavy-soil lawns effectively. Adjust your watering times to find the cycle that works best for your conditions, and jot the information down for future reference.

Aerating a Hard-packed Lawn

Grass roots need oxygen from the soil in order to live. Plants in a healthy lawn get all the oxygen they need because earthworms tunnel through the soil, feeding on the organic matter and keeping the soil loose enough to absorb air, fertilizer, and water. If your soil is low in organic matter or if it's heavily compacted by use, however, your lawn may benefit from aeration. This is accomplished by punching many small holes in the turf, to encourage air and water to enter the root zone.

Do You Need to Aerate?

To test for soil compaction, try to push a big screwdriver or a sturdy stake into the soil. If it goes in only

with difficulty, the lawn is too hard and you should aerate it, ideally once in the spring and again in the early fall when it is growing well. If you do it only once, fall is the best time for cool-season grasses and spring for warm-season ones.

Aerate a struggling lawn once or twice a year for a year or two, then every 2 years after that to keep it in peak condition.

Even if your lawn isn't heavily compacted, consider aerating it every few years to prevent problems from forming.

Use a spading fork to aerate small sites.

For small lawn areas, you can use a simple manual aerating tool that you press into the soil with your foot.

If you have a large lawn area to aerate, consider renting a power-driven core aerating machine.

Aerating Equipment

Different types of aerators are available from garden-supply stores, either for sale or rent. A hand-held aerator that resembles a fork with tubular tines is fine for a small lawn, but for a larger site, a walk-behind aerator is more practical. To aerate a very large lawn, use a power-driven model.

Most aerators either have hollow or open tines. Hollow tines pull out cores of grass and soil and drop them on the lawn; open tines scoop out soil and grass. The empty holes allow air, water, and fertilizer to reach deep into the soil, and the cores quickly decompose and become part of the lawn.

Some models simply have spikes that punch holes in the soil. Since they don't remove any soil, spikes are not quite as effective as hollow or open tines. But on a small lawn, aerating with a spading fork, hand spiking tool, or even special spiking shoes (golf shoe spikes are too short) can serve the purpose.

Aerating How-to

Aerate your lawn after a soaking rain, or water the lawn well the night before to soften the soil and make the job easier. Run the aerator in rows, as you would the lawn mower. If the tool leaves cores on the soil, rake them up for the compost pile (if you find them objectionable) or leave them on the lawn; they'll break down in a week or two. After aerating, scatter a $1/4$-inch (6 mm) layer of sifted compost over the lawn to add organic matter and nutrients.

Handling Thatch

Lawn thatch is a mystery to some homeowners: everyone says it's a problem, but many don't really know what it is. Thatch consists of a tight mass of undecomposed organic matter—stems, stolons, rhizomes, roots, and leaves—that has accumulated over a period of years. Thatch is not simply piled up grass clippings, although a layer of thatch can keep clippings from reaching the soil and breaking down.

If you prod your lawn with a finger and find it soft and spongy, and you can't reach the soil, it has thatch. A little thatch isn't bad, but a thatch layer of over $^1/_2$ inch (1.25 cm) is undesirable for several reasons.

- Thatch crowds the grass crowns, interfering with healthy vigorous growth.
- Thatch prevents water from reaching the soil. It holds the moisture near the plants, encouraging pest and disease problems.
- Thatch leads to shallow rooting, so lawn grasses are more susceptible to drought damage.

Cool-season bent grasses and certain warm weather grasses—hybrid bermuda, St. Augustine, and zoysia—are most likely to form thatch because their stoloniferous roots run above the ground. But thatch can form on just about any turf, especially those treated with chemical fertilizers. Unless lawns of bluegrass and other creeping grasses are properly fertilized, aerated, and mowed, they too may develop thatch.

Raking your lawn vigorously with a metal or bamboo leaf rake can help remove a buildup of thatch.

Dispatching with Thatch

If the thatch layer is not too thick, you can get rid of it gradually without a major dethatching job. A good start is to aerate the lawn with a core aerator at least twice a year, then spread organic fertilizer and water the lawn generously to encourage the grasses to root below the thatch. After each mowing, rake and remove all of the grass clippings (put them in your compost pile) for at least one season so they won't compound the problem. Several times during the growing season, sprinkle a compost activator over the area to help break up the accumulation.

Since it can take a few years to get your lawn in shape using this method, you may want to do it faster by using a dethatching rake or renting a dethatching mower, also called a vertical mower. A dethatching mower has metal blades that rotate vertically, cutting into and yanking out the thatch.

The best time to remove thatch is before the grass starts growing in spring. Set the tool blades so they barely touch the soil surface. It's better to cut out only a little at one time if the thatch is deep. After removing the pieces, rake and compost them.

Prevent future thatch by mowing properly (only removing the top one-third of the grass.) Aerate the soil every few years; give the lawn a vigorous once-a-year raking between aerating times. Hold off on high-nitrogen lawn fertilizers; excess nutrients may contribute to thatch build-up.

Removing only the top one-third of the grass at each mowing will produce small clippings that break down quickly.

Fertilizing for Good Lawn Growth

Unlike vegetables and many other crops, turf grasses growing in healthy, well-drained, humus-rich soil need little additional fertilizer. The grass clippings you leave on the lawn recycle many of the nutrients. The decomposing clippings also add organic matter and encourage earthworms, which aerate the soil and leave fertile castings in their wake.

seaweed

Even though many lawns get along just fine without additional fertilizing, almost all will benefit from an annual feeding. Those that are heavily used or that have bare spots or thin, anemic-looking grass are especially good candidates for fertilizing each year. Kentucky bluegrass and certain warm-weather grasses can become disease-prone if they lack nutrients.

Choosing a Fertilizer

The best lawn fertilizers release a small but steady supply of nutrients over a long period. The slow nutrient release will help your lawn grow slowly and steadily all season long, without encouraging a growth spurt that leads to more frequent mowing.

Natural fertilizers from plants, animals, and rocks—including manures, bonemeal, granite dust, rock phosphate, seaweed, alfalfa meal, and granite dust—are excellent sources of slow-release nutrients; some also

Watering with seaweed extract or fish emulsion will give your lawn a nutrient boost and promote good growth.

Sifted compost is excellent for fertilizing lawn grasses as well as flower beds.

add organic matter that helps to improve the structure of the soil. Homemade or commercial compost is another natural fertilizer that supplies nutrients and good soil conditioning.

Although chemical fertilizers are lower priced and often contain larger amounts of nutrients than most organic fertilizers, they are not the best choices for feeding your lawn. They release nutrients, especially nitrogen, so quickly that they are likely to "burn" grasses if you add too much. Fast-acting fertilizers can also harm earthworms and other beneficial soil organisms.

How Much to Apply

A complete soil test will tell you exactly what nutrients your lawn needs. If you don't want to bother with a test, however, you can usually get good results by following the recommended application rates on a package of commercial balanced organic fertilizer. Spread dry fertilizer any of these three ways:
- By hand. It's not particularly accurate, but it's fast and easy, especially for very small areas.
- With a rotary broadcast (or cyclone) spreader. These spreaders fling fertilizers far and wide, covering a 6-foot (1.8 m) swath on each pass. Rotary spreaders are an efficient way to cover

large lawn areas quickly and evenly.
- With a drop spreader. Drop spreaders are the best choice for applying fertilizers accurately. You can adjust the openings at the bottom of the spreader to match the material you're using and application rate you want (follow the directions that come with the spreader). Drop spreaders usually cover an area about 2 feet (60 cm) wide on each pass.

If you use homemade or commercial compost, sift it through a wire screen first to remove large lumps. (Running the compost through a shredder first can help if the compost is very lumpy.) Scatter the sifted compost with a shovel, or apply it with a standard fertilizer spreader. Spread $^1/_4$ to $^1/_2$ inch (6 to 12 mm) of compost evenly over the lawn. Apply the sifted compost in late summer for cool-season grasses or in spring for warm-season grasses.

Scattering fertilizer by hand is probably the best option for small areas, but it can give spotty results if you don't spread the material evenly.

Feeding Times

If your lawn needs nutrients, plan your fertilizing schedule around the kind of grass you're growing.

Cool-season Grasses Fall is the best time to add fertilizer to cool-season grasses. They grow vigorously then and store nutrients, which they'll release in the spring for slow, steady growth. If you live where fall seasons are long, feed the lawn lightly twice, once in early fall and again just before the grass becomes dormant. If hard frosts come early in your climate, omit the second feeding, but if the lawn is in poor condition, give it another light feeding in the spring just as growth starts.

Warm-season Grasses Fertilize warm-season lawn grasses in spring when they are just beginning to grow. Some, like bermuda grass and zoysia, can benefit from an extra application of fertilizer in August or September. Avoid feeding your lawn later in the fall, though, or you'll encourage a flush of new growth when the grass should be slowing down for the winter season.

If you're applying granular fertilizers, use a drop spreader to get even coverage.

Green Up Your Grass

If you want your lawn to look top-notch, give it a boost with a liquid feeding of seaweed extract or fish emulsion. Fresh or dried livestock manure, soaked in water for several days and diluted to the color of weak tea, is another fast-acting liquid fertilizer. (Strain the liquid through cheesecloth or a nylon stocking to prevent it from clogging the sprayer.)

Apply any of these liquid fertilizers to your lawn with a sprinkling can, a backpack sprayer, or a hose applicator. To get the greenest lawn on the block, make three applications: one in early spring, one in midsummer, and one in late summer.

Handling Turf Troubles

With good care, your lawn can shrug off problems like weeds, insects, and diseases without much help from you—possibly even before you know there is a problem. But if these pesky turf troubles start invading your yard, there are steps you can take to control them.

Identifying the Problem

It's relatively easy to tell if weeds are a problem in your lawn, since most look quite different from the grass. Pest and disease damage, however, can be a little trickier to identify, since less-than-ideal growing conditions can cause similar symptoms.

If your grass is weak in spite of good care, first think about the site. Is the lawn getting shaded out by growing trees? Does a septic tank, large

If you want to keep lawn weeds to a minimum, make sure your grass has the conditions it needs for vigorous growth.

rock, or old paving material lie close to the surface, interfering with good drainage? Was there salt spray on the site from the ocean or winter roads?

There isn't much you can do to change your site, so the next best thing is to change your plants. Replace struggling lawn areas with groundcovers that are better adapted to shade, wet soil, or whatever the challenge is.

If the site is sunny, well drained, and not especially wet or dry, then start looking closely for signs of pests or diseases. In this section, you'll find descriptions of some of the most common lawn attackers. If you can't figure out what's causing the problem, jot down some notes about what the problem looks like; then ask your local Cooperative Extension agent or garden-center staff to help you identify the cause.

Controlling Weeds

Insects flourish during dry seasons, and diseases proliferate most rapidly during warm, humid ones, but weeds grow in all kinds of weather.

Some weeds prefer certain soil conditions. Control these weeds by changing the growing conditions. For instance, yellow dock, horsetails, foxtail, and ox-eye daisies thrive in poorly drained areas; either improve the drainage or replace the lawn with moisture-tolerant groundcovers. Sorrels, mosses, wild strawberries, and ferns are among the weeds that enjoy acidic soils. To help control them, apply lime to keep

Preventing Lawn Problems

Preventing diseases, pests, and weeds is always easier than trying to find remedies after they attack. Here are some tips to help you keep your lawn naturally healthy.

- Plant the right grasses for your soil and climate, including some that are endophyte-enhanced to fight insects.
- Keep soil pH between 6.5 and 7 by adding lime or sulfur as needed.
- Aerate the lawn at least once every 2 years to promote vigorous growth.
- Apply organic fertilizer containing nitrogen if the grass isn't growing well.
- Avoid walking on the lawn as much as possible when it's wet to minimize soil compaction and prevent root damage.
- In the South, many lawn grasses become dormant and brown in the winter but weeds continue to grow. To keep the lawn green and discourage weeds, overseed warm-season turf with ryegrass or another cool-season grass in the fall.

the pH from 6.5 to 7. Weeds such as bindweed, quack grass, and plantain grow on hard-packed soils. To discourage them, aerate the lawn; if foot traffic has caused the compaction, install paths.

To eliminate every possible weed in your lawn would require either full-time work or chemical sprays that are neither practical nor ecological. Hand-digging is a safe but time-consuming option for disposing of weeds. Soap-based organic herbicides are available, but they may kill your grass as well as the weeds.

Fortunately, the simple act of mowing can go a long way toward preventing weed problems. Set the mower high for the first mowings of the summer, so the tall grasses will shade the seeds of crabgrass and other annuals and prevent their germination. Return the mower blade to the height recommended for your particular grass until the final mowings in the fall; then set it high again so the taller blades of grass will shade out any late-germinating perennial weeds.

Coping with Pest Problems

In any healthy lawn, you'll find many worms and insects, both friends and foes of the grasses there. Unless there is a population explosion of the bad guys, they cause little harm. You should welcome the earthworms, of course, and the predators that devour the harmful bugs. Keep your eyes open for signs of pests, so you can take appropriate control measures to prevent serious damage.

Pests that can damage lawn grasses include chewing insects, such as armyworms that attack the foliage, and grubs, which kill turf by devouring the roots. White grubs are the larvae of May/June beetles, Japanese beetles, chafers, and other beetles that lay their eggs in lawns. Besides feeding on the grass roots, they attract larger hungry creatures, such as

If top-quality turf is not a priority, you may decide that you can live with some weeds.

moles and skunks. Eliminate grubs, and you'll also discourage the four-legged pests.

For clues to recognizing the damage caused by several pesky lawn-attacking insects, see "Spotting Common Lawn Pests" on page 50.

Choosing a Control   The best way to control several common lawn pests is to plant a grass mixture containing at least 50 percent endophyte-enhanced seeds. Endophytes are fungi that kill chinch bugs, sod webworms, billbugs, armyworms, aphids, and certain other insects. They don't control grubs or Japanese beetles, and they are not recommended for areas where animals graze.

Besides damaging your lawn, grubs can also attract digging animals such as moles and skunks.

Small piles of soil don't indicate pest problems; they're signs of healthy earthworm activity.

Fescues and perennial rye cultivars are currently the only grasses that contain endophytes. Since the shelf life of the fungi is approximately 9 months, buy only fresh seed and store it in a cool, dry spot. Starting new lawns with these cultivars can help prevent pest damage; overseeding can convert existing pest-prone lawns into healthier, problem-resistant turf.

If pest problems become worrisome, there are organic insecticides that can help. Look in stores or catalogs that sell organic garden supplies for products such as neem (azadirachtin), horticultural oils, pyrethrin, sabadilla, and insecticidal soap. Milky disease powder—containing spores of the bacteria *Bacillus popilliae*—is a biological control that you apply to the soil, where it infects and kills grubs. Beneficial nematodes also help to control grubs, cutworms, and other lawn pests. All of these products are offered under various trade names. Always check the label to be sure the product controls the pests you have, and follow application directions carefully.

With good regular care, most home lawns are fairly resistant to pest and disease problems.

Combating Diseases

A variety of bacteria, viruses, fungi, mildews, and blights may attack lawns, especially when the grasses are stressed. Providing a site with abundant sunlight

---

Spotting Common Lawn Pests

Here are some clues to help you spot some common insects and their damage before problems get out of hand.

- **Armyworms:** Large greenish brown, white-striped caterpillars that devour grass blades, leaving bare patches. Spray affected areas with parasitic nematodes or BTK (*Bacillus thuringiensis* var. *kurstaki*). Reseed or overseed with endophyte-containing grasses.
- **Billbugs:** Larvae (white grubs) feed on roots; adults (brown weevils) eat the crowns. Both cause yellow or brown patches in turf. Aerate, remove thatch, water deeply, and add organic matter. Plant resistant cultivars.
- **Chinch bugs:** Adults have dark bodies with a triangular pad between white, folded wings. Nymphs are bright red with a white band across their backs. Both feed on plant juices, causing yellowed, round patches in the lawn. To control, soak sod with soapy water (1 ounce of liquid dish soap to 2 gallons [8 l] of water); then lay a flannel sheet over the treated area to trap the pests as they emerge from the soil. Pick up the shee and rinse it out with soapy water to kill the pests. Water well to rinse out of the treated area. Reseed or overseed with resistant cultivars.
- **Mole crickets:** These large, light brown insects have short forelegs and shovel-like feet. They tunnel under the lawn and feed on roots, causing irregular streaks of brown grass. Apply parasitic nematodes, watering thoroughly before and after the application.
- **Spider mites:** These tiny, 8-legged creatures feed on foliage, causing yellowed grass blades and thin, browned turf. Spray serious infestations with insecticidal soap.
- **Webworms:** Webworm moths often invade lawns in early spring, laying eggs that hatch into night-feeding caterpillars. These larvae cut off grass blades at the base of the plant, causing small, irregular dead spots. Spray with BTK or drench the soil with parasitic nematodes; spray with pyrethrin as a last resort.
- **White grubs:** These curved, fat, whitish beetle larvae chew on grass roots, causing patches of loose, browned turf. Treat the lawn with milky disease spores or parasitic nematodes.

Some pests, including Japanese beetles and spider mites, can attack garden plants as well as turf grass.

and good air circulation is the best way to avoid these diseases, since most blights, mildews, rots, and other fungal and bacterial diseases thrive in dark, damp conditions. To encourage strong, naturally problem-resistant growth, keep the soil nutrients and pH balanced and add ample organic matter with a yearly application of sifted compost.

If diseases strike, the best control is usually raking out the diseased grass and overseeding with a disease-resistant cultivar. For descriptions of several common diseases and other recommended controls, see "Dealing with Turf Diseases."

Red thread is a disease that thrives in cool, wet weather. Avoid problems by choosing resistant grass cultivars.

Dealing with Turf Diseases

Don't let lawn diseases destroy your yard's good looks! Keep your eyes open for the first signs of damage, and start control measures right away to stop diseases before they spread. Along with the controls suggested below, replant or overseed damaged areas with disease-resistant cultivars.

- **Brown patch:** Plants die within a circular area. Common on bentgrass and warm-season grasses, but may affect others as well. Aerate, remove thatch, and top-dress with sifted compost to add organic matter.
- **Dollar spot:** Kills grass in small, tan circles on cool-weather grasses and in larger circles on warm-season grasses. Aerate; top-dress with sifted compost. Apply a high-nitrogen organic fertilizer; spraying with seaweed extract may also help.
- **Fusarium blight:** Shows as irregular patches of wilted turf that change from reddish brown to tan. Aerate and remove thatch; raise mowing height in summer.
- **Leaf spot:** Leaf blades with streaks or discolored markings are probably under attack by various fungi. Build soil fertility; mow high in summer. Top-dress with sifted compost.
- **Pythium blight:** Most common in warm, wet conditions, this blight causes the turf to look wilted and greasy, possibly with a cottony appearance. Aerate and remove thatch. Reduce nitrogen fertilization.
- **Rusts:** This fungus causes orange and brown leaf discolorations and thinning of the turf. Fertilize with seaweed extract or a high-nitrogen fertilizer. If you must water your lawn, do it in early morning so the grass will dry quickly. Mow regularly.

Lawn Care through the Year

Most gardeners have enough on their mind without having to remember when they're supposed to aerate their lawn or add fertilizer. If you're not sure what you need to do each season to keep your lawn looking great, this handy month-by-month calendar tells you just what to do and when to do it.

December and January

• In the North, avoid filling gas tanks of snowblowers or snowmobiles on the lawn; spilled fuel can lead to damaged spots in spring. Other than that, there's not much to do during the winter months.

February

• While homeowners in the North are still shoveling sidewalks and driveways, Southerners can rake the grass, pull weeds, and fill low spots with topsoil.
• Make sure mower blades are sharpened for spring.

March and April

• As soon as the snow disappears, rake and clean up winter debris and repair any snowplow damage.
• Check for snow mold—gray or pink fuzzy areas on grass blades—and treat severe cases with raking and light fertilization. If the fungus appears each year, aerate the lawn regularly, and reseed the affected sections with a fungus-resistant cultivar.

Spring is a good time to repair damaged lawn areas. Loosen the soil and sow seed or lay pieces of sod.

• Keep off wet soil as much as possible.
• When the soil has dried out somewhat, rake the lawn to remove dead grass and light thatch. Gather the material you rake up and use it as part of your first spring compost pile.
• Plant a new lawn from seed, sod, sprigs, or plugs.
• Patch up and reseed any bare spots or worn-out areas in an established lawn.
• In the South, if you planted a winter grass in the fall, cut it very short to give the warm-season grasses a head start as they begin to grow again. Then aerate and fertilize your lawn to get the warm-season grass growing vigorously.
• In the North, apply fertilizer only if the grass is thin and struggling to fill in.

If snow mold appears, rake the lawn to remove damaged grass and fertilize lightly to promote healthy growth.

Dig out weeds as you spot them, before they set seed, and you'll dramatically reduce future weed problems.

In midsummer, mowing is the main lawn care activity that you'll need to think about.

- As soon as the soil dries out, it's time to start mowing. Mow a new lawn closely for the first cutting to encourage it to thicken up. Mow established lawns high for the first two or three cuttings, then set the mower to the recommended height for your type of grass.

May

- Inspect the lawn for diseases and sprouting weeds, and take necessary measures to control them before they get out of control.
- Mow fast-growing grass often so you don't need to remove the clippings from the lawn.
- Sharpen your mower blade if the lawn looks browned and tattered a day or two after you mow.

June

- If you've planted a new lawn, water it often.
- Dig out dandelions (make sure you get the taproots, too!) and don't let them go to seed in nearby areas.
- Check now and throughout the summer for diseases and insects, and apply organic controls if necessary.
- Choose a watering strategy before dry weather arrives: Either water regularly to keep grass lush and green, or avoid watering and let the grass go dormant for the summer.

July and August

- If you've done everything right, the midsummer lawn should be nearly care-free, except for mowing. Take time to enjoy your lawn.
- Continue to dig out the worst weeds; if insects or diseases become numerous, fight them with the appropriate organic control.
- Water warm-season grasses if necessary.
- Mow grasses high if drought is a problem, and

stop mowing entirely if the lawn is becoming dormant (turning brown).

September

- In the North, give the lawn its annual dose of fertilizer early in the month.
- Start a new lawn or repair your old one, including some endophyte-enhanced grasses in the seed mixture for pest control.
- Dethatch and aerate cool-season lawns if needed.
- Stop mowing as soon as moderately hard frosts begin, leaving the grass fairly high at the last mowing.
- In the South, if you plan to sow a winter grass next month, fertilize and mow the grass lower now. Mow it high if you don't plant winter grass.
- Consider replacing unused or problem-prone lawn areas with easy-care ornamental grasses and groundcovers.

October and November

- Don't let fallen leaves stay on the lawn and smother the grass. Either collect them for the compost pile, rake them into shrub borders, or shred them for use as a mulch on the perennial border or berry patch.
- Stop mowing when moderately hard frosts begin.
- Change the oil in your mower, drain the gas tank, and sharpen blades for winter storage. Clean and oil other lawn equipment.
- In the South, plant winter grass for weed control and winter color as soon as the lawn begins to go dormant.

A heavy layer of fallen leaves can smother your grass. Rake the leaves off and use them for compost or mulching.

GROWING ORNAMENTAL GRASSES

rnamental grasses is a loosely defined term that describes any grass-like plants that are attractive enough for planting in a landscape. This group includes the bamboos, rushes, and sedges, along with the true grasses. Unlike the more familiar and sedate lawn and meadow grasses, ornamental grasses grow in a diverse array of sizes, shapes, textures, and colors. In the landscape, they are often in motion, shimmering and swaying in the breeze with faint rustling sounds. As they catch the early morning or late afternoon light, their graceful forms create spectacular silhouettes against the sky or other backgrounds.

The expression "green as grass" doesn't apply to these ornamentals, since they can wear many different colors as well as spots and streaks of white, yellow, and gold. As the season progresses, a plant may change from spring green to bright summer red, fall yellow, and, finally, wintertime shades of beige. Grasses with an interesting inflorescence (cluster of flowers) are especially showy throughout their seasonal transformation.

Just as the sizes of grasses vary from low-growing, 4-inch (10 cm) tall groundcovers to the 20-foot (6 m) giant reed (*Arundo donax*), their habits also differ considerably. Some grow upright; others are mounded or arching. Clumping types, such as pampas grass (*Cortaderia selloana*), grow in large tufts; running kinds, including many bamboos, spread quickly by aboveground stolons or underground rhizomes.

Compared to trees and shrubs, ornamental grasses are inexpensive. And unlike many landscape plants, they need almost no care except cutting back. Insects and diseases don't bother most of them, and they require little fertilizer. Some grasses tolerate drought and heat well, so they often need no watering. Whenever you want to increase your plantings or share with friends, it's usually easy to divide them.

In this chapter, you'll learn all the basics of adding these beautiful, adaptable, easy-care grasses to your yard. "Great Grass Relatives" on page 56 discusses other ornamental grass–like plants, including bamboo, sedges, and rushes, that can add excitement to your garden. "Landscaping with Ornamental Grasses" on page 58 offers loads of great ideas for using grasses throughout your garden—in flower borders, as screens, as groundcovers, and in containers.

"Buying and Planting Ornamental Grasses" on page 62 covers the basics of getting your new plants off to a good start; "Nurturing Your Ornamental Grasses" on page 64 tells how to keep them healthy and looking good. Once you discover how easy grasses are to grow, you'll want lots more; "Propagating Ornamental Grasses" on page 68 will give you all of the techniques you need. Starting on page 70, you'll find the "Guide to Ornamental Grasses," an encyclopedic directory of 38 great grasses with information on choosing and caring for them.

Unlike lawn grasses, which have been selected for uniform growth, ornamental grasses come in an exciting range of shapes, sizes, and colors. These beautiful plants will fit into almost any part of your yard.

Spreading bamboos can be useful for protecting the soil on tough, sloping sites where other plants fail.

Planting creeping bamboos along a road or driveway will help to control the spread, at least in one direction.

Great Grass Relatives

Along with the more traditional true grasses, easy-to-grow bamboos, sedges, and rushes can be attractive, exotic additions to your home landscape.

The Bamboos

Bamboos give landscapes in the temperate zones a tropical, graceful appearance as they sway in the breeze. The plants come in an astonishing array of sizes and forms, with hollow woody canes (culms) ranging from less than 1 foot (30 cm) tall up to a giant 100 feet (30 m) tall.

Bamboos in the genus *Bambusa* are tropical or semi-tropical plants and are of little use in Northern

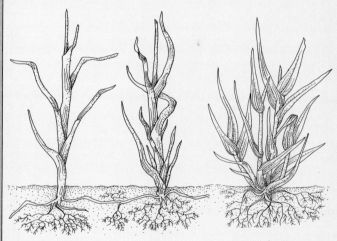

Some grasses and their relatives spread quickly by surface or underground runners. Others form dense clumps.

climates. Many other genera of bamboo are hardy to Zone 6, however. Some can grow in even cooler climates with protection, although their foliage may die back over the winter. For a listing and description of some particularly cold-tolerant species, see "A Sampler of Hardy Bamboos."

These attractive plants produce beautiful, often colorful stems and airy green or variegated foliage. They need virtually no care once they are established, although a mulch to keep them from drying out will help them get started. They grow in both sun and partial shade and are seldom bothered by diseases or insects. Different types are suitable for mass plantings, screening, and erosion control; several species make great groundcovers. Some can be showy container plants for the terrace, too.

Bamboos have a reputation for being invasive and impossible to eradicate once established. In many cases, this distinction is well deserved. If you want to plant a bamboo where invasiveness could be a problem, choose kinds designated as "clump forming" and place them where they won't interfere with other plantings.

Be wary of bamboo species that rapidly form vigorous rhizomes (runners) and impenetrable thickets of roots. Plant them only where it's not a problem if they spread rampantly, or surround them with a thick concrete barrier at least 2 feet (60 cm) deep in the soil. You can also control their spreading habits somewhat by cutting back or mowing the new shoots to the ground as soon as they appear.

The Sedges and Rushes

"Sedge" is the common name for the many *Carex* species, as well as plants in some related genera. Sedges look much like true grasses, but you can tell them apart from the grasses by their pith-filled stems that are triangular when cut in cross-section.

Most sedges enjoy shade and moist locations, although a few prefer full sun and tolerate drought. They vary in hardiness within Zones 4 to 9 and in growth habit from upright to weeping. Many have colored foliage in shades of yellow, orange, and red as well as in silvery blues and iridescent greens; some are striped with silver, gold, yellow, or white.

Sedges are excellent accent plants in a border or rock garden or beside a pond. Many low-growing types make good groundcovers. Some—like blue sedge (*Carex glauca*)—even tolerate light foot traffic and can substitute for lawn grasses in shady areas. Some sedges can be invasive, however, so choose their homes carefully.

Rushes are usually grouped with sedges as close cousins of the true grasses. Unlike the grasses and sedges, though, rushes have cylindrical, solid, stiff stems. The two species most commonly grown in gardens are the true or bog rushes (*Juncus* spp.) and the wood rushes (*Luzula* spp.). Both are ideal for moist spots that are difficult habitats for other plants. Bog rushes are great for water gardens or marshy areas; they have colorful stems and very showy seed heads. Wood rushes tend to be low-growing and make good groundcovers beneath shrubs; they can even be useful as lawn substitutes in shady spots.

Sedges look much like true grasses. They are ideal for moist, shady locations, where grasses might grow poorly.

A Sampler of Hardy Bamboos

The bamboos listed below are hardy in Zone 6 and sometimes in even cooler zones with winter protection. A winter mulch of 4 to 8 inches (10 to 20 cm) of leaves or straw is helpful to protect young plants from cold temperatures; plants tend to become more cold-tolerant as they get established.

- *Fargesia nitida* (fountain bamboo): Greenish purple stems grow to 20 feet (6 m) tall. An evergreen clump-former.
- *Phyllostachys aureosulcata* (yellow-groove bamboo): Green canes with yellow grooves between stem joints (nodes). A spreader that can grow to 30 feet (9 m) where the tops are hardy.
- *P. nigra* (black bamboo): A runner with canes that turn black as they mature and can reach 25 feet (7.5 m). Prefers light shade.
- *Sasa palmata*: Large, leathery leaves to 15 inches (37.5 cm) long. Can grow 5 to 7 feet (1.5 to 2.1 m) tall and is extremely invasive; adapts well to container growing.
- *S. veitchii* (Kuma bamboo): A spreader that grows 3 to 5 feet (1 to 1.5 m) tall. Green leaves develop light tan edges in winter.
- *Shibataea kumasaca*: Grows to about 3 feet (90 cm) tall, with shiny green leaves. It can spread, but tends more toward clumping.

Wood rushes (*Luzula* spp.) appreciate shade and moist soil, but they can adapt to drier conditions.

Landscaping with Ornamental Grasses

Whether you need drifts of plants in a dry, sunny border, a groundcover for a shady nook, a rock garden specimen, or a container plant for a roof garden, you'll find a suitable ornamental grass for the spot. These adaptable, easy-care plants serve all kinds of landscape functions, from screening unpleasant views to providing four-season interest in the flower garden.

Grasses for Challenging Sites

Ornamental grasses are great replacements for more traditional shrubs and groundcovers on difficult sites. Drought-tolerant types stop erosion on steep, dry slopes. Short species line pathways nicely, serve as neat edgings in front of gardens or shrubs, or act as substitutes for lawn grasses. Many do well in wet places; some even grow in water. Salt-tolerant species—such as switch grass (*Panicum virgatum*) and dune grass (*Elymus arenarius*)—thrive at the seashore or on a roadside, where salt spray or salt-laden runoff from winter roads would destroy turf grass or evergreen shrubs. Medium-sized grasses make attractive foundation plantings where snow sliding from the roof could break the limbs off shrubs.

Upright arching grasses such as variegated Japanese silver grass (*Miscanthus sinensis*) are ideal for flower borders.

Grasses as Screens and Hedges

Tall ornamental grasses—those that grow 4 feet (1.2 m) or more—can provide a welcome change of texture and color from more rigid shrubs and trees. In large yards, big grasses like pampas grass (*Cortaderia selloana*) and eulalia grasses (*Miscanthus* spp.) provide spectacular backgrounds

Some grasses have a low, mounding habit.

Blue lyme grass (*Elymus arenarius* 'Glaucus') is super for seaside gardens, since it adapts well to sand and salt.

There's nothing like the tall, leafy stems of giant reed (*Arundo donax*) for an eye-catching landscape feature.

Low-growing grasses such as variegated hakone grass (*Hakonechloa macra* 'Aureola') are great as groundcovers.

Graceful mounds of fountain grass (*Pennisetum alopecuroides*) make wonderful garden accents.

for shorter grasses, shrubs, and flowering plants.

Tall-growing grasses also make excellent quick screens to provide privacy, eliminate unpleasant views, and cut down on street noise. Such screens can divide a larger area into separate "rooms" and also protect more delicate plants from being buffeted by wind storms. Most grasses become fully established for screening purposes within 2 to 3 years—far more quickly than a standard hedge. This makes them ideal for new gardens where you need fast-growing plants to get an almost immediate effect. Grasses can also fill space while slower-maturing shrubs are getting started.

White-striped ribbon grass (*Phalaris arundinacea* var. *picta*) spreads quickly by runners and can become invasive.

Consider the Spread

Some people are wary of planting ornamental grasses, fearful that—like quack grass—they will overtake the property. "Give them an inch, and they'll take a yard," wary homeowners think. But that reputation is deserved only by a few particularly fast-spreading species, such as blue lyme grass (*Elymus arenarius* 'Glaucus').

Clump-forming grasses are less likely to be invasive than those that expand by rhizomes or stolons. Some, however— including pampas grass (*Cortaderia selloana*), fountain grasses (*Pennisetum* spp.) and, to a lesser extent, northern sea oats (*Chasmanthium latifolium*)—can spread by reseeding.

Before you choose a grass, always check whether it is a clump-former or a runner and whether it tends to reseed. Since some plants are rank spreaders in certain climates but well behaved in others, find out how the grass has performed for other gardeners in your area, if you're concerned about a plant's potential invasiveness. Keep fast-creeping grasses confined by paved paths, metal or plastic edging strips, or other solid barriers.

Grasses in the Flower Garden

Ornamental grasses blend beautifully into traditional flower borders. Annuals and perennials add vibrant colors to the subtle, muted tones of many grasses. The grasses, in turn, supply all-season interest and soothing backgrounds for delicate flowers.

Choose companions for your grasses based on the growing conditions you have available. In sunny areas, good choices include chrysanthemums, delphiniums, peonies, poppies, gas plant (*Dictamnus purpureus*), lupins (*Lupinus* spp.), and shasta daisies (*Chrysanthemum* x *superbum*). Under trees, plants like ferns, hostas, and lily-of-the-valley (*Convallaria majalis*) combine well with shade-loving sedges. In dry locations, colorful rock garden plants—including maiden pinks (*Dianthus deltoides*) and woolly yarrow (*Achillea tomentosa*)—are ideal with low-growing grasses. And in wet places, rushes (*Juncus* spp.) form naturally beautiful combinations with water-loving

Spiky grasses make great accent plants.

perennials such as blue flag iris (*Iris versicolor*).

Grasses look great with flowers in all parts of the garden. Spring bulbs such as daffodils, crocus, grape hyacinths, snowdrops, and tulips make a colorful display early in the season; as they fade, the fast-growing grasses neatly camouflage the dying bulb foliage. In semiwild areas, wildflowers combine beautifully with the less showy grasses, including broomsedge (*Andropogon virginicus*), tufted hairgrass (*Deschampsia caespitosa*), switch grass (*Panicum virgatum*), and prairie cord grass (*Spartina pectinata*).

Grasses with bright foliage go well with deep green evergreen shrubs or gray-leaved perennials. The unusual red-leaved Japanese blood grass (*Imperata cylindrica* 'Red Baron') is spectacular against a background of greenery, for example. Clumps of grasses with variegated, yellow, or silvery blue foliage are particularly striking when they accompany plants with green or gray leaves.

The cool color of blue oat grass (*Helictotrichon sempervirens*) combines well with bright flowers.

For a delicate effect, try the fuzzy spikes of fountain grass (*Pennisetum* spp.) with a creeping pink verbena.

Grasses for Containers

Many small- and medium-sized grasses are attractive in pots, urns, and planters. Northern gardeners can enjoy spectacular grasses that are hardy only in Zones 8 and 9 by growing them outdoors in pots during the summer, then moving them to a cellar or cool greenhouse for the winter.

Plants in containers need more water than those in the ground because their roots can't reach moisture in the soil. In very hot weather, check plants daily and water as needed to keep the soil evenly moist. Since frequent watering leaches nutrients out of the soil, give container-grown grasses a topdressing of compost or organic fertilizer during the summer.

In mild climates, you can leave the containers outdoors all winter as long as you never let the soil dry completely. In colder regions, either store the containers indoors or tip them on their sides, so water can't collect and drown the roots. Then bury them beneath a pile of leaves, evergreen boughs, or similar materials.

When rescuing buried plants from outdoor storage in the spring, wait until all frosts are over before uncovering them. If the plants have started to grow, put them in a sheltered, shaded spot for a few days until the foliage has hardened enough for them to withstand sunlight.

Grasses make exciting container plants. You may need to bring pots of cold-tender types indoors for the winter.

Great Grasses for Every Garden

With so many grasses to choose from, it can be a challenge to decide which to grow. Here is a quick-reference list to help you spot the grasses best adapted to your conditions. You'll learn more about these in detail in the "Guide to Ornamental Grasses," starting on page 70.

Grasses for Shady Sites

Carex spp. (sedges)
Chasmanthium latifolium (northern sea oats)
Deschampsia caespitosa (tufted hairgrass)
Hakonechloa macra 'Aureola' (golden variegated hakone grass)
Hystrix patula (bottlebrush grass)
Luzula nivea (snowy wood rush)
Phalaris arundinacea var. *picta* (white-striped ribbon grass)

Grasses for Dry Sites

Bouteloua curtipendula (side oats gramma)
Erianthus ravennae (ravenna grass)
Helictotrichon sempervirens (blue oat grass)
Koeleria glauca (large blue hairgrass)
Schizachyrium scoparium (little bluestem)
Sorghastrum nutans (Indian grass)
Sporobolus heterolepis (prairie dropseed)

Grasses for Moist Sites

Arrhenatherum elatius var. *bulbosum* (bulbous oat grass)
Arundo donax (giant reed)
Briza media (quaking grass)
Calamagrostis acutiflora 'Stricta' (feather reed grass)
Carex elata 'Bowles Golden' ('Bowles Golden' sedge)
Miscanthus sinensis (Japanese silver grass)
Panicum virgatum (switch grass)
Phalaris arundinacea var. *picta* (white-striped ribbon grass)
Spartina pectinata (prairie cord grass)

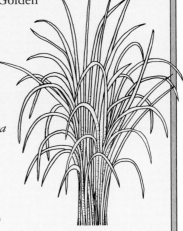

Blue oat grass (*Helictotrichon sempervirens*) is a cool-season grass with evergreen or semi-evergreen leaves.

Give your grasses plenty of room so they can develop their graceful, natural shapes without crowding.

Buying and Planting Ornamental Grasses

As with any aspect of gardening, success with ornamental grasses starts with good plants and good planting. Before you buy, you'll want to make sure the grasses you've chosen are healthy and well adapted to

the growing conditions your yard has to offer. Once you get them home, proper planting will help to get your carefully chosen ornamental grasses off to the best possible start.

Buying Great Grasses

If you're new to growing ornamental grasses, the best place to shop is a local nursery with a display garden that shows the appearance and behavior of the mature plants. You'll be able to see which grasses grow well in your area (including those that grow *too* well!) and how they look through the year.

Once you've experimented with a few of the common grasses, you'll probably want to find a bigger selection than you can see locally. At that point, consider ordering from one of the ornamental grass mail-order sources listed in garden magazines for the best selections of the newest cultivars.

When you're ready to buy grasses, you'll generally find them sold either growing in containers or bareroot (dormant plants with no soil around the roots). Most garden centers sell grasses growing in containers. Although some mail-order sources ship grasses in small pots, they are just as likely to send them bareroot.

When you have a choice between the two, you'll probably find that the grasses growing in pots are more expensive. On the plus side, you know that the growing potted plants are alive and that the roots are intact. You can also plant container-grown grasses any time the soil isn't frozen. If you want an immediate landscape effect, buying potted plants is the best way to get big grasses that will grow and fill in quickly.

When you receive bareroot grasses in the mail, you'll probably unpack what appear to be lifeless handfuls of dead grass. But have faith—if you care for them

Understanding Grass Growth Cycles

Grasses tend to divide easily into one of two broad groupings: warm-season grasses and cool-season grasses. Knowing which kind of grass you have will help you understand how it will perform in your garden.

Warm-season grasses make new growth in spring, flower in summer, turn beautiful colors in fall (just as some deciduous trees do), and go dormant in winter. Their muted, deciduous foliage usually stays intact over the winter, helping to insulate the plant and direct water away from the crown.

Cool-season grasses tend to be evergreen or semi-evergreen but may be deciduous in cold climates. They start to grow in late winter or early spring, flower in mid- to late-spring, then become dormant or grow very slowly in the summer. They often look brown and tattered toward the end of the summer, but then they begin to grow again at a lively pace in the fall. In warm climates, cool-season grasses even continue growing in the winter.

Planted at close spacings, clumping grasses such as blue fescue (*Festuca cinerea*) make attractive groundcovers.

according to the shipping directions, they should soon revive and begin to grow. Even small bareroot grasses can grow quickly to reach their full mature height within 2 to 3 years. Spring is the best time to plant bareroot grasses, though if you live in a mild climate, you can plant them whenever they are available.

Preparing the Soil

If you plan to plant a large area, prepare the spot as you would for a flower bed or vegetable garden. Strip off any existing sod with a spade; then dig or till the earth at least 6 inches (15 cm) deep, making sure no lumps of sod are left. Unless you know that the soil is very fertile, dig in some organic matter, too—about a medium-sized wheelbarrowful of compost or aged manure for each 1,000 square feet (93 sq m) of garden area.

If you're planting only a few clumps of grasses here and there, dig a hole for each plant as if you were setting out a shrub or tree. Make each hole large enough to eliminate the surrounding grass and weeds that would compete with the grass. Mix a few handfuls of compost and a tablespoon or two of organic fertilizer with the soil you have removed from the hole before putting it back around the plant.

Whether you're planting many grasses or only a few, always eliminate any weedy competitors before setting in the new plants. Most ornamental grasses, especially young ones, find it difficult to

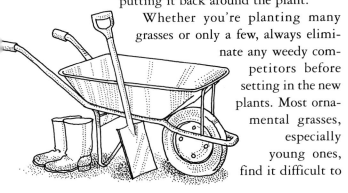

Mulch It!

Mulching your grasses is a great way to promote strong, healthy growth. Organic mulches suppress weeds, hold moisture in the soil, prevent wide fluctuations in soil temperature, protect against winter damage, and, as they decompose, add humus and nutrients to the soil. Water grasses immediately after you plant them, then apply 1 to 2 inches (2.5 to 5 cm) of mulch.

cope with quack grass (*Agropyron repens*), bermuda grass (*Cynodon dactylon*), and other aggressive pests. Even lawn grasses can become problems if they spread into ornamental grass plantings. Once weedy grasses mingle with your good grasses, it's a real challenge to get them separated again.

Spacing and Planting

You can determine the spacing of ornamental grasses by gauging their mature size, a factor that's easier to determine for clump grasses than for those that spread by rhizomes and stolons. The spacing suggestions in the "Guide to Ornamental Grasses," starting on page 70, will give you a good idea of how much room to provide. In moist, fertile soil, you may want to space plants a little farther apart to allow for faster growth; drier, infertile soils may call for slightly closer spacing.

In general, space the grasses as far apart as their height at maturity. For example, allow 3 feet (90 cm) of width for a plant that grows 3 feet (90 cm) tall. The planting will seem sparse the first year, but as the grasses grow, they'll quickly fill in the gaps. Planting clumps too close together is not only expensive but you'll also need to thin them later if each is to attain its full, mature beauty. Plant grasses closer together than suggested if you need a fast-growing cover, a tight screen or hedge, or quick erosion control. Tall grasses—those over 5 feet tall (1.5 m)—also look better at closer spacings.

When you plant, set the grass at the same depth it grew originally. If it was in a container, make the top of the soil in the container level with the ground surface. If you're planting bareroot grasses, set the crown—the point where the leaves join the roots—even with the soil surface. Firm the soil around each plant, leaving a slight depression to catch rain and waterings. Then water thoroughly and apply an organic mulch over the roots. After planting, water frequently to keep the soil evenly moist for a few weeks.

Nurturing Your Ornamental Grasses

When you've planted your carefully chosen ornamental grasses in the right location, most will need little care except for an annual cutting back and, eventually, division. Although pests may occasionally appear, grasses are remarkably insect-free and disease-resistant. Here you'll find all the basics of growing healthy, great-looking grasses in all parts of your landscape.

Watering Wisely

Like any garden plant, grasses benefit from regular watering their first season. After that, if you've chosen grasses that are naturally adapted to the soil conditions you have to offer, their watering needs should be minimal.

If you do plan to water established grasses, it's worth installing a drip irrigation system or laying a soaker hose so the water will come out at soil level. Overhead irrigation with sprinklers or hoses wastes water to evaporation and can damage the showy flowers and seed heads. The grass foliage can also deflect the water from falling on the soil, where it's needed.

Adding Necessary Nutrients

Grasses generally need little supplemental fertilizer to grow well year after year. A mulch of compost or shredded leaves will provide a small but steady supply of nutrients. Applying too much fertilizer may delay flowering or cause weak, floppy foliage; the extra-lush growth may also demand more frequent division to keep the clumps healthy.

Cutting down the tough leaves and stems of pampas grass calls for heavy-duty tools, such as sturdy loppers.

Whenever the plants aren't growing well, however, mix a heaping tablespoon of dry organic fertilizer (3-3-3 or a similar formula) into the soil around each medium-sized plant in early spring. Use a bit less for a smaller plant, a little more for a large clump. Also renew the organic mulch as it breaks down during the year to keep it about 1 to 2 inches (2.5 to 5 cm) deep.

Shearing, Clipping, and Pruning

Although grasses will survive perfectly well without cutting back and most eventually cast off their dead foliage, an annual trim will help to keep your ornamental grasses healthy and attractive.

The best time for cutting is generally in late winter or early spring, just before or just as the new growth begins to peek through the earth. Cut warm-season grasses to 3 to 4 inches (7.5 to 10 cm) above the ground, but no closer; snip cool-season types at about two-thirds their height, since many do not recover well if they are pruned more closely.

In cool climates, some gardeners prefer to tidy up and cut their grasses in late fall. This helps to prevent reseeding, but you lose the beautiful winter shapes, colors, sounds, and movement. In warm climates, cutting grasses in the fall stimulates the new growth to begin, making the plants more

Watering during dry spells will keep 'Red Baron' blood grass (*Imperata cylindrica* 'Red Baron') looking its best.

Many grasses, including Japanese silver grass (*Miscanthus sinensis*), last well into winter; cut them down in spring.

Mulching with compost or some other organic material gives your grasses a small but steady supply of nutrients.

attractive throughout the winter months. In hot, dry places where dried foliage is a fire hazard, you should cut down the grasses as soon as they become dormant. The flowers of spring-blooming species often look better if you clip them off below the top of the foliage after they're past their prime.

For cutting light, thin grasses, use grass shears, hand pruners, or hedge shears. If you have a large number of clumps to cut, however, use a string trimmer or power hedge clippers to speed the process. To chop off tough kinds such as pampas grass (*Cortaderia selloana*), you may also need long-handled loppers or a power weed trimmer with a metal blade. Whatever tools you use, keep them sharp; heavy grasses are tough on clippers of all sorts. Some grasses can also be tough on your skin, so it's smart to wear sturdy gloves, long sleeves, and long pants to protect yourself from the sharp edges.

You may want to use some of the prunings in dried arrangements. Add the others to the compost pile or use them for mulch to protect perennials over winter or cover the soil in your vegetable garden.

Dividing—By Choice or Necessity

One of the great things about grasses is that they can often live in one spot for years without special care. There are, however, some cases where you will need to divide your plants. When species with vigorous rhizomes or stolons spread too rapidly, it will be necessary to remove their offshoots to keep them within bounds. Some clump-forming grasses tend to deteriorate and become overgrown and unhealthy as they age; if they become discolored or die in the center, it is time to dig them up and split them into smaller sections.

You may also want to divide plants to enlarge your own supply or to give them to friends. From one large clump, you can make many small divisions or a few big ones. To find complete details on separating grass clumps to rejuvenate old plantings or make more new ones, see "Multiplying by Dividing" on page 69.

Dividing your grasses every few years will keep them healthy and give you more plants to fill your garden.

Dealing with Pests and Diseases

If you grow grasses and groundcovers in healthy soil with the light and moisture they need, they are rewardingly trouble-free. When the growing conditions are less than ideal, plants are generally less vigorous and more prone to pest and disease problems. In this section, you'll learn about the possible difficulties your plants can face and how to control them.

Prevention: The First Line of Defense To encourage good health and resistance to pests, never allow the plants to become stressed. Also, don't let them get overcrowded by each other or by weeds. Ample sunshine and good air circulation around plants will help to keep the foliage dry, preventing many disease problems. Encourage insect-eating birds by providing birdhouses and growing trees and shrubs of different heights nearby so each bird can have its favorite nesting place.

Battling Bugs and Slimy Slugs Aphids, beetles, mealybugs, lace bugs, scale, slugs, snails, spider mites, and caterpillars affect a wide variety of plants, occasionally even the grasses. Aphids, scales, and other sucking insects not only weaken plants by sucking out their juices but also are the leading spreaders of plant viruses. Beetles, weevils, caterpillars, and other chewing insects, as well as slugs and snails, eat holes in the leaves, often working out of sight at night. Grubs and nematodes feed on the roots.

Avoid spraying unless absolutely necessary, so you won't disturb any beneficial insects. If it becomes

Average garden soil is ideal for most grasses. Too much fertilizer can lead to lush, disease-prone leaves.

necessary, however, choose the safest sprays available. *Bacillus popilliae,* commonly known as milky spore powder and sold under various trade names, helps control the grubs that feed on plant roots; you apply the powder to the soil. Beneficial nematodes also help control root-feeding pests. Another bacteria, *Bacillus thuringiensis* (BT), can be sprayed on leaves to control leaf-chewing caterpillars.

For serious infestations, most garden centers carry an assortment of other natural pest-control products, including neem (azadirachtin), horticultural oils, sabadilla, pyrethrin, and insecticidal soaps. These products are sold under various trade names. Check the labels to see which pests they control, and follow the application instructions carefully.

Dealing with Diseases Most grasses stay gratifyingly disease-free, but there are a few problems that can crop up.

Rust, a fungal disease that appears as orange spots on the leaves, is a common problem on some grasses. It probably won't kill your plants, but it can weaken them and make them more susceptible to other problems. Prevent the spread by removing infected leaves as you see them. Clean up and destroy any infected leaves and stems at the end of the season. If rust is a serious problem every year, spray plants with wettable sulfur several times during the growing season.

Other common diseases that can attack grasses and

Birds will do much of your pest control work for you in exchange for the food and shelter your grasses supply.

Spacing your grasses properly and dividing overgrown clumps will help to prevent many disease problems.

Slug and Snail Control Strategies

Many grasses aren't prone to slug or snail damage, but some—like the sedges—can be quickly chewed to shreds. Sand or diatomaceous earth scattered around the plants will provide an irritating surface that discourages these slimy creatures; reapply the materials after a rain.

Trap pests by laying boards or shingles on the ground, smooth sides down; in early morning, crush two boards together or drown the critters in warm, soapy water. Slugs apparently like the yeasty flavor of beer—you can drown some of them by sinking shallow dishes of it around the garden, so the rim is at ground level. Empty the traps regularly.

groundcovers include bacterial and fungal leaf spots, causing streaking or discolored markings on leaves. Anthracnose, most common in wet weather, causes reddish brown spots with yellow markings. Crown rot causes decay at the base of the plant; poor drainage is often to blame here. Fungal powdery mildew produces a white or gray, powdery appearance on the leaves.

Allowing ample space between plants is an important part of discouraging disease development. Overcrowding leads to shading and poor air circulation, so foliage stays wet longer. Overhead watering also wets the leaves, providing ideal conditions for disease development; ground-level watering is a better approach.

If diseases do strike, remove all affected parts immediately. Dig out and destroy badly infected plants. (Burn them if you can; otherwise, bury them in an out-of-the-way spot or dispose of them with household trash. Never compost diseased plants.) Wait several years before replanting the same species in that spot; grow something else there instead.

Handling Animal Pests Moles, mice, woodchucks, gophers, and rabbits frequently lunch on grasses and groundcovers. White-tailed deer and moose sometimes eat grasses and groundcovers, but usually only when their normal browse is scarce.

A well-trained dog helps to control animals, as does placing smelly items such as bloodmeal, perfumed soaps, and human hair around the area. A cat can help you cope with voles, mice, and—if your kitty is a mighty hunter—even rabbits. In gopher territory, you may need to plant your grasses in large, sunken, mesh baskets made from hardware cloth to protect the roots and crowns from damage.

Garden-supply catalogs and hardware stores sell other pest controls, such as electronic devices that emit high-frequency, pest-repelling noises. When large animals are persistent, a tall fence is sometimes the only viable way to protect your plantings.

Most grasses are surprisingly problem-free. Animals such as mice and rabbits are probably the most serious pests.

Propagating Ornamental Grasses

Few plants are easier to propagate than grasses. You can grow new plants of many species from seed. Or, if you already have a grass and want more of it, dividing is a quick and inexpensive way to expand your planting.

Growing from Seed

It's fun to start ornamental grasses from seed if you want many plants and aren't in a hurry. Growing from seed is best suited for species grasses, like little bluestem (*Schizachyrium scoparium*) and northern sea oats (*Chasmanthium latifolium*). The seedlings of named grass cultivars—such as *Miscanthus sinensis* 'Zebrinus' or *Panicum virgatum* 'Heavy Metal'—seldom share the special characteristics that make their parents great garden plants.

Large seed companies have a good selection of common grasses. Some kinds can be sown directly into the garden; others you'll want to start indoors in late winter. The seed catalog or packet will give you the information you need. The "Guide to Ornamental Grasses," starting on page 70, also offers details on propagating 38 popular grasses.

For outdoor planting, start with a well-tilled or spaded bed of light, loose soil. Dig out any existing

Spreading grasses such as white-striped ribbon grass are easy to propagate—just dig up a section and transplant.

weed and grass roots. If your soil is heavy or lacks humus, dig or till in some well-decomposed compost. Smooth the bed, scatter the seeds lightly over the soil surface, and cover it with a thin layer of either sand or perlite.

For indoor planting, store seeds in paper envelopes in a cool, dry, dark place, and plant them in late winter in flats filled with seed-starting medium. Cover the seeds with a light layer of sand or perlite, then place them in an east-facing window.

Whether you've planted indoors or out, keep the soil moist until the seeds germinate, which may take from less than a week to 3 months or more. Water carefully, so you don't wash out the fine seeds.

Wait until frosts are over to move the indoor seedlings outside. As soon as the indoor seedlings are large enough to handle easily, transplant them to a temporary outdoor bed.

Allow young grasses to grow throughout the

Growing Grasses from Seed

Starting grasses from seed is fun and easy. You can buy seeds of many grass species or gather and plant ripe seed from your own grasses. Here are some of the best perennial grass species that grow well from seed.

Chasmanthium latifolium (northern sea oats)

Erianthus ravennae (ravenna grass)

Festuca cinerea (blue fescue)

Holcus lanatus (velvet grass)

Koeleria glauca (large blue hairgrass)

Pennisetum alopecuroides (fountain grass)

Sorghastrum nutans (Indian grass)

Spodiopogon sibericus (frost grass)

Sporobolus heterolepis (prairie dropseed)

If you pot up divisions, set them in the shade for a few days and keep them moist to help them recover.

To get new divisions off to a good start, water with a liquid fertilizer such as fish emulsion at planting time.

summer. The following spring, transplant the stronger clumps to wherever you want them to grow permanently. Leave any weak ones to grow in the nursery bed for another season.

Multiplying by Dividing

Division is the way to go when you want additional plants of a named grass cultivar or if you need to rejuvenate an existing clump. Besides providing you with many new clumps to replant or share, dividing your grasses will help to keep the clumps healthy and vigorous.

When to Divide The best time to divide most grasses is just as they begin to grow in early spring, but you can divide cool-season grasses successfully in the fall and winter as well. If your grasses are vigorous, it is even possible to split them during a rainy period in summer without harming them. You can divide those that grow in wet places nearly anytime, as long as you cut back their foliage by two-thirds before replanting. If you divide during the growing season, keep the replanted clumps well watered, and shade them with a large paper bag or box for a few days, until they're established.

How to Divide Grasses that spread by rhizomes—like white-striped ribbon grass (*Phalaris arundinacea var. picta*)—are easy to

Make sure each division has roots and some leaves.

divide. Simply dig out a section of the plant with a spade, being certain it has both top sprouts and roots. Replant the entire section, or, if it is large, cut it apart and plant the divisions.

One way to divide a clump is to drive a sharp spade into the crown while it's still in the ground. Some grasses are so tough and grow in such tight groups that you may need a hatchet to break them apart. Lift out some of the plant sections and leave the remainder in the ground. To increase your plantings, set the sections out intact, or, if you want even more plants, chop them into several smaller sections before replanting. If you have all the grasses you want, either discard the removed portions in a place where they won't grow and spread or share them with friends.

If you want to get the most possible divisions, dig the entire clump and carefully divide it into small sections. Wash the soil from the roots so you can see exactly what you are doing. Cut the clump into small pieces with a knife, making sure you have top sprouts and roots on each division. Plant the divisions into pots or a nursery bed. Fill the hole where you removed the original one with compost or topsoil.

Plant all divisions right away. Water them thoroughly right after planting and then as needed for the first few weeks to keep the soil evenly moist.

Agropyron magellanicum   Gramineae

BLUE WHEAT GRASS

Blue wheat grass produces handsome clumps of eye-catching, narrow, blue leaves. The summer flower spikes are attractive in the garden and in arrangements.

TYPE OF PLANT: Cool-season, clumping perennial grass.

BEST CLIMATE AND SITE: Zones 5–9. Moist, well-drained soil. Full sun. Blue wheat grass does well on coastal slopes but not in hot, dry areas or wet soil.

HEIGHT AND SPREAD: Height 1–1^1/$_2$ feet (30–45 cm); similar spread.

DESCRIPTION: Blue wheat grass is one of the bluest grasses. It forms dense clumps of foliage that are dormant in cold climates and evergreen in warm regions. The blue-green, June flower spikes turn from blue-green to straw-colored. *Agropyron magellanicum* is also known as *Elymus magellanicus*.

GROWING GUIDELINES: Set plants 2 feet (60 cm) apart in spring or fall. Cut brown foliage back to about 4 inches (10 cm) in late fall or early spring. Propagate by seed in spring or by division in fall or early spring.

LANDSCAPE USES: The blue color and spiky texture is attractive with low shrubs or perennials. Blue wheat grass is also a good companion for low-growing evergreens in a foundation planting. The flower spikes make good fillers in dried arrangements.

OTHER SPECIES:

A. scabrum, New Zealand blue grass, forms a mat of very blue foliage. It is less hardy than blue wheat grass. Zones 8–10.

Alopecurus pratensis var. *aureus*   Gramineae

YELLOW FOXTAIL GRASS

A single plant of yellow foxtail grass adds a bright splash of color to beds and borders. In a mass planting, this grass creates a dramatic landscape feature.

TYPE OF PLANT: Cool-season, spreading perennial grass.

BEST CLIMATE AND SITE: Zones 6–9. Grows best in cool climates. Prefers soil that is evenly moist but not dry or overly wet for long periods. Full sun; partial shade in hot areas.

HEIGHT AND SPREAD: Height to about 1 foot (30 cm); spread 8–12 inches (20–30 cm). Flowering stems grow to 2 feet (60 cm) tall.

DESCRIPTION: This low-growing, mostly evergreen grass has wide, bright yellow-green stripes on light green leaves. The foxtail-like flower head, soft to the touch, appears in late spring. Yellow foxtail grass is a slow spreader and non-invasive.

GROWING GUIDELINES: Set plants 18–24 inches (45–60 cm) apart in spring or early fall. To get a new flush of leaves, cut back foliage if it becomes discolored by rust or if it looks tattered by mid-summer. Cut back browned leaves in late fall. Fertilize if growth is poor, and water in dry weather. Propagate by division in spring or fall.

LANDSCAPE USES: Use a single specimen to add a spot of color or in masses for an eye-catching landscape feature. Yellow foxtail grass is a good choice for grouping with spring bulbs.

Andropogon gerardii   Gramineae

BIG BLUESTEM

Big bluestem is a tall, warm-season grass that's a natural choice for prairie and meadow gardens. It is also excellent alone as an accent plant or in groups as a screen.

TYPE OF PLANT: Warm-season, clumping perennial grass.

BEST CLIMATE AND SITE: Zones 4–9. Moist, well-drained soil. Full sun.

HEIGHT AND SPREAD: Height of leaves to 2 feet (60 cm); clumps to 3 feet (90 cm) or more. Flowering stems grow 6–7 feet (1.8–2.1 m) tall or more.

DESCRIPTION: This heat-loving grass has blue-toned, deciduous foliage. Purplish flower clusters in late summer are followed by unusual, three-branched seed heads that give the plant another of its common names, turkey foot. In fall, the foliage turns a bronze color that lasts into winter.

GROWING GUIDELINES: Set plants 3 feet (90 cm) apart in spring. Established plants are drought-tolerant, but they'll be larger and more vigorous if you water them during dry spells. Cut back to 6 inches (15 cm) in early winter. Propagate by division in spring.

LANDSCAPE USES: Grow big bluestem as a single specimen in a border or in groups in mass plantings. Groups are also useful as background screens and for preventing erosion on slopes. The flowers are attractive in dried arrangements.

CULTIVARS: 'Champ' grows to 6 feet (1.8 m) and prefers light soil. 'Kaw' blooms late and is best for planting in the South. 'Pawnee' has a weeping habit and grows to 6 feet (1.8 m) tall.

Andropogon glomeratus   Gramineae

BUSHY BLUESTEM

Grow bushy bluestem for its showy flower plumes and purplish fall color. Steady soil moisture is important for the best growth, especially in hot, sunny sites.

TYPE OF PLANT: Warm-season, clumping perennial grass.

BEST CLIMATE AND SITE: Zones 5–10. Moist, fertile soil. Prefers full sun; tolerates light shade.

HEIGHT AND SPREAD: Height 1–2 feet (30–60 cm); similar spread. Flowering stems grow 2–3 feet (60–90 cm) tall.

DESCRIPTION: Bushy bluestem is grown for its dense clusters of fluffy, cotton-like flowers above clumps of attractive green foliage in late summer. In late fall the seed heads become orange, and the leaves turn purplish.

GROWING GUIDELINES: Set plants 24–30 inches (60–75 cm) apart in spring. Cut them back to about 6 inches (15 cm) by late winter. Propagate by seed or division in spring.

LANDSCAPE USES: Bushy bluestem grows best near streams and in wetlands. It will grow in containers if you keep the soil moist. It looks equally wonderful as a specimen plant or in masses. Use the flowers or seed heads in arrangements. Be aware that bushy bluestem reseeds readily in moist areas and can become invasive under those conditions.

OTHER SPECIES:

A. scoparius, little bluestem, grows 18–24 inches (45–60 cm) tall and has orange-toned foliage. This drought-resistant grass is excellent in dry gardens or containers. Zones 4–9.

Arrhenatherum elatius var. *bulbosum* 'Variegatum' Gramineae

BULBOUS OAT GRASS

Variegated bulbous oat grass takes its name from the bulbous nodes at the base of the stems. The white-and-green striped leaves are showiest in spring and fall.

TYPE OF PLANT: Cool-season, clumping perennial grass.

BEST CLIMATE AND SITE: Zones 4–9. Grows best in cool climates. Fertile, well-drained, acid soil. Full sun or light shade.

HEIGHT AND SPREAD: Height to 1 foot (30 cm); spread to 2 feet (60 cm).

DESCRIPTION: This clump-forming grass is mostly grown for its blue-green leaves that are attractively striped with white. In cool climates, variegated bulbous oat grass looks good all season, with small spikes of oat-like flower spikes in summer. In warm-summer areas, the plant may go dormant in summer, but it will produce a mound of fresh leaves in fall.

GROWING GUIDELINES: Set plants 1–2 feet (30–60 cm) apart in spring or fall. Leaves are susceptible to rust, which causes orange spots; treat with wettable sulfur and cut back discolored leaves. Divide in spring or fall. If plants turn brown during summer dry spells, cut back the foliage; new growth will appear when cool weather returns.

LANDSCAPE USES: Variegated bulbous oat grass is great as an accent in rock gardens or as an edging for a flower border. In cool climates, you could plant it in masses as a groundcover. In warm climates, grow it with other groundcovers or bushy perennials to fill the space when plants go summer-dormant.

GIANT REED

Giant reed may not reach flowering size in cool climates; in warm areas, long flower clusters form silky plumes late in summer and last well into winter.

TYPE OF PLANT: Warm-season, spreading perennial grass.

BEST CLIMATE AND SITE: Zones 7–10. Well-drained soil. Full sun.

HEIGHT AND SPREAD: Height 6–20 feet (1.8–6 m); spread unlimited.

DESCRIPTION: Giant reed produces wide leaves to 2 feet (60 m) long on tall, fast-growing canes. The leaves are evergreen in frost-free areas. Plants spread by short, creeping rhizomes (underground runners). Fast-growing giant reed supplied early Southwest settlers with building material for fences and roof thatching; it is still used for reeds in musical instruments.

GROWING GUIDELINES: Set plants 5 feet (1.5 m) apart in spring. Propagate by dividing clumps in spring. In areas where the plant turns brown in winter, cut the dead stems to the ground in winter.

LANDSCAPE USES: Giant reeds are striking as specimens or as background plants for flower borders. They are also useful as screens and windbreaks, especially in seaside gardens. Giant reed can be invasive in warm climates, so choose its location carefully.

CULTIVARS: 'Variegata' has showy yellow- to white-variegated leaves and grows 6–12 feet (1.8–3.6 m) tall. Zones 8–10.

SIDE OATS GRAMMAGRASS

Side oats grammagrass takes its name from the arrangement of delicate individual flowers on one side of the flowering stem. It looks great in meadows and as a groundcover.

TYPE OF PLANT: Warm-season, clumping perennial grass.

BEST CLIMATE AND SITE: Zones 4–9. Prefers fertile, well-drained soil, but grows well in nearly all conditions. Full sun.

HEIGHT AND SPREAD: Height to 2 feet (60 cm); similar spread. Flowering stems grow 6–15 inches (15–37 cm) tall.

DESCRIPTION: This durable plant forms clumps of fine, gray-green leaves. The flowers are purple or reddish in early summer and eventually dry to a tan color in winter.

GROWING GUIDELINES: Set plants 2 feet (60 cm) apart in spring or fall. They will tolerate drought and can even take occasional mowing when established. Cut back the dead leaves in late fall. Propagate either by seed or division in spring.

LANDSCAPE USES: Side oats grammagrass is beautiful in meadow plantings and useful for erosion control on banks. It also makes an attractive groundcover.

OTHER SPECIES:

B. gracilis, blue grammagrass or mosquito grass, is an upright grower to 2 feet (60 cm) tall. Its odd flowers resemble mosquito larvae. It is sometimes mixed with buffalo grass in a mowed lawn in the Southeast. Blue grammagrass adapts well to dry soil. Zones 3–9.

Briza media   Gramineae   Calamagrostis x *acutiflora* 'Stricta'   Gramineae

QUAKING GRASS

FEATHER REED GRASS

The flowers of quaking grass tremble in the slightest breeze, adding movement to flower borders and rock gardens. Cut plants back in midsummer to promote new leaves.

TYPE OF PLANT: Cool-season, clumping perennial grass.

BEST CLIMATE AND SITE: Zones 4–10. Grows well in a wide range of soil types, but prefers moist, humus-rich soil. Full sun; tolerates light shade.

HEIGHT AND SPREAD: Height 1–2 feet (30–60 cm); clumps to about 1 foot (30 cm) wide. Flowers bloom on 2–3-foot (60–90 cm) tall stems.

DESCRIPTION: Quaking grass is an easy-to-grow plant. The tiny, showy, heart-shaped, bright green florets shake in the breeze in late spring, giving the grass its name. They turn purple, then golden yellow in summer. The leaves are green in spring but turn straw-colored by summer.

GROWING GUIDELINES: Set plants 1–2 feet (30–60 cm) apart in spring or fall. Don't fertilize. Cut back the old flower heads and unsightly old foliage to a few inches above the crown in midsummer to encourage fresh leaves to grow from the base. Cut back again in late fall. Propagate by division in spring or fall, or sow seed in spring.

LANDSCAPE USES: Quaking grass is good for edgings, rock gardens, and flower borders. It can also be useful as a groundcover for low-maintenance areas. The flowers are delightful in arrangements.

OTHER SPECIES:

B. maxima, big quaking grass, is an annual that grows 1–2 feet (30–60 cm) tall.

One of the most spectacular grasses, feather reed grass has an upright habit and stiff, narrow leaves that are evergreen in warm climates and deciduous in cold regions.

TYPE OF PLANT: Cool-season, clumping perennial grass.

BEST CLIMATE AND SITE: Zones 5–9. May not bloom well in hot climates. Tolerates most soil types, but prefers those that are moist and humus-rich. Full sun or light shade.

HEIGHT AND SPREAD: Height 18–24 inches (45–60 cm); spread to about 2 feet (60 cm). Flowering stems may rise to 6 feet (1.8 m) tall.

DESCRIPTION: Flowers appear in late spring or early summer on erect, tall spikes and consist of 1-foot (30 cm) long, pinkish green clusters that later become beige. Seed clusters form in July and last well into winter.

GROWING GUIDELINES: Set plants 2–3 feet (60–90 cm) apart in spring or fall (spring is best in Northern areas). Cut back by late winter. Divide in spring in cool climates and in spring or fall in warmer ones.

LANDSCAPE USES: Feather reed grass is an excellent tall accent plant. Its rich, golden, late-summer colors make spectacular screens or masses in backgrounds. Its flowering stems sway in the slightest breeze, adding movement to the garden.

CULTIVARS: 'Karl Foerster' is similar to *C. acutiflora* 'Stricta', feather reed grass, but blooms earlier with more fluffy inflorescence. It is also more compact.

Calamagrostis arundinacea var. *brachytricha*   Gramineae

FALL-BLOOMING REED GRASS

The purplish pink flower plumes of fall-blooming reed grass add a graceful touch to the late-season garden and last well into the winter months.

TYPE OF PLANT: Warm-season, clumping perennial grass.

BEST CLIMATE AND SITE: Zones 6–9. Grows well in most soil types, but prefers rich, moist sites. Full sun to light shade. In hot climates, light shade and extra moisture are beneficial.

HEIGHT AND SPREAD: Height to 3 feet (90 cm); spread to 3 feet (90 cm) or more. Flowering stems rise to 5 feet (1.5 m) tall.

DESCRIPTION: The rich green, deciduous foliage turns bright yellow in late summer. The tall, flowering stems are topped with 1-foot (30 cm) long, lavender-pink, foxtail-shaped flower spikes in late summer or early fall. The spikes turn golden tan when cold weather arrives and persist into winter.

GROWING GUIDELINES: Set plants 2–3 feet (60–90 cm) apart in spring or fall. Cut down by early spring. Propagate by division in spring or fall.

LANDSCAPE USES: Fall-blooming reed grass is attractive in groups or as single accents. For extra interest, combine it with late-season perennials, such as asters and goldenrods (*Solidago* spp.).

OTHER SPECIES:

C. nutkaensis, Pacific reed grass, grows 2–3 feet (60–90 cm) tall. Its purplish flowers bloom on 3–4-foot (90–120 cm) stems. It is a good grass for wet coastal areas and for erosion control, but it is susceptible to rust in wet weather. Zones 8–10.

Carex elata 'Bowles Golden'   Cyperaceae

'BOWLES GOLDEN' SEDGE

Grow 'Bowles Golden' sedge as an accent plant, or use it in masses near a pond, water garden, or quiet stream that reflects the bright color.

TYPE OF PLANT: Clump-forming sedge.

BEST CLIMATE AND SITE: Zones 5–9. Acid soil, always moist or in very shallow water. Half day of sun or light, all-day shade.

HEIGHT AND SPREAD: Height to 2 feet (60 cm); spread 2–5 feet (60–150 cm).

DESCRIPTION: This outstanding foliage plant has bright, golden, semi-evergreen leaves with green edges. Brownish flowers appear in late spring.

GROWING GUIDELINES: Set plants 2–3 feet (60–90 cm) apart in spring in wet spots or even in shallow water up to 4 inches (10 cm) deep. Plants prefer acid soil, so avoid using lime or wood ashes around them. Remove brown leaves as needed. Propagate by division in spring.

LANDSCAPE USES: 'Bowles Golden' sedge is effective as single accents in water or bog gardens.

OTHER SPECIES: Many other garden-worthy sedges are available; here are a few of the best.

C. comans 'Bronze', bronze New Zealand hair sedge, has fine, brownish white foliage. Height 1–6 feet (30–180 cm). Zones 7–9.

C. glauca, blue sedge, is a good blue-toned groundcover that forms a low-growing, 6-inch (15 cm) tall mat. Zones 5–9.

C. morrowii 'Variegata', silver-variegated Japanese sedge, grows well in shade and wet meadows. Height 1 foot (30 cm). Zones 5–9.

NORTHERN SEA OATS

JOB'S TEARS

Northern sea oats adapt to either sunny or shady sites. The flattened seed heads dangle from the stem tips starting in summer and lasting into winter.

TYPE OF PLANT: Warm-season, clumping perennial grass.

BEST CLIMATE AND SITE: Zones 5–9. Moist soil rich in humus. Full sun; prefers partial shade in warm climates. Quite salt-tolerant.

HEIGHT: Height 2–3 feet (60–90 cm) in leaf and flower; clumps expand quickly to 2 feet (60 cm) and then spread slowly.

DESCRIPTION: The stems of this native American grass are covered with bamboo-like, light green foliage that becomes coppery in fall and brown in winter. Flat, green flower spikes appear in summer on stem tips that droop from the weight. The seed heads turn copper-colored in fall and last into winter. Northern sea oats are also commonly known as wild oats.

GROWING GUIDELINES: Set plants 2 feet (60 cm) apart in spring. Cut back dead foliage in early spring or fall to prevent self-sown seedlings, which can be prolific. Propagate by seed, by transplanting self-sown seedlings, or by division in spring.

LANDSCAPE USES: Attractive flowers and foliage make this grass a fine choice for planting as an accent or in masses, especially in moist, lightly shaded spots. Northern sea oats also grow well in containers, and they are excellent in fresh or dried arrangements.

Job's tears is grown for its hard, bead-like seeds. It is perennial in very warm climates, but it will grow as an annual in the rest of the United States.

TYPE OF PLANT: Warm-season, clumping, tender perennial grass.

BEST CLIMATE AND SITE: Zones 9–10; grows as an annual in colder climates. Moist to wet, rich soil. Full sun.

HEIGHT AND SPREAD: Height to 6 feet (1.8 m); clumps to about 2 feet (60 cm) wide.

DESCRIPTION: Job's tears is probably one of the first grasses ever grown as an ornamental. Its hard seeds were once used as beads in necklaces and rosaries. Coarse, shiny, upright leaves to 12 inches (30 cm) long surround the stems. Flowers are short, gray tassels that appear in midsummer. The $1/4$-inch (6 mm), light green seeds turn white or black and drop when ripe.

GROWING GUIDELINES: Plant seed indoors in late winter or outdoors in late spring after soaking for 24 hours for better sprouting. Job's tears is extremely sensitive to cold, so wait until after the last frost date to set out seedlings 2 feet (60 cm) apart. Water during dry spells to keep the soil evenly moist.

LANDSCAPE USES: Job's tears makes a good living screen in warm climates. In most areas, it is grown as an accent plant in cutting gardens or vegetable gardens for its ornamental seeds.

Cortaderia selloana   Gramineae

PAMPAS GRASS

Pampas grass is one of the showiest and most popular ornamental grasses where it is hardy. Wear long sleeves, long pants, and gloves when working around the sharp leaves.

TYPE OF PLANT: Warm-season, clumping perennial grass.

BEST CLIMATE AND SITE: Zones 8–10. Fertile, well-drained soil. Prefers full sun; takes light shade.

HEIGHT AND SPREAD: Height 5–12 feet (1.5–3.6 m); spread to 12 feet (3.6 m). Flowering stems may be 8–15 feet (2.4–4.5 m) tall.

DESCRIPTION: Plants form neat clumps of sharp-edged leaves that are usually deciduous in fall. Spectacular, plume-like, 1–3-foot (30–90 cm) flower heads, either white or pink, rise on tall spikes in midsummer and last until late fall.

GROWING GUIDELINES: Set plants 5–8 feet (1.5–2.4 m) apart in spring in a spot where each can reach its huge, full beauty without being crowded. They tolerate dry soil but do better with adequate moisture, so you may want to water the clumps during dry spells. Cut back the foliage every year or two in early spring. Propagate plants by division in spring. Some plants sold as _C. selloana_ are actually weedy relatives (like _C. jubata_), which reseed prolifically and spread aggressively into native plantings. Look for cultivars of _C. selloana,_ or buy the species from a reputable nursery to be sure you're getting the right plant.

LANDSCAPE USES: Plants make dramatic tall screens or backgrounds and elegant single specimens. The plumes are wonderful as cut flowers.

Deschampsia caespitosa   Gramineae

TUFTED HAIRGRASS

Tufted hairgrass is one of the earliest grasses to bloom in spring. The flowers change from green to gold to bronze as they age. This grass combines well with ferns.

TYPE OF PLANT: Cool-season, tufted perennial grass.

BEST CLIMATE AND SITE: Zones 4–9. Grows best in cool climates. Moist, well-drained, fertile soil. Prefers partial shade.

HEIGHT AND SPREAD: Height to about 2 feet (60 cm); spread to 2 feet (60 cm) or more. Flowering stems grow to 3 feet (90 cm) tall.

DESCRIPTION: Tufted hairgrass forms mounds of narrow, deep green foliage. The leaves are evergreen in Zones 8–9 but turn brown over winter in cool climates. Airy flower clusters 20 inches (50 cm) long and 8 inches (20 cm) wide rise on long stems above the foliage.

GROWING GUIDELINES: Set plants 2–3 feet (60–90 cm) apart in spring or fall. Cut off flowers before seeds form to control spreading. Cut down dead foliage in winter. Seedlings vary in color and form, so propagate by division in spring or fall.

LANDSCAPE USES: The attractive blooms make an excellent early accent in the flower border. Tufted hairgrass is also good for meadow plantings and groundcovers, especially in damp areas bordering streams and ponds.

OTHER SPECIES:

D. flexuosa, crinkled hairgrass, has evergreen foliage and shiny flower clusters in June that turn yellowish brown. Best in areas with cool summers and acid soil. Height to 2 feet (60 cm). Zones 4–8.

BLUE LYME GRASS

RAVENNA GRASS

Blue lyme grass has fast-spreading rhizomes that can form large colonies in fertile soil. It is drought-tolerant, but regular watering will keep the plant looking its best.

TYPE OF PLANT: Cool-season, spreading perennial grass.

BEST CLIMATE AND SITE: Zones 4–9. Adapts to many different soil types as long as it has good drainage; grows well on sand dunes. Full sun or light shade.

HEIGHT AND SPREAD: Height 1–3 feet (30–90 cm); spreads quickly to 2 feet (60 cm), then grows more slowly.

DESCRIPTION: Blue lyme grass forms masses of metallic blue leaves that have an arching habit. The foliage usually turns yellow to tan over winter in cool climates; in warm areas, plants may grow year-round. The inconspicuous blue-gray flowers bloom erratically throughout summer and turn beige in fall.

GROWING GUIDELINES: Set plants 2 feet (60 cm) apart in spring or early fall. If you need to keep blue lyme grass under control, plant it in bottomless buckets sunken into the soil or grow it in containers. If foliage looks tattered in midsummer, cut it back to the ground to stimulate dense, colorful new growth. In cool climates, cut down discolored foliage in winter. Propagate by dividing the plants in spring.

LANDSCAPE USES: Plant this garden favorite as a dramatic specimen in flower beds, borders, and containers, where its blue foliage combines well with many flower colors. It is also a handsome choice for edging ponds and streams.

Enormous and vigorous, ravenna grass resembles pampas grass (Cortaderia selloana) but is more cold-hardy. The flowers and leaves are attractive in arrangements.

TYPE OF PLANT: Warm-season, clumping perennial grass.

BEST CLIMATE AND SITE: Zones 5–10. Well-drained, moist, fertile soil. Full sun.

HEIGHT AND SPREAD: Height of foliage to 5 feet (1.5 m); spread 3–5 feet (90–150 cm). The flower spikes bloom on 8–12-foot (2.4–3.6 m) tall stalks.

DESCRIPTION: Silky, silvery flowers with purple tones appear on tall spikes in early fall. They turn cream-colored and last into winter. The gray-green foliage changes to orange, rust, and purple in fall.

GROWING GUIDELINES: Set plants 3–5 feet (90–150 cm) apart in spring. Ravenna grass tolerates dry conditions once established, but regular watering during dry spells will keep the foliage looking respectable. The flower spikes may break in strong winds; stake plants or avoid watering to encourage shorter, stronger stems. Plants may not bloom in very cold climates; in warm climates, they may self-sow prolifically. Cut back dead leaves and stems by late winter. Propagate by seed or divide clumps in early spring.

LANDSCAPE USES: Grow ravenna grass in masses, as a tall screen, or as a specimen in large gardens.

OTHER SPECIES:

E. strictus, narrow plume grass, has excellent fall color and is especially effective near ponds and streams. Zones 5–9.

Festuca cinerea　　　　　Gramineae

BLUE FESCUE

The leaf color of blue fescue can range from dark green to bright blue, depending on the cultivar. Most plants will produce spiky clumps of blue-gray foliage.

TYPE OF PLANT: Cool-season, clumping perennial grass.

BEST CLIMATE AND SITE: Zones 4–9. Moist, well-drained soil. Full sun; light shade in hot climates. Plants are drought-resistant but grow poorly in hot, humid conditions.

HEIGHT AND SPREAD: Height 8–12 inches (20–30 cm); clumps spread to 2 feet (60 cm).

DESCRIPTION: Blue fescue is noted for its rounded mounds of beautiful silver-blue, spiky, evergreen foliage. The gray-green flowers are not especially noteworthy. Blue fescue is also sold as *F. glauca, F. ovina,* and *F. ovina* 'Glauca'.

GROWING GUIDELINES: Set plants 1–2 feet (30–60 cm) apart in spring or fall. Cut back in early spring or fall to promote tidy, new growth. Individual plants are short-lived; divide and replant every 2–3 years to keep plants looking their best. Blue fescue may self-sow readily, and the seedlings may range in color from blue to green; clipping off the flower spikes can prevent reseeding. Start species plants from seed or division and cultivars by division in early spring.

LANDSCAPE USES: The showy foliage color and interesting texture make blue fescues attractive accent plants for borders and rock gardens. They are also useful as edgings, groundcovers, container plants, and seaside plantings.

Hakonechloa macra 'Aureola'　　　Gramineae

VARIEGATED HAKONE GRASS

Variegated hakone grass forms slow-spreading clumps of elegant, bamboo-like leaves. The yellow-striped foliage takes on pink or reddish tints in fall.

TYPE OF PLANT: Warm-season, slow-spreading perennial grass.

BEST CLIMATE AND SITE: Zones 6–9. Moist, well-drained, fertile soil. Light shade.

HEIGHT AND SPREAD: Height 18–24 inches (45–60 cm); spread to 2 feet (60 cm) or more.

DESCRIPTION: Variegated hakone grass is a well-behaved, low-growing, arching, deciduous grass. Its star feature is its soft, bright yellow, bamboo-like leaves that are striped with green in summer and reddish in fall. Clumps get larger with age but are not invasive. Inconspicuous flowers bloom in late summer.

GROWING GUIDELINES: Set plants 2 feet (60 cm) or more apart in spring or early fall. Keep them out of full sun, and water during dry spells to keep the soil evenly moist at all times. Propagate by division in spring.

LANDSCAPE USES: This handsome grass is lovely either as a single specimen plant or massed in a shady spot. It is good for edgings, in containers, and as groundcover under trees. It is a favorite for oriental gardens because of its bamboo-like appearance.

OTHER SPECIES:

H. macra, hakone grass, has light green leaves. It is an attractive border plant and more vigorous in areas with hot summers than 'Aureola'. One of the best groundcover grasses. Zones 7–9.

BLUE OAT GRASS

Blue oat grass is one of the most beautiful blue-leaved species for gardens in cool, dry climates. It tends to grow poorly in areas with hot, humid summers.

TYPE OF PLANT: Cool-season, clumping perennial grass.

BEST CLIMATE AND SITE: Zones 5–8. Well-drained, fertile, not-too-acid soil. Full sun or partial shade.

HEIGHT AND SPREAD: Height 20–24 inches (50–60 cm); spread to 20 inches (50 cm). Flowers grow on 3–4-foot (90–120 cm) tall stems.

DESCRIPTION: Blue oat grass has attractive, blue, narrow, pointed leaves that are evergreen (or semi-evergreen in cool climates). Oat-like, bluish white flowers rise on long stems in early summer and later turn golden.

GROWING GUIDELINES: Set plants out in spring or late summer at least 2 feet (60 cm) apart. Blue oat grass can stand some dryness once established, but plants don't thrive in hot, humid climates and may get root rot in poorly drained soil. Cut back to about 3 inches (7.5 cm) in early spring to keep plants neat. Rust may be a problem if the plants get too much shade. Propagate by seed or division in spring.

LANDSCAPE USES: The striking blue foliage makes blue oat grasses beautiful accent plants in rock gardens or flower borders. They are also effective when planted in masses.

VELVET GRASS

Velvet grass forms a low, dense, spreading clump that can become invasive. Give it room to creep, or plant it in a bottomless pot sunken in the soil to control the spread.

TYPE OF PLANT: Cool-season, spreading perennial grass.

BEST CLIMATE AND SITE: Zones 5–9; grows best in cool climates. Moist, fertile, well-drained soil. Full sun or partial shade.

HEIGHT AND SPREAD: Height 1–2 feet (30–60 cm); spread 2 feet (60 cm). Flowering stems 2–3 feet (60–90 cm) tall.

DESCRIPTION: Velvet grass is distinguished by its soft, gray-green, semi-evergreen leaves. Spikes of pretty white flowers rise above the leaves and bloom for most of the summer. In warm areas, velvet grass often goes dormant in summer.

GROWING GUIDELINES: Set plants 2 feet (60 cm) or more apart in spring or fall. Water plants in dry weather to keep them growing actively, or let them go dormant and cut back browned leaves. Velvet grass is susceptible to rust, which may be difficult to control; remove infected leaves as you see them. Propagate by seed or division in spring or fall.

LANDSCAPE USES: Velvet grass is useful as a meadow grass or groundcover. It looks especially nice with spring bulbs. It also is a fairly good lawn grass where foot traffic is light. When crowded into flower beds and borders, velvet grass tends to sprawl and crowd other plants.

CULTIVARS: 'Variegatus', variegated velvet grass, grows only 8 inches (20 cm) tall.

Hystrix patula Gramineae

BOTTLEBRUSH GRASS

Bottlebrush grass is a charming native grass for shady gardens. Enjoy the flowers in the garden through the summer, or pick them before they open for arrangements.

TYPE OF PLANT: Cool-season, clumping perennial grass.

BEST CLIMATE AND SITE: Zones 5–9. Moist, well-drained, fertile soil. Full sun (with moisture) to light shade.

HEIGHT AND SPREAD: Height 1–2 feet (30–60 cm); spread to 1 foot (30 cm). Flowering stems 2–4 feet (60–90 cm) tall.

DESCRIPTION: Bottlebrush grass is grown for its brushy spikes of greenish flowers that rise above hummocks of dark green foliage. It blooms throughout the summer; the seed heads turn brown and fall apart in early fall.

GROWING GUIDELINES: Bottlebrush grass grows poorly in dry, sunny locations, so set plants in moist soil 1–2 feet (30–60 cm) apart. It self-sows easily, so plant where reseeding isn't a problem. Cut back in fall or early spring. Propagate by seed or division in spring or fall.

LANDSCAPE USES: Bottlebrush grass is a good accent plant for lightly shaded borders. It is especially attractive in woodlands and shady meadow gardens. If cut before they open, the flower spikes are interesting in arrangements.

Imperata cylindrica 'Red Baron' Gramineae

'RED BARON' BLOOD GRASS

If possible, site 'Red Baron' blood grass where the morning or late afternoon sun can shine through it; backlighting can really make the red color glow.

TYPE OF PLANT: Warm-season, slow-spreading perennial grass.

BEST CLIMATE AND SITE: Zones 6–9. Fertile, moist, well-drained soil. Full sun; partial shade in hot climates.

HEIGHT AND SPREAD: Height 12–18 inches (30–45 cm); spread to 2 feet (60 cm).

DESCRIPTION: This Japanese grass has spectacular foliage, especially in spring and fall. It starts green with red tips in spring but gradually becomes more red; by summer's end, it is deep blood red. The leaves turn copper in late fall, and the color endures throughout winter. Unlike the species, the cultivar 'Red Baron' does not flower, so it does not set seed and is not invasive.

GROWING GUIDELINES: Set plants 1–2 feet (30–60 cm) apart in spring or early fall. Red color is best in full sun, except in hot climates, where plants need partial shade during the heat of the day. Blood grass tolerates drought, but watering during dry spells will prevent leaf tips from turning brown. Propagate in spring by division.

LANDSCAPE USES: Blood grass is dramatic as a mass planting. It also adds a colorful touch to flower borders or containers. Blood grass makes a unique background for a low border.

Juncus effusus   Juncaceae

SOFT RUSH

Soft rush grows in stiff, upright clumps and thrives in wet soil and shallow water. The foliage is evergreen in most areas; it may turn brownish in cold-winter climates.

TYPE OF PLANT: Clump-forming rush.

BEST CLIMATE AND SITE: Zones 5–9. Moist soil to shallow water. Partial shade.

HEIGHT AND SPREAD: Height 2–3 feet (60–90 cm); spread to 2 feet (60 cm) or more.

DESCRIPTION: Soft rush forms distinct clumps of spiky, dark green stems. Flowers appear in early summer and last until fall. Plants are evergreen in warm climates; in cool areas, the foliage turns brown in winter.

GROWING GUIDELINES: Set plants 2–3 feet (60–90 cm) apart in spring or early fall in wet locations. Cut back foliage in late summer if it becomes unsightly. Plant seed or divide in spring.

LANDSCAPE USES: Soft rush is useful in masses or as accent plants along streams, bog gardens, and water gardens—wherever the soil stays moist. Soft rush naturalizes easily in low-maintenance areas.

CULTIVARS: 'Spiralis', corkscrew rush, is a garden novelty with unusual, highly twisted foliage.

Koeleria glauca   Gramineae

LARGE BLUE HAIRGRASS

Large blue hairgrass is a short-lived perennial that tends to die out in the center as it ages. Divide and replant clumps every 2 or 3 years to keep them vigorous.

TYPE OF PLANT: Cool-season, clumping grass.

BEST CLIMATE AND SITE: Zones 6–9; can survive in colder areas with dependable winter snow cover. Well-drained, somewhat alkaline soil with average fertility. Full sun.

HEIGHT AND SPREAD: Height 6–12 inches (15–30 cm) for leaves; similar spread. Flowering stems to 18 inches (45 cm) tall.

DESCRIPTION: The narrow, flat, blue-green leaves grow upright in tight clumps. Striking blue-green flower clusters rise above the foliage in late spring; they later change to a buff color.

GROWING GUIDELINES: Set plants 1 foot (30 cm) apart in spring or early fall. Cut back leaves and flower stems in midsummer to encourage new growth. Propagate by seed in spring or division in spring or fall.

LANDSCAPE USES: Single specimens are good accent plants in the front of borders. In groups they make effective edgings and good companion plants for low-growing evergreens. Large blue hairgrass is also an interesting pot plant for a terrace or deck. The flowers are beautiful in arrangements.

OTHER SPECIES:

K. macrantha, June grass, height 18 inches (45 cm); thrives in dry, rocky soil and has blue-green foliage with glossy green flowers in early summer. Goes dormant early. Zones 4–9.

Luzula nivea   Juncaceae

SNOWY WOODRUSH

Grow snowy woodrush with ferns for an easy-care planting beneath trees. It also makes a wonderful companion for crocuses and other spring bulbs.

TYPE OF PLANT: Tufted but spreading perennial rush.

BEST CLIMATE AND SITE: Zones 4–9. Not fussy, but does best in moist, humus-rich soil. Tolerates full sun in cool climates; needs light shade in warm regions.

HEIGHT AND SPREAD: Height 9–12 inches (22–30 cm); spread to 12 inches (30 cm). Flowering stems to 2 feet (60 cm) tall.

DESCRIPTION: Among the best of the woodrushes, snowy woodrush has gray-green, grass-like, usually evergreen leaves covered with soft, white hairs. In spring, creamy white flowers stand in rounded clusters above the foliage clump; they dry later to brownish tan.

GROWING GUIDELINES: Set plants 1 foot (30 cm) apart in spring or late summer. Cut back leaves in winter if they turn brown. Propagate by division in spring.

LANDSCAPE USES: Snowy woodrush is an attractive groundcover in light shade. Or use it as a flowering accent in spring for the front of the border. Flowers dry well for winter arrangements.

OTHER SPECIES:

L. sylvatica, greater woodrush, height to 18 inches (45 cm). Does well in dry or wet shade, especially in woodland plantings. Glossy, evergreen leaves with white hairs. Yellowish flowers in early spring change later to brown. Zones 5–9.

Milium effusum 'Aureum'   Gramineae

GOLDEN WOOD MILLET

Golden wood millet is a shade-loving perennial grass grown for its yellow flowers and yellow leaves. It is especially eye-catching in large clumps or masses.

TYPE OF PLANT: Cool-season, clumping perennial grass.

BEST CLIMATE AND SITE: Zones 6–9. Moist, fertile soil. Light shade.

HEIGHT AND SPREAD: Height 6–18 inches (15–45 cm) in leaf; spread to 2 feet (60 cm). Flowers on stems to 2 feet (60 cm) tall.

DESCRIPTION: In spring, open, airy clusters of golden yellow flowers bloom above loose clumps of arching, evergreen leaves. The leaves are bright yellow in spring and later fade to greenish yellow.

GROWING GUIDELINES: Set plants 1–1 1/2 feet (30–45 cm) apart in spring or late summer. Golden wood millet enjoys cool spots, so provide additional shade and moisture in hot climates. Cut off flower heads before seeds form so they won't produce seedlings. Propagate by division in spring.

LANDSCAPE USES: Golden foliage and blooms make this plant an effective, captivating accent in the shady border. It's also good for rock gardens or in shady spots combined with ferns, hostas, and other shade-loving perennials. The flowers are excellent in both fresh and dried arrangements.

JAPANESE SILVER GRASS

Japanese silver grass, also commonly called eulalia grass, is one of the best large ornamental grasses. It is especially attractive near streams and ponds.

*Maiden grass (***M.** sinensis 'Gracillimus') *is popular for its narrow leaves and graceful arching habit. Coppery flower heads appear above the foliage in fall.*

TYPE OF PLANT: Warm-season, clumping perennial grass.

BEST CLIMATE AND SITE: Zones 5–9. Light, moist, humus-rich soil. Full sun.

HEIGHT AND SPREAD: Height 3–5 feet (90–150 cm) for foliage; spread to 3 feet (90 cm) or more. Flowering stems can grow 6–10 feet (1.8–3 m) tall.

DESCRIPTION: Large clumps of long, pointed, sharp-edged leaves show a silvery color in early summer; later they turn beautiful fall reds, yellows, rusts, and browns. Decorative flower plumes in hues from silver to reddish purple bloom above the foliage from midsummer through early fall.

GROWING GUIDELINES: There are many cultivars of *M. sinensis,* and their cultural requirements differ somewhat. Check the catalog description or plant label for specific information. In general, set plants 2–4 feet (60–120 cm) apart in spring. Provide light shade and extra water in hot climates. Stake the tall, floppy kinds if necessary, and divide in spring when the plant clumps begin to die in the center. Most cultivars are pest-resistant, but some are susceptible to mealybugs and rust, although neither problem usually becomes serious. Propagate the species by seed or division, and propagate cultivars by spring division only.

LANDSCAPE USES: The large cultivars are excellent for screens, hedges, and background plantings, especially in large gardens. Choose compact cultivars for accenting flower beds and borders. Combine the grass with asters, goldenrods (*Solidago* spp.), and other fall-blooming perennials to create a stunning fall show.

CULTIVARS: 'Autumn Light', height to 10 feet (3 m), is hardy and late-blooming. 'Cabaret', height to 6 feet (1.8 m), has wide, green leaves with white stripes in the center; the flowers bloom pink in September, then become cream-colored. 'Gracillimus', maiden grass, height to 6 feet (1.8 m), is a popular, upright grower with narrow, silvery leaves that turn buff or orange in fall. 'Morning Light', one of the best cultivars, grows to 4 feet (1.2 m) with narrow, white-edged leaves and reddish bronze fall flowers that later turn to a cream color. 'Purpurascens', flame grass, height to 4 feet (1.2 m), has green leaves with a reddish tint that later becomes bright orange, then reddish brown; Zones 7–8. 'Silberfeder', Japanese silver grass, height to 7 feet (2.1 m), has gorgeous silvery flowers. The variety 'Strictus', porcupine grass, height to 6 feet (1.8 m), has coppery flowers in fall and stiff green leaves that are banded with yellow; Zones 4–9. 'Zebrinus', zebra grass, is similar but has a more open, arching form.

Molinia caerulea   Gramineae

PURPLE MOOR GRASS

The old foliage of purple moor grass disappears nicely by itself in fall by breaking off at the base of the stems. The flowers are excellent in fresh or dried arrangements.

TYPE OF PLANT: Warm-season, clumping perennial grass.

BEST CLIMATE AND SITE: Zones 4–9. Moist, fertile, acid soil. Full sun; tolerates light shade.

HEIGHT AND SPREAD: Height to 1 foot (30 cm); similar spread. Flowering stems grow to 2 feet (60 cm) tall.

DESCRIPTION: Purple moor grass produces mounds of arching, narrow, light green leaves. Yellow or purple, spiky blooms appear in midsummer on stems above the foliage; the seed heads become wheat-colored as they mature.

GROWING GUIDELINES: Set plants 2 feet (60 cm) apart in spring. Cut back any remaining foliage in winter. Propagate by division or seed in early spring.

LANDSCAPE USES: Purple moor grass is a good accent plant, especially for fall color. It tolerates coastal locations, so try it in seaside gardens.

CULTIVARS: 'Variegata', variegated moor grass, has showy, yellow-striped, 12–18-inch (30–45 cm) leaves. Purplish green flowers bloom 12 inches (30 cm) above the leaves. This is an excellent small plant for accenting borders or as an edging.

OTHER SPECIES:
M. caerulea subsp. *arundinacea* has larger leaves and taller flowers, both of which turn golden yellow in fall. Height 2–3 feet (60–90 cm). Zones 4–9.

Panicum virgatum   Gramineae

SWITCH GRASS

Switch grass is a versatile native species that adapts to many different growing conditions. It is excellent for naturalizing and erosion control as well as for gardens.

TYPE OF PLANT: Warm-season, clumping perennial grass.

BEST CLIMATE AND SITE: Zones 5–9. Prefers fertile, moist conditions but tolerates many soil types from dry seashores to wet bogs. Full sun; tolerates light shade.

HEIGHT AND SPREAD: Height of foliage to about 3 feet (90 cm); spread 3–5 feet (90–150 cm). Flowering stems grow 4–8 feet (1.2–2.4 m) tall.

DESCRIPTION: Switch grass forms clusters of pinkish to buff-brown, feathery flowers in midsummer. The flowers bloom on tall stems over clumps of long, deep green, narrow, deciduous leaves. In fall, the flowers turn brown and foliage turns beige.

GROWING GUIDELINES: Set plants 3–5 feet (90–150 cm) apart in spring or fall. Cut leaves and stems back by early spring. Propagate by division in spring.

LANDSCAPE USES: Switch grass is a good accent plant in the garden. It tolerates damp soil, so it's useful beside streams and in moist areas. Both the foliage and flowers are excellent in arrangements.

CULTIVARS: 'Haense Herms', red switch grass, height to 3 feet (90 cm) in leaf and to 4 feet (1.2 m) in flower. It is more compact and upright-growing than the species, with a bright, fiery, orange color in fall. 'Heavy Metal', height to 3 feet (90 cm), has stiff, metallic blue leaves in a tight, upright clump.

Pennisetum alopecuroides   Gramineae

FOUNTAIN GRASS

Fountain grass is one of the most beautiful and adaptable of all ornamental grasses. The showy seed heads cascade, like a fountain, over mounds of glossy green leaves.

TYPE OF PLANT: Warm-season, clumping perennial grass.

BEST CLIMATE AND SITE: Zones 5–9. Prefers fertile, moist, well-drained soil but adapts well to other soil types. Full sun; tolerates light shade.

HEIGHT AND SPREAD: Height of foliage to 3 feet (90 cm); similar spread. Flowering stems grow to 4 feet (1.2 m) tall.

DESCRIPTION: Fountain grass blooms in midsummer, with creamy white to pinkish flowers in 4–10-inch (10–25 cm) long clusters shaped like little foxtails. The seed heads later turn reddish brown and remain until fall.

GROWING GUIDELINES: Set plants 2–3 feet (60–90 cm) apart in spring. Keep them watered in dry weather for best growth. Cut off seed heads in fall to keep them from spreading their seeds throughout the garden. Cut back dead leaves by early spring. Propagate the species by division or seed and cultivars by spring division only.

LANDSCAPE USES: Fountain grasses are excellent single accent plants in borders. Try them in foundation plantings, or grow them in drifts as a groundcover. Fountain grasses are a good choice for coastal plantings, too, since they tolerate wind.

CULTIVARS: 'Hameln' is a compact form that grows 2–3 feet (60–90 cm) tall. Ideal for small gardens in Zones 6–8.

Phalaris arundinacea var. _picta_   Gramineae

WHITE-STRIPED RIBBON GRASS

White-striped ribbon grass can be invasive. Grow it where its creeping habit isn't a problem, or plant it in a bottomless bucket sunken into the soil to control the spread.

TYPE OF PLANT: Warm-season, spreading perennial grass.

BEST CLIMATE AND SITE: Zones 4–9. Wide range of soil types, but does best in moist, fertile soil. Light shade.

HEIGHT AND SPREAD: Height 2–3 feet (60–90 cm); spread unlimited. Flowering stems grow to 4 feet (1.2 m) tall.

DESCRIPTION: Grow white-striped ribbon grass for the white-striped foliage that gives it the amusing common name gardener's garters. The flowers are pretty white spikes in early summer. In fall, leaves turn buff-colored.

GROWING GUIDELINES: For groundcover, set plants 1–2 feet (30–60 cm) apart in spring. For other uses, one plant is probably all you need, as this grass spreads rapidly by rhizomes (underground runners). Leaves may turn brown in hot sun. Cut back sprawling plants in summer to stimulate dense, new growth. Weed out all-green shoots. Propagate by division in spring.

LANDSCAPE USES: White-striped ribbon grass is an excellent spreading groundcover. It's helpful for erosion control where other plants won't grow well. It will grow in shallow water up to 4 inches (10 cm) deep, so it is good for pond edging.

CULTIVARS: 'Feesey's Form' has handsome, white-striped foliage touched with pink.

Schizachyrium scoparium   Gramineae

LITTLE BLUESTEM

Little bluestem is a good groundcover for large areas, for erosion control on dry slopes, and for naturalizing in meadows— wherever its reseeding habit isn't a problem.

TYPE OF PLANT: Warm-season, clumping perennial grass.

BEST CLIMATE AND SITE: Zones 3–10. Any soil that is not soggy. Full sun.

HEIGHT AND SPREAD: Height of foliage to about 1 foot (30 cm); spread to about 1 foot (30 cm). Flowering stems grow to 3 feet (90 cm) tall.

DESCRIPTION: This common North American native has light green, somewhat hairy, deciduous leaves. The plant is not especially showy in summer, but the cool temperatures of fall transform its green leaves into shades of copper and bright orange. Spiky flowers in midsummer become attractive seed clusters in fall.

GROWING GUIDELINES: Plant about 2 feet (60 cm) apart in spring. Cut back dead leaves and stems by early spring. Propagate by seed or divide the clumps in spring.

LANDSCAPE USES: Little bluestem can make a fine accent plant in the border if you remove the seed heads by late summer to prevent reseeding. The flowers and foliage are handsome in arrangements.

CULTIVARS: 'Blaze' has bright fall colors ranging from orange-pink to purple, and it holds the color all winter.

Sorghastrum nutans   Gramineae

INDIAN GRASS

One of the most handsome North American native grasses, Indian grass once covered the prairies. Grow it for its feathery flower clusters and showy fall color.

TYPE OF PLANT: Warm-season, clumping perennial grass.

BEST CLIMATE AND SITE: Zones 4–9. Prefers deep, rich, loamy, moist soil; tolerates drought once established. Full sun; tolerates light shade.

HEIGHT AND SPREAD: Height of foliage to 3 feet (90 cm); spread to 2 feet (60 cm). Flowering stems grow to 6 feet (1.8 m) tall.

DESCRIPTION: Neat clumps of light green to nearly blue foliage turn yellow, then burnt orange in fall and stay attractive into winter. The 12-inch (30 cm), feathery flower clusters bloom in late summer in rosy shades that later turn gold and orange.

GROWING GUIDELINES: Set plants 2 feet (60 cm) apart in spring. Cut back by early spring. Propagate by collecting and spreading seed or by dividing plants in spring.

LANDSCAPE USES: Indian grass is excellent for mass plantings, naturalizing, and as a groundcover on slopes for erosion control. It will reseed prolifically in moist areas. If you cut off the flower heads in early fall (to prevent reseeding), Indian grass makes a good accent plant for late-season color in flower borders. The flowers are superb in fresh or dried arrangements.

CULTIVARS: 'Holt' blooms earlier than the species and has showy seed clusters and beautiful fall color. 'Sioux Blue' has blue-gray foliage and a more upright growth habit.

PRAIRIE CORD GRASS

FROST GRASS

Prairie cord grass is a beautiful background plant for flower beds and borders. It will spread in moist soil but is more restrained on dry sites.

TYPE OF PLANT: Warm-season, spreading perennial grass.

BEST CLIMATE AND SITE: Zones 4–9. Fertile, moist to wet soil, in fresh or salt water. Full sun to light shade.

HEIGHT AND SPREAD: Height 2–5 feet (60–150 cm); spread to 2 feet (60 cm) in dry areas or unlimited in moist sites. Flowering stems grow to 6 feet (1.8 m) tall.

DESCRIPTION: This deciduous, native grass has long, narrow, glossy, arching leaves. The leaves are light green to blue in summer; they turn bright yellow and dry to burnt orange in late fall. One-sided, beige, feathery flower clusters appear in mid-summer.

GROWING GUIDELINES: Set plants 3–4 feet (90–120 cm) apart in spring or fall. Cut back dead foliage in winter. Propagate by seed or division in spring.

LANDSCAPE USES: Prairie cord grass is ideal as an aggressive groundcover in marshy areas and for erosion control in windy coastal regions. Single specimens grow more slowly in dry borders and make good background plants.

CULTIVARS: 'Aureomarginata', variegated cord grass, has green leaves with thin gold edges. It is somewhat invasive but good for erosion control on the banks of streams and ponds.

Frost grass forms upright clumps of short, broad leaves that often turn reddish in fall. It grows well in shade but can adapt to full sun if the soil is evenly moist.

TYPE OF PLANT: Warm-season, clumping perennial grass.

BEST CLIMATE AND SITE: Zones 5–9. Well-drained, moist, fertile soil. Full sun to light shade; needs shade in warm climates.

HEIGHT AND SPREAD: Height 2–3 feet (60–90 cm); spread 2 feet (60 cm) or more. Flowering stems grow to 4 feet (1.2 m) tall.

DESCRIPTION: This upright-growing grass has bamboo-like, dark green, arching leaves that grow in compact clumps. Often tinged with red in late summer, the leaves turn deep wine red by fall. The 12-inch (30 cm), loose, purplish flower clusters rise in midsummer and later turn a wheat color; they are particularly striking when covered with frost. Frost grass is also known as graybeard grass.

GROWING GUIDELINES: Plant 2 feet (60 cm) apart in spring in a damp area. Cut back dead foliage in winter. Propagate by seed in spring or by division in spring or fall.

LANDSCAPE USES: Alone or in groups, frost grass is useful as a compact accent in flower borders. It is especially handsome in winter in climates where it doesn't get too cold or too hot.

Sporobolus heterolepis   Gramineae

PRAIRIE DROPSEED

Prairie dropseed is a drought-resistant grass that grows in fountains of narrow leaves. It takes a few years to reach full size, so buy large plants if you can find them.

TYPE OF PLANT: Clumping perennial grass with both warm-season and cold-season grass tendencies.

BEST CLIMATE AND SITE: Zones 3–9. Dry, rocky soil. Full sun.

HEIGHT AND SPREAD: Height to 1 foot (30 cm); spread to 2 feet (60 cm) or more. Flowering stems grow 2–3 feet (60–90 cm) tall.

DESCRIPTION: Prairie dropseed forms arching, bright green clumps that turn golden in fall and creamy brown by winter. Fragrant, 6-inch (15 cm), drooping flower clusters appear in mid- to late-summer and last through fall.

GROWING GUIDELINES: Set out plants 2 feet (60 cm) apart in spring or fall. Cut back dead foliage in winter. Propagate by seed or division in spring or fall.

LANDSCAPE USES: Prairie dropseed is an excellent groundcover for large, dry areas. It also is appealing as a single specimen in dry flower borders, where you can enjoy its light fragrance. The seeds attract birds.

OTHER SPECIES:

S. airoides, alkali dropseed, height 2–3 feet (60–90 cm). Has dense, gray-green clumps of leaves that turn yellowish, then straw-colored for winter. Clusters of pink flowers rise 2 feet (60 cm) above the foliage in June; they later turn golden and are effective until winter. This tough grass tolerates dry weather and many soil types. Zones 8–10.

Stipa gigantea   Gramineae

GIANT FEATHER GRASS

Giant feather grass is especially stunning where its handsome flower plumes are backlit by the morning or late afternoon sun. The seed heads remain showy until fall.

TYPE OF PLANT: Cool-season, clumping perennial grass.

BEST CLIMATE AND SITE: Zones 7–9. Well-drained, fertile soil. Established plants are somewhat drought-tolerant; must have excellent drainage wherever rainfall is heavy. Full sun.

HEIGHT AND SPREAD: Height of foliage to 2 feet (60 cm); clumps spread to 2 feet (60 cm) or more. Flowering stems grow to 5 feet (1.5 m).

DESCRIPTION: Giant feather grass forms dramatic clumps of arching, rolled, evergreen leaves. Golden flowers hang from tall stems that rise 2–3 feet (60–90 cm) above the gray-green foliage in late spring.

GROWING GUIDELINES: Set out plants 2–3 feet (60–90 cm) apart in spring or fall. If needed, cut back the foliage to about 6 inches (15 cm) by early spring. Propagate either by early-spring or fall division, which can be difficult with the tight-growing clumps, or by seed, which may take 3 months or more to germinate.

LANDSCAPE USES: Giant feather grass looks great in masses as a screen or singly as a dramatic, tall specimen. The cut flowers are captivating in fresh or dried arrangements.

OTHER SPECIES:

S. capillata, height to 2 feet (60 cm), with feathery blooms that grow 2 feet (60 cm) above the foliage in midsummer. Zones 6–9.

GARDENING WITH GROUNDCOVERS

In the broadest sense, just about any plant that spreads its leaves over the soil can be called a groundcover. From the tundra to the tropics, mosses, ferns, grasses, vines, flowers, shrubs, and trees spread over the planet, shielding the earth from erosion and building the soil as they decompose.

In gardening circles, however, the term "groundcover" is most often used to describe low, spreading plants—usually those that grow less than 2 feet (60 cm) tall. That still includes a wide range of plants, from spreading grasses and sedges to creeping perennials and suckering shrubs.

You'll find no end to the ways you can use these versatile plants in your yard. They'll help you reduce your lawn space or even replace a lawn to save money, work, and energy. In a dry, sunny climate, drought-tolerant species such as succulents are indispensable for creating a water-saving landscape; in damp areas, water-loving plants are just as handy to absorb water.

Some groundcovers attractively blanket steep banks to stop erosion and cover rough or rocky areas that are difficult to mow. Shade-lovers border woodland paths or cover low-light areas beneath trees and between buildings. Flat, creeping types fill in the gaps between paving stones and tumble attractively between the crevices in garden walls and steps. Fast-growing vines can quickly cover unsightly stumps, unattractive rocks, or debris you want to hide. Whatever the job, one groundcover or another can do it for you.

Apart from the practical benefits of these plants, the reason most gardeners plant groundcovers is because they add beauty to the landscape. They display interesting and handsome foliage shapes and textures and sometimes attractive flowers or berries as well. Many, such as creeping phlox (*Phlox stolonifera*) and rock cotoneaster (*Cotoneaster horizontalis*), also provide masses of glorious color. Others make a stunning undercarpeting for taller bulbs, perennials, shrubs, and trees. A combination of different groundcover plants can change your lawn from a bland, one-dimensional green carpet into a mosaic of interesting three-dimensional patterns and colors.

In this chapter, you'll learn the basics of selecting, planting, and growing groundcovers to accent all parts of your yard. "Landscaping with Groundcovers" on page 92 covers some of the many ways you can use these tough, adaptable plants to deal with challenging garden sites. "Choosing the Right Groundcovers" on page 96 explains how to pick the best plants for each particular spot. "Ferns in Your Garden" on page 98 highlights tips for landscaping with these lovely leafy species.

When you're ready to get started in the yard, read "Buying and Planting Groundcovers" on page 100 to get your new plants off to a good start. "Caring for Groundcovers" on page 102 tells how to follow through to keep the garden looking great. Once you've tried a few groundcovers, you'll probably want many more; "Propagating Groundcovers" on page 104 tells how to expand your plantings without draining your bank account. At the end of this chapter, starting on page 106, you'll find the "Guide to Groundcovers," a quick-reference encyclopedia for over 90 great groundcovering plants.

Just about any low-growing, spreading plant can make a great groundcover. Silvery lamb's-ears (*Stachys byzantina*) is commonly grown with other plants in borders, but it also looks super planted in masses.

Spotted lamium is a fast-spreading creeper with silver-striped leaves that brighten up shady spots.

Landscaping with Groundcovers

To many people, the word "groundcover" brings to mind boring beds of plain green ivy, periwinkle, or pachysandra. But with so many wonderful plants to choose from, groundcovers definitely don't need to be dull. Even with the most common ones, you can create pleasant, appealing plantings to beautify a garden setting or deal with a difficult site.

Choosing Groundcovers for Garden Challenges

Well-chosen groundcovers are among the most versatile and easy-care garden plants you can grow. Unlike lawn grasses, groundcovers don't need much regular maintenance: Just plant them, weed or mulch a few times for the first year or two, and then let the plants do the work. The individual entries in the "Guide to Groundcovers," starting on page 106, will tell you which conditions each plant is best suited to handle. Following you'll find in-depth information on using groundcovers to solve three of the most troublesome garden challenges: shade, slopes, and wet spots.

Groundcovers for Shady Sites Shady plantings are natural choices for woodlands and forests, but they

Made for the Shade

Many leafy and flowering groundcovers adapt well to life in less-than-ideal light. If you have a spot that gets plenty of filtered light but no direct sun, try some of the species listed below. For more information on any of these plants, look them up in the "Guide to Groundcovers," starting on page 106. Ferns are also naturals for shady sites: see "Ferns in Your Garden" on page 98 for details.

Aegopodium podagraria 'Variegata' (variegated bishop's weed)

Ajuga reptans (ajuga)

Asarum europaeum (European ginger)

Astilbe chinensis var. *pumila* (Chinese astilbe)

Euonymus fortunei (wintercreeper)

Galium odoratum (sweet woodruff)

Hedera helix (English ivy)

Hosta hybrids (hostas)

Lamium maculatum (spotted lamium)

Liriope spicata (creeping lilyturf)

Pachysandra procumbens (Allegheny pachysandra)

Pachysandra terminalis (Japanese pachysandra)

Saxifraga stolonifera (strawberry geranium)

Tiarella cordifolia (Allegheny foamflower)

Tolmeia menziesii (piggyback plant)

Vancouveria hexandra (American barrenwort)

Vinca minor (common periwinkle)

Waldsteinia fragarioides (barren strawberry)

are, of course, not limited to those spots. Sunlight is also scarce on the north side of buildings, between buildings, beneath lawn trees, and behind tall hedges, fences, or garden walls. It is difficult to grow many flowering plants and evergreens in these spots, but shade-loving groundcovers are ideal there. Japanese pachysandra (*Pachysandra terminalis*) and common periwinkle (*Vinca minor*) tolerate shade especially well, as do ferns and many less common foliage plants and wildflowers. You'll find a list of some of the best choices in "Made for the Shade."

Groundcovers to Cope with Slopes Sloping sites are another common landscaping challenge. Grassy slopes can be downright difficult, and even dangerous, to mow. Or perhaps you have an ugly, rocky slope where even grass won't grow. Besides being maintenance headaches, slopes are also prime targets for soil

erosion. The runoff from heavy rains can easily carry top-soil down a bare slope, depositing the dirt on paths and paving at the bottom. That makes more work for you, as you have to clean up the debris after each rain.

If your property has a troublesome slope, groundcovers are a good solution. To stabilize the soil, you need species that transplant easily and spread quickly. Drought tolerance is a plus, especially on hot, sunny sites; slopes tend to be dry, since water runs off instead of soaking in. Fortunately, there are some beautiful flowering plants—such as moss pinks (*Phlox subulata*), two-row sedum (*Sedum spurium*), and showy sundrops (*Oenothera speciosa*)—that are well adapted to life on dry, rocky slopes. "Super Groundcovers for Slopes" offers a list of more tough plants for these challenging sites, along with tips on getting them established for quick cover.

Groundcovers for Moist Soils Wet spots can be a real landscaping hassle. They may be just moist enough that you can't get the mower in to trim until midsummer; or they're so wet that grass won't grow there at all. Instead of struggling with the site, just plant species that like "wet feet." Certain ferns, Japanese primroses (*Primula japonica*), and creeping Jenny (*Lysimachia nummularia*) are a few of the groundcovers that thrive in soggy soil. Combine them with moisture-loving perennials and shrubs such as turtleheads (*Chelone* spp.), blue flag (*Iris versicolor*), winterberry holly (*Ilex verticillata*), and summersweet (*Clethra alnifolia*) for interesting effects.

English ivy is a dependable, easy-to-grow groundcover that's ideal for protecting the soil on shaded slopes.

On gentle slopes, make shallow basins to trap moisture.

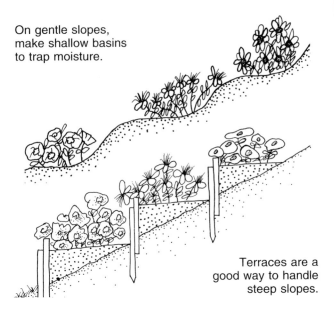

Terraces are a good way to handle steep slopes.

Super Groundcovers for Slopes

Fast-spreading groundcovers are excellent choices for slopes that are too steep or rocky to mow. Set plants out a little closer than normal for quick cover, and mulch between them to protect the soil until they fill in. For more information about the plants listed below, see the entries in the "Guide to Groundcovers," starting on page 106.

Achillea tomentosa (woolly yarrow)
Ajuga reptans (ajuga)
Coronilla varia (crown vetch)
Cotoneaster horizontalis (rockspray cotoneaster)
Euonymus fortunei (wintercreeper)
Hedera helix (English ivy)
Hemerocallis fulva (tawny daylily)
Hypericum calycinum (St.-John's-wort)
Juniperus horizontalis (creeping juniper)
Pachysandra terminalis (Japanese pachysandra)
Parthenocissus quinquefolia (Virginia creeper)
Potentilla fruticosa (shrubby cinquefoil)
Rosa rugosa (rugosa rose)
Stephanandra incisa (lace shrub)
Vinca minor (common periwinkle)

Dalmatian bellflower (*Campanula portenschlagiana*) and blood-red cranesbill make a pretty garden picture.

Combining Groundcovers for Great-looking Gardens

Groundcovers offer a wealth of solutions to landscaping problems, but they're more than just practical—they're beautiful as well. Combining flowering and foliage groundcovers with each other and with bulbs, perennials, shrubs, and other plants can give your yard year-round appeal. For innovative ideas and inspiration about using groundcovers, visit public gardens and nurseries that have display gardens, and study landscape photos in books and magazines. Since it's a great deal easier to correct mistakes before you've actually planted anything, plan your landscape on paper first and try to visualize how different groundcovers will look after they've grown a few years. To help your planning, the "Guide to Groundcovers," starting on page 106, offers color photographs and suggested landscape uses for over 90 excellent groundcover species.

Weaving Groundcover "Tapestries" Although one species and color all by itself can be appropriate in a small space, large, solid splotches of one groundcover are likely to be visually monotonous. For a more exciting landscape, intermingle plants of different species or different cultivars of the same species, combining various colors, heights, textures, and forms. An area covered with two or more different plants can change frequently during the gardening season, as each blooms in turn and as the foliage changes colors in the fall.

Even if you grow only a single groundcover species, you can often choose among many different cultivars, with varying flower and foliage colors. Moss pinks, for instance, can have pink, blue, magenta, or white flowers; heaths and heathers (*Erica* and *Calluna* spp.) can have gold, yellow, orange, bronze, or red foliage, as well as flowers in white, cream, pink, lavender, or red. Many leafy groundcovers also have showy leaves striped with white, cream, or yellow. A bed that features several compatible flower and foliage colors can be an eye-catching accent instead of a humdrum mass planting.

To combine groundcovers effectively, choose kinds that are similar in vigor, such as English ivy (*Hedera helix*) with common periwinkle, or foamflower (*Tiarella cordifolia*) with creeping phlox (*Phlox stolonifera*). Otherwise, a vigorous spreader is likely to overpower the weaker one. When plants are evenly matched, the different species can weave in and out of each other's spaces in a natural way.

For a colorful combined planting, use various flowering groundcover species that provide a continuous change of bloom throughout the season. A bank covered with naturalized spring bulbs, for example, could be overplanted with moss pink (*Phlox subulata*), maiden pinks (*Dianthus deltoides*), and blood-red cranesbill (*Geranium sanguineum*) for later bloom.

Good Groundcover Companions Groundcovers not only look great with each other but they also group well with other garden plants. They provide a finishing touch by "tying" together mixed plantings of

For a soft look, combine light yellow daylilies (*Hemerocallis* hybrid) with silvery artemisia (*Artemisia* spp.).

shrubs, trees, flowers, and grasses. Groundcovers are also perfect foils for many bulbs, providing an interesting background for the blooms and covering the yellowing bulb foliage afterward. Tall spring-blooming bulbs such as daffodils and tulips are complemented by a backdrop of ivy or accented by a spring-blooming groundcover such as Bethlehem sage (*Pulmonaria saccharata*). Tiny spring bulbs, such as snowdrops (*Galanthus* spp.), squills (*Scilla* spp.), and crocuses, are ideal company for low-growing groundcovers like fringed bleeding heart (*Dicentra eximia*), cranesbills (*Geranium* spp.), and creeping phlox (*Phlox stolonifera*). Taller herbaceous groundcovers that bloom later, such as Chinese astilbe (*Astilbe chinensis* var. *pumila*) and tawny daylilies (*Hemerocallis fulva*), also go well with spring bulbs.

Summer bulbs, particularly hybrid lilies, can be good pals with wintercreeper (*Euonymus fortunei*), certain ferns, and other low-lying groundcovers that provide welcome summer shade to the bulb roots. Many fall-blooming bulbs, including spider lily (*Lycoris* spp.) and autumn crocuses (*Colchicum* spp.), have foliage only in spring and then become dormant. When they flower in the fall, a background of groundcover greenery is particularly welcome.

Groundcovering shrubs such as creeping junipers (*Juniperus horizontalis*), shrubby cinquefoil (*Potentilla*

Short-stemmed bulbs such as grape hyacinths (*Muscari* spp.) can carpet the ground under daffodils and other tall bulbs.

fruticosa), and cotoneasters (*Cotoneaster* spp.) are beautiful in groupings of one species or combined with taller shrubs and trees or lower groundcovers and bulbs. Vigorous groundcovers like ajuga (*Ajuga reptans*) and common periwinkle (*Vinca minor*), which could crowd out more delicate perennials and grasses, are ideal companions for sturdy shrubs such as lilacs, shrub roses, hydrangeas, and viburnums.

Underplant flowering shrubs such as daphnes (*Daphne* spp.) with groundcovers that bloom in compatible colors.

Groundcovers for Easy-care Landscaping

If you're searching for ways to reduce yard work, look no further—groundcovers are the answer. Here are a few ways these tough, adaptable plants can do your work for you.

- **Eliminate tedious trimming.** Grow groundcover plantings around trees and shrubs and along paths and walkways to get rid of hand trimming.
- **Decrease weeding.** Include groundcovers in new perennial or shrub plantings to prevent weeds from taking hold while the plantings get established and fill in.
- **Minimize mowing.** Plant groundcovers to replace unused lawn areas and fill in around exposed tree roots and rocky areas.
- **Reduce raking.** Groundcover plantings under trees can trap fallen leaves, so you have less raking to do. As a plus, the decomposing trapped leaves will release nutrients and organic matter to nourish the groundcovers.

Choosing the Right Groundcovers

Choosing a groundcover for your property is a lot like picking out carpeting for your house. Your choice should be attractive, with colors and textures that will go with the surroundings and that you'll enjoy living with for a long time. Plus, it should be easy to install and maintain.

Unlike the inanimate carpeting, however, groundcovers also need to match the growing conditions that your site has to offer. If the plants you choose can't get the amount of light or water they need, they'll neither thrive nor spread, and you'll have wasted both time and money.

Consider the Climate

The first criterion for a good groundcover is that it be suitable for your climate. Some groundcovers only thrive in hot, dry climates; others prefer cool summers and plenty of humidity. Fortunately, many of them adapt well to a wide range of climates.

If you're not sure that the groundcovers you're interested in will grow in your area, compare their hardiness ratings with that of your own zone. You'll find the hardiness rating (such as Zones 5 to 9) in the catalog description, on the plant tag, or in the individual entries in the "Guide to Groundcovers," starting on page 106. See the "USDA Plant Hardiness Zone

Hostas are tough, dependable perennial groundcovers that can adapt to a wide range of climates.

Map" on page 154 to figure out which hardiness zone you live in.

Think about the Site

You will also want to know if the spot where you're planting is sunny or shady and whether the soil is wet or dry, fertile or poor. Most plants aren't fussy about whether soil is acid or alkaline, but if you choose one that is sensitive about pH, test the soil before you plant, then add lime to raise the pH or sulfur to lower the pH as needed. You'll find the particular site preferences of each plant in the "Guide to Groundcovers," starting on page 106.

Although some groundcovers will grow in nearly any spot, many prefer specialized habitats. Low-growing, creeping plants such as mazus (*Mazus reptans*) and pearlwort (*Sagina subulata*) thrive when covering a shady terrace or filling spaces between flag-stones in a path, but they would shrivel up and die on a hot, dry slope. Woody shrubs like junipers or shrubby cinquefoil (*Potentilla fruticosa*) can

The evergreen leaves and showy flowers of Lenten rose (*Helleborus orientalis*) add welcome color in early spring.

If you enjoy fragrant flowers, consider sweet violet as a groundcover for a cool, moist, shady spot.

For loads of color, it's hard to beat the sunny blooms of shrubby cinquefoil. It blooms all summer long.

effectively cover the poor soil on a dry hillside but would drown quickly in a bog.

Weigh Your Wants and Needs

After you've determined that a particular ground-cover is suitable for your climate, soil, and light conditions, make sure that it has the height and color you're looking for. Check the individual plant descriptions in the "Guide to Groundcovers," starting on page 106, to discover the traits of the plants that interest you.

A mixture of different thymes makes a beautiful, fragrant, and useful groundcover for a sunny site.

As you're choosing, don't forget to consider the extraspecial features that turn an ordinary ground-cover planting into a real landscape feature. Several spreaders, for instance, have fragrant flowers, including sweet violet (*Viola odorata*), rugosa rose (*Rosa rugosa*), and lily-of-the-valley (*Convallaria majalis*).

Even without fragrance, flowering groundcovers can add a nice touch of color to your landscape. Try bright, spring flowering moss phlox (*Phlox subulata*) for a sunny slope or showy Japanese primrose (*Primula japonica*) for a wet area. Bethlehem sage (*Pulmonia saccharata*) adds both pink-and-blue spring flowers and silver-spotted leaves. A few groundcovers offer the bonus of fragrant foliage, among them several popular herbs such as thyme, chamomile, and lavender cotton (*Santolina chamaecyparissus*). Thyme and chamomile tolerate light foot traffic, and their scents waft up whenever you walk over them.

If you are a very practical gardener, you may want to consider plants that are also productive. Thyme is a popular culinary herb; chamomile flowers or rugosa rose fruits (hips) make a tasty tea. Berry-producing plants that attract birds include partridgeberry (*Mitchella repens*) and bearberry (*Arctostaphylos uva-ursi*).

Ferns in Your Garden

For all-season variety and foliage interest, ferns are hard to surpass as groundcovers. In early spring, their small, tight fiddleheads uncurl, gradually becoming the rich green fronds that brighten shady summer woods. In fall, the deciduous ferns turn glorious shades of yellow, russet, and red; evergreen species keep their color year-round. The plants vary enormously in size, form, and texture. Some are small, delicate, and lacy; others are tall, statuesque, and formal.

Most ferns enjoy a cool, shady woodland setting or a moist spot bordering a pond or stream. They combine well with many other plants that grow in the same habitats, including hostas, foamflowers (*Tiarella cordifolia*), European wild ginger (*Asarum europaeum*), spotted lamium (*Lamium maculatum*), and creeping phlox (*Phlox stolonifera*). The beauty of ferns is highlighted when you plant them near or within a carpet of common periwinkle (*Vinca minor*), pachysandra (*Pachysandra* spp.), or some other low-lying groundcover.

Many ferns make ideal companions for crocuses and other early-blooming spring bulbs. As the bulb blossoms fade, the emerging foliage of the ferns effectively camouflages their dying leaves. Hay-scented fern (*Dennstaedtia punctilobula*) and other sun-tolerant species are good companions for lilies. They serve as a luscious green background for the blooms, then hide the unattractive stems of the lilies after the flowers fade.

Once ferns are established in a good location, they are among the most trouble-free and rewarding garden plants.

Planting and Caring for Ferns

Ferns are often more fussy than other groundcovers about where they grow. Most ferns prefer moist soil that is rich in humus and somewhat acid. Royal fern (*Osmunda regalis*), for example, likes a wet spot and will grow even in standing water. Other species are adapted to sun, drought, or alkaline soil. When ferns fail, it is usually because someone planted them in the wrong site. Check the catalog description or plant tag, or ask at your local garden center to find out if a particular fern is suited to the conditions you have to offer.

Many nurseries grow a fine assortment of popular ferns, so it usually isn't difficult to locate a good selection. Choose potted plants, if you can. If you buy one dug from a nursery row, make sure you get a ball of

Planting a Fern

Dig a planting hole that's big enough to hold all the roots.

Mix compost with the soil you removed; fill around the roots.

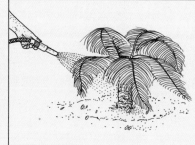

After planting, water well to thoroughly moisten the soil.

The upright form of many ferns is an excellent accent for carpets of low-growing, mat-forming groundcovers.

soil around the roots. Plant potted ferns any time the ground isn't frozen. Move or divide established clumps only in early spring or late fall.

To plant, dig a hole large enough to hold the roots without bending them. Mix compost or leaf mold with the soil you removed before putting it back in the hole and firming it around the root ball. After planting, water heavily to thoroughly moisten the soil. Mulch with compost, shredded leaves, or some other organic material. If the plants are in leaf, continue to water every other day until they begin to produce new fronds.

Royal fern is a super choice for soggy spots, grown alone or as background for other water-loving plants.

A Sampler of Easy-to-grow Ferns

With so many wonderful species to choose from, you could create a garden full of ferns and still have some left to try. Below is a list of just a few of the most popular and beautiful ferns you can grow. Most of the species listed prefer shade and moist soil; any exceptions are noted.

- *Adiantum pedatum,* maidenhair fern, grows 12 to 20 inches (30 to 50 cm) tall. One of the most attractive ferns, with black, wiry stems. Zones 3 to 8.
- *Athyrium nipponicum* 'Pictum' (also listed as *A. goeringianum* 'Pictum') is commonly known as Japanese painted fern. The gray fronds with wine red stems grow to 14 inches (35 cm) tall. Zones 3 to 8.
- *Dennstaedtia punctilobula,* hay-scented fern, reaches 15 inches (45 cm) tall. This tough fern grows in dry soil in sun or shade where other ferns do poorly; it can be invasive in better conditions. The fronds smell like dry hay when crushed. Zones 3 to 8.
- *Matteuccia struthiopteris,* ostrich fern, can grow as tall as 6 feet (1.8 m). The tightly coiled emerging spring fronds (known as fiddleheads) are considered a gourmet treat. Ostrich fern spreads quickly by rhizomes and grows in sun or shade as long as the soil is moist and fertile. Zones 2 to 8.
- *Osmunda regalis,* royal fern, grows 2 to 6 feet (60 to 180 cm) tall. The best fern for a wet spot in sun or light shade; royal fern grows even in still, shallow water. Zones 3 to 9.
- *Polystichum acrostichoides,* Christmas fern, forms neat, compact clumps of leathery, dark green, evergreen fronds reaching 10 to 20 inches (25 to 50 cm). Zones 3 to 9.
- *Woodsia obtusa,* blunt-lobed woodsia, grows 6 to 18 inches (15 to 45 cm) tall. It performs well in shady sites with dry soil. Zones 4 to 9.

Buying and Planting Groundcovers

Once you've chosen the right groundcover for your site and needs, it's time to start planning for planting. Buying healthy plants is one important part of success with the groundcovers; the other is creating the best possible planting site so your groundcovers will thrive.

Getting Your Groundcovers

Groundcover plants are available from many sources and in many different forms. Mail-order firms usually sell bareroot, dormant (not actively growing) plants in spring or fall, packed either in moss or shredded newspaper and wrapped in plastic or paper. Some mail-order sources, as well as most garden centers and nurseries, offer plants growing in pots, in packs of 4 to 8, or in flats (shallow trays containing many plants). Some nurseries may dig clumps from their sales beds while you wait.

Creeping lilyturf (*Liriope spicata*) spreads rampantly, so you can probably find someone who's willing to share some.

Potted plants cost the most, but they're generally well rooted and easy to handle. They're a good option if you have a small space to fill or if you need to plant during the growing season and can afford the extra cost. Nursery-dug clumps are usually cheaper and can be planted any time during the growing season, but you'll need to deal with them right away to prevent the clumps from drying out. Bareroot stock is the cheapest, but it also needs the most care to get off to a good start. It is usually available only in spring or fall. If you set out any groundcovers in the fall, do it at least 1 month before the ground freezes so they'll become firmly established and not suffer winter damage.

Other Sources Friends, neighbors, and community plant sales are also excellent sources of groundcovers. After a few years, most gardeners have extra plants to share. The most readily available groundcovers are likely to be fast-spreading, invasive kinds, however, so be careful where you plant them. ("Space Invaders" lists some potentially invasive groundcovers.)

Starting from Seed If you're in no rush to fill an area or if you need to cover a lot of territory with a small budget, consider growing your groundcovers from seed. Some easy ones to grow are crown vetch (*Coronilla varia*), St.-John's-wort (*Hypericum calycinum*), pearlwort (*Sagina subulata*), mother-of-thyme (*Thymus serpyllum*), fringe cups (*Tellima grandiflora*), and creeping lilyturf (*Liriope spicata*). Start the seeds in outdoor seedbeds in spring or in pots or trays indoors in late

winter. Thin the seedlings and transplant them into pots or nursery beds as soon as they are large enough. Plant them in their final location after a year or two.

Planting Groundcovers

The first step is to remove any existing vegetation. Clear out any weeds—take the tops and as much of the root system as you can. If the area is in grass, use a spade or rent a sod cutter to strip off the turf. (Use the turf pieces to patch holes in the remaining lawn or compost them.) Or, if you're not in a hurry, cover the area with multiple layers of newspapers topped off with mulch, and let the mulch smother the weeds for a year before planting.

When you're just setting out a few larger groundcover plants, such as junipers or roses, you could get

If you choose to grow houttuynia for its colorful leaves, consider giving it a fairly dry spot to control the spread.

If you're planting on rocky slopes, you may need to dig individual planting holes for your groundcovers.

away with digging individual planting holes. In most cases, though, you'll get the best groundcover growth by providing a loose, well-prepared bed. Till the area or dig it thoroughly. Also work in a 1- to 2-inch (2.5 to 5 cm) layer of compost, shredded leaves, or other organic matter. Smooth the area with a rake, water it to settle the soil, and you're ready to plant.

Set the plants into the soil at the depth they grew originally, following the suggested spacings in the "Guide to Groundcovers," starting on page 106. For container-grown or nursery-dug clumps, set them so the soil level right around the clump matches the soil level of the bed. On bareroot stock, set the crown (the point where the roots meet the leaves and stems) right at ground level. Leave a slight indentation in the soil around each plant to catch waterings and rainfall.

After planting, soak the groundcovers with water that contains a weak solution of organic liquid fertilizer, such as fish emulsion. Surround each plant with 1 inch (2.5 cm) of organic mulch (such as chopped leaves or shredded bark) to protect the soil and hinder weed growth. Unless you get a good, soaking rain, water thoroughly at least twice a week—or more often in hot, dry areas—until the plants start producing new growth and filling in. Add some liquid fertilizer to the water once a week for the first month. If the area looks sparse and the plants are slow to spread, you may want to put in temporary plantings of annuals to keep the space attractively covered for the first year or two.

Space Invaders

Groundcovers are, by definition, spreaders. In most cases, that's why you plant them in the first place. However, there are a notorious few that can spread too much, romping through lawn and flower beds until they become nearly impossible to eradicate.

Unfortunately, it's sometimes hard to predict how a given groundcover will grow on your site. Some species behave beautifully in certain locations but go wild in others where the growing conditions suit them perfectly. The individual entries in the "Guide to Groundcovers," starting on page 106, offer hints on predicting how a particular plant may react to your yard's growing conditions.

Listed below are some groundcovers that may be too vigorous to keep in a small planting. Try these in an out-of-the-way area or in a particularly tough spot where nothing else wants to grow.

Aegopodium podagraria (bishop's weed)
Ajuga reptans (ajuga)
Antennaria dioica (pussy-toes)
Campanula rapunculoides (creeping bellflower)
Cerastium tomentosum (snow-in-summer)
Chamaemelum nobile (chamomile)
Coronilla varia (crown vetch)
Hedera helix (English ivy)
Houttuynia cordata (houttuynia)
Hypericum calycinum (St.-John's-wort)
Lamiastrum galeobdolon (yellow archangel)
Lamium maculatum (spotted lamium)
Liriope spicata (creeping lilyturf)
Lysimachia nummularia (creeping Jenny)
Mazus reptans (mazus)
Oenothera speciosa (showy evening primrose)
Opuntia humifusa (prickly pear)
Sedum acre (goldmoss stonecrop)
Viola odorata (sweet violet)

Mulch is especially important for weed control in clumping groundcovers, such as hellebores (*Helleborus* spp.).

Caring for Groundcovers

Few garden plants require less routine care than well-chosen, established groundcovers. A little attention is all they need to look splendid all season long.

Dealing with Weeds

Until newly planted groundcovers cover the soil completely, their worst enemies are likely to be weeds—particularly weedy grasses. To minimize problems, be certain that the site is weed-free before you plant. Then, to inhibit the growth of weed seeds that are already in the soil, renew the organic mulch annually for the first few years. If any weeds pop up through the mulch, pull them out before they get a strong roothold. Edging strips between lawn areas and groundcover plantings will keep the grass from mingling with the groundcover and causing a real maintenance headache.

Once your low-growing groundcovers have become fully established, weeds usually aren't a major problem. Higher, shrubby groundcovers like junipers and cinquefoils (*Potentilla* spp.) may be more open

and weed-prone; continue mulching them to prevent weeds from getting started. Ideally, you should pull any weeds that appear before they flower and spread their seeds. At least one midseason weeding session can help you catch most young weeds and keep them from getting established.

Watering

A number of attractive, easy-to-grow groundcovers are remarkably drought-tolerant. If you've chosen groundcovers that are adapted to your growing conditions, you probably won't need to water them at all. Even though low-growing, shallow-rooted plants may suffer during dry periods, most will recover after the first rain. If the dry period lasts longer than a few weeks, however, consider watering to thoroughly moisten the top few inches of soil.

Fertilizing

Unless the soil is poor, most established groundcovers need little additional fertilizer. When your plants aren't growing well and seem malnourished, however, give them a light feeding each year in early spring, before they begin to grow. Scatter a dry organic fertilizer over the area, following the application directions on the package. If it doesn't rain within a few

Installing edging strips is an easy way to keep grasses from creeping into groundcovers. Without edgings, you'll have to weed regularly to keep the plants separate.

days after you spread the fertilizer, use a hose or sprinkler to wash it into the soil. Plants growing in light, sandy soil will need more frequent fertilizing than those growing in clay or heavy loam.

Dividing

In their natural habitats, groundcovers grow more slowly as they become crowded, so they seldom need division. In ideal garden conditions, however, your groundcovers may keep growing and spreading quickly, until they start crowding each other and competing for light, water, and nutrients. Clump-forming groundcovers, such as daylilies (*Hemerocallis* spp.) and hostas, are more likely to need renewal than those that spread by rhizomes or stolons, such as ajuga (*Ajuga reptans*) and Japanese pachysandra (*Pachysandra terminalis*). If dead spots appear in the midst of a clumping plant, it is time to divide it; you'll find complete details in "Dividing Groundcovers" on page 104.

Pruning

As shrubby groundcovers age, a little pruning and thinning can help to keep the plants vigorous and full. Prune most woody groundcovers, including junipers and roses, in early spring, before they put out new growth.

Trimming can rejuvenate vining groundcovers.

Cut down the tops of hardy geraniums (*Geranium* spp.) and other deciduous groundcovers in fall or spring.

Spreading groundcovers such as sundrops (*Oenothera* spp.) may need to be divided in spring if they get too crowded.

Trim as needed to shape the growth and to remove shoots that are too upright. Also remove dead or broken branches and any winter-damaged shoots.

A few vining groundcovers, including English ivy (*Hedera helix*) and wintercreeper (*Euonymus fortunei*), occasionally become thickly matted and need help. Renew such a planting by cutting it back with the lawn mower set high, at about 4 inches (10 cm), before the plants begin to grow in early spring.

Fall Care

Most low-growing groundcovers need a minimum of fall maintenance. For neatness sake, you may want to cut down tall-growing types such as cranesbills (*Geranium* spp.) and catmints (*Nepeta* spp.) after they turn brown, but it does no harm to leave the tops intact as a protective winter mulch. In the spring, it's easy to rake away the dead foliage.

Coping with Pests and Problems

Although diseases and insects do not cause major problems for most groundcovers, almost any plant growing in large numbers could become an inviting target. Cotoneasters (*Cotoneaster* spp.) are susceptible to a bacterial disease called fire blight, especially in the South. Junipers may get blights; roses are vulnerable to both diseases and insects. Any deer, Japanese beetles, and gypsy moths in the area will feed on most plants. "Dealing with Pests and Diseases" on page 66 covers basic information on controlling common garden problems. The individual plant entries in the "Guide to Groundcovers," starting on page 106, offer specific tips for keeping your plants healthy.

Tawny daylilies are tough, durable plants. You can divide them just about any time the ground isn't frozen.

Propagating Groundcovers

Although many groundcovers are naturally rapid spreaders, you may occasionally want additional plants to cover a new area or to share with friends. It's easy to propagate nearly all groundcovers by division. When you want large numbers, consider growing them from seeds, layers, or stem cuttings. For details on when and how to propagate specific groundcovers, check the individual entries in the "Guide to Groundcovers," starting on page 106.

Dividing Groundcovers

The simplest way to propagate clumps of herbaceous perennials, most vines, and many suckering shrubs is to divide them. It is also a reliable way to get plants exactly like the originals.

When to Divide The best time to divide most plants is in early spring, when they are just coming back to life. Some groundcovers—like tawny daylilies (*Hemerocallis fulva*) and ajuga (*Ajuga reptans*)—are so vigorous, however, that you can divide them successfully nearly any time during the growing season. To help them recover quickly, cut two-thirds of the tops off, keep them watered, and provide shade from the sun for a few days.

How to Divide Clump-formers When you want only a few new plants or need to renew an overgrown clump, divide it by driving a sharp spade downward through the center. Lift out a portion and leave the remainder undisturbed in the ground. Fill the hole left with soil and compost, then top it with mulch. Cut the removed part or parts into smaller sections, making sure each one has both top growth and roots.

To get the largest possible number of plants, dig the entire clump. Wash the soil off the roots so you can better see what you are doing. Carefully cut the clump into as many pieces as you want, being sure to leave tops and roots on each section. If your divisions are large, with a few plants in each section, plant them immediately where you want them to grow permanently. If you've divided down to single plants, it's usually best to grow them in a separate nursery bed for a season before setting them out in their permanent spot.

How to Divide Spreading Groundcovers The sprawling stems of creepers, such as common periwinkle (*Vinca minor*) and wintercreeper (*Euonymus fortunei*), form roots easily. Dig up these rooted sections and cut or pull them apart.

Certain woody plants, including roses, creeping mahonia (*Mahonia repens*), and sweet box (*Sarcococca hookeriana* var. *humilis*) send up suckers from their roots. You can dig up these new rooted plants and move them to other parts of the garden. In early spring, before they start to grow, cut the tops of the suckers back to about half. Then dig them carefully, making sure you get most of the roots, and plant them in their new spot.

Aftercare After planting, water the new divisions thoroughly; add some liquid fertilizer, such as fish emulsion, to the water to give plants a real boost. Spread a mulch 1 inch (2.5 cm) deep around the plants, and keep them watered until they start producing new growth.

Layering Plants

Layering is another good method of getting new plants just like the originals. You can layer all kinds of plants with creeping or vining stems as well as many woody shrubs, including shrubby cinquefoil (*Potentilla fruticosa*), rugosa rose (*Rosa rugosa*), and creeping junipers (*Juniperus horizontalis*). Choose a low-growing branch, strip the foliage from the middle section, and cut off a small piece of bark from the underside. Dust the exposed section with a rooting

When layering stems, you may need to hold them down with a rock.

hormone (available at your local garden center), and bend the stem down to the ground. Cover the middle section with 1 to 2 inches (2.5 to 5 cm) of soil, leaving the end of the branch sticking out. You may need to place a stone over the layered portion to hold it in place.

Some shrubs may take a year to form roots, but others develop them within a few months. After 2 months, dig around the layered area carefully to see if any roots have formed; if not, wait a few more months and check again. When a mass of roots has developed, cut the stem from the parent, but let it remain in place to grow more roots. The following spring, dig up the rooted layer and plant it where you want it to grow.

Taking Stem Cuttings

Division is the easiest way to get a good supply of new plants from an established planting. But if you only have a few groundcover plants and need more, stem cuttings may be a good way to go. You can successfully root cuttings from many kinds of woody vines and shrubs, as well as herbaceous groundcovers like mother-of-thyme (*Thymus serpyllum*), common periwinkle), and moss phlox (*Phlox subulata*).

Common periwinkle is a fast-spreading groundcover that's easy to propagate by layering, cuttings, or division.

Propagate shrubby groundcovers such as sun rose (*Helianthemum nummularium*) by cuttings or layering.

In early summer to midsummer, cut off sprouts of new growth from 3 to 5 inches (7.5 to 12.5 cm) long. Remove the bottom leaves and any flowers or flower buds. Dip the ends into a rooting hormone. Stick the bases of the cuttings halfway into pots or flats (shallow trays) filled with a moistened mixture of half perlite and half vermiculite. Cover the cuttings with a clear plastic bag (prop up the bag so the plastic doesn't rest on the cuttings), and place them in a warm, brightly lit place out of direct sunlight.

Remove the bottom leaves from your cuttings.

Keep the cuttings moist until they form roots. You can tell when a good clump of roots has formed because the cutting will resist your gentle pull. Transplant each rooted cutting into a small pot. When its roots fill the pot, plant it in its permanent location. Never let the cuttings dry out during any part of the process.

Starting Plants from Seed

Another way to get large numbers of both herbaceous and woody groundcovers is to grow them from seed, although the woody types may take a long time to sprout and grow. Since only species plants will come true from seed, always propagate named cultivars by layers, cuttings, or division. For more information on growing a garden full of groundcovers this way, see "Starting from Seed" on page 100.

Achillea tomentosa   Compositae

WOOLLY YARROW

Woolly yarrow is a low-growing groundcover that thrives in sunny, dry sites. It withstands light foot traffic, so you can even mow it and use it as a small-scale lawn substitute.

BEST CLIMATE AND SITE: Zones 3–7. Grows poorly in hot, humid areas. Well-drained soil. Full sun.

HEIGHT AND SPREAD: Height of foliage to 2 inches (5 cm); spread to 1 foot (30 cm). Flower height 6–8 inches (15–20 cm).

DESCRIPTION: Woolly yarrow forms spreading mats of aromatic, hairy, gray-green foliage. The leaves may be evergreen in warm climates. Small, vivid yellow flowers bloom in flat, 1-inch (2.5 cm) clusters from early summer to midsummer.

GROWING GUIDELINES: Set plants 1 foot (30 cm) apart in spring or fall. This yarrow spreads so quickly, even in poor, dry soil, that it may become invasive. Grow it where the spread isn't a problem, or surround the planting with an edging. Cut down the flowering stems after bloom to keep the planting neat. Propagate the species by seed or division and the cultivars by division in spring.

LANDSCAPE USES: Woolly yarrow is a great groundcover for dry slopes and an attractive edging where it can be controlled. Some of the cultivars are popular for rock gardens.

CULTIVARS: 'Aurea' has bright yellow flowers. 'Nana' is only 4 inches (10 cm) tall in bloom.

OTHER SPECIES:
A. *ptarmica* 'The Pearl' grows to 2 feet (60 cm) tall and has clusters of white flowers. Fast-spreading; Zones 2–9.

Aegopodium podagraria 'Variegata'   Umbelliferae

VARIEGATED BISHOP'S WEED

Fast-spreading variegated bishop's weed, also called silver-edged goutweed, has attractive toothed leaves marked with green and white. It's easy to grow but can become invasive.

BEST CLIMATE AND SITE: Zones 3–9. Grows in a wide variety of soil types, both fertile and poor. Full sun to shade.

HEIGHT AND SPREAD: Foliage and flower height to 12 inches (30 cm); spreads indefinitely.

DESCRIPTION: A useful groundcover where nothing else will grow, variegated bishop's weed spreads by creeping roots and seeds and is difficult to keep within bounds. In early summer, tiny white flowers bloom in flattened clusters up to 3 inches (7.5 cm) wide.

GROWING GUIDELINES: Set plants 18–24 inches (45–60 cm) apart. Plant any time during the growing season. Surround the planting with a sturdy edging to keep it from taking over your yard. The leaves may turn brown in sunny spots; cutting back in midsummer encourages fresh new growth and improves the appearance. Weed out any all-green plants. Propagate by division in spring or fall. Friends may admire its handsome foliage, but be sure they understand how invasive the plant can be before you share; otherwise, you may lose your friends!

LANDSCAPE USES: Choose variegated bishop's weed for difficult shady or sunny areas, slopes, and areas near paved paths where little else will grow. Combine with vigorous types of ferns, hostas, daylilies, or shrubs.

Ajuga reptans   Labiatae

AJUGA

The short, spinach-like leaves of this excellent, low-growing groundcover spread rapidly to form a solid carpet. Many colorful cultivars of ajuga are available.

BEST CLIMATE AND SITE: Zones 3–8. Thrives in well-drained garden soil. Full sun to partial shade (shade is especially important in hot climates).

HEIGHT AND SPREAD: Height of foliage to 3 inches (7.5 cm); spread unlimited. Flower height to about 6 inches (15 cm).

DESCRIPTION: The leaves are usually dark green; cultivars are available with purple, bronze, or variegated foliage. Ajuga is evergreen in warm areas but tends to turn brown by midwinter in cold climates. Spikes of ¼-inch (6 mm) blue or purple flowers bloom in spring or early summer.

GROWING GUIDELINES: Set plants 12–15 inches (30–37.5 cm) apart any time during the growing season. They need little maintenance. Don't give them fertilizer; otherwise, the lush growth will be prone to fungal disease. Propagate by division any time during the growing season.

LANDSCAPE USES: Plant ajuga as a flowering groundcover under trees and shrubs and on slopes. It will easily invade lawns, creating a maintenance headache where you need to keep the two separate; use an edging strip to avoid the problem. Ajuga can also overwhelm less vigorous plants, so it's not a good choice for edging flower beds or borders.

CULTIVARS: 'Bronze Beauty' has deep purple flowers and bronze leaves. 'Burgundy Glow' has burgundy new foliage that ages to white and deep pink.

LADY'S-MANTLE

PUSSY-TOES

Lady's-mantle is superb as a carpet beneath trees. It also looks great in borders and rock gardens, but there you'll want to snip off the spent flowers to prevent reseeding.

BEST CLIMATE AND SITE: Zones 3–8. Grows well in light-textured, well-drained, humus-rich, fertile soil. Grows well in partial shade; tolerates full sun in the North.

HEIGHT AND SPREAD: Height of foliage 9–12 inches (22.5–30 cm); spread to 2 feet (60 cm). Flower height to 15 inches (37.5 cm).

DESCRIPTION: Grow lady's-mantle for its attractive mounds of soft, silvery gray, deeply lobed, rounded foliage. The large leaves can grow up to 6 inches (15 cm) wide. Small, greenish yellow, petal-less flowers bloom in airy clusters in late spring and early summer.

GROWING GUIDELINES: Set plants 20 inches (50 cm) apart in spring. If leaves look tattered by midsummer, cut plants to the ground to get a flush of new growth. Plants self-sow easily and can become weedy; cut off the spent flowers to prevent seed formation, or grow the plants where reseeding isn't a problem. Propagate by division in spring or fall or by seed in summer.

LANDSCAPE USES: Lady's-mantle looks wonderful alone or combined with other vigorous perennials in flower borders. The chartreuse blooms look especially nice with blue or purplish flowers, such as catmints (*Nepeta* spp.) or violet sage (*Salvia* x *superba*). They also make an excellent, long-lasting cut flower.

Pussy-toes is a charming little groundcover for a dry, sunny site. The rosettes of hairy, silver-green leaves are topped with pink-tipped, off-white flowers in early summer.

BEST CLIMATE AND SITE: Zones 4–7. Dry, sandy, poor soil. Full sun.

HEIGHT AND SPREAD: Height of foliage to 10 inches (25 cm); spreads over a wide area in time. Flower height to 1 foot (30 cm).

DESCRIPTION: Pussy-toes gets its name from the tiny, off-white, pink-tipped flowers that resemble a cat's foot. The blooms appear atop leafless stalks in early summer above rosettes of hairy, silver-green, 1-inch (2.5 cm) wide leaves.

GROWING GUIDELINES: Set plants 6 inches (15 cm) or more apart in light soil in spring or fall. Plants are generally maintenance-free, but they self-sow readily and tend to become invasive, so cut off the flowers before they form seed if you wish to prevent spreading. Pussy-toes is easy to propagate by spring-sown seed or by spring division.

LANDSCAPE USES: A planting of pussy-toes will spread to form a good cover for hot, dry spots in sunny wild areas or rock gardens. The flowers dry well for winter bouquets.

CULTIVARS: 'Rosea' has rosy pink flower heads and whitish leaves.

Arabis caucasica　　　　Cruciferae

WALL ROCK CRESS

The spreading, evergreen mounds of wall rock cress are accented with masses of sweetly scented white flowers in spring. Cut plants back after bloom to promote compact growth.

BEST CLIMATE AND SITE: Zones 3–7. Fertile, well-drained soil. Full sun.

HEIGHT AND SPREAD: Height of foliage 4–6 inches (10–15 cm); spread to 18 inches (45 cm). Flower height to 1 foot (30 cm).

DESCRIPTION: Wall rock cress forms spreading mounds of grayish green, 1-inch (2.5 cm), toothed leaves. In spring, the mounds are smothered in clusters of small, fragrant, white, four-petaled flowers.

GROWING GUIDELINES: Set plants 1 foot (30 cm) apart. Cut plants back by half after bloom to remove the spent flowers and to promote compact new growth. Propagate by division in fall, by seed in spring, or by cuttings in early summer.

LANDSCAPE USES: Wall rock cress is an ideal ornamental to place in rock gardens or in crevices in a stone wall. It makes a good edging plant and is ideal for the front of a flower border. The white flowers are a nice complement to spring-flowering bulbs.

CULTIVARS: 'Compinkie' has rosy pink flowers on 6–8-inch (15–20 cm) stems in spring. 'Flore Pleno', with double flowers, stays in bloom longer than the species.

OTHER SPECIES:

　　A. procurrens grows in sun or light shade. Clusters of tiny white flowers in spring rise 1 foot (30 cm) above mats of shiny green leaves. Needs excellent drainage and tends to rot in humid areas. Zones 5–7.

Arctostaphylos uva-ursi　　　　Ericaceae

BEARBERRY

Bearberry, also called kinnikinnick, is a native American evergreen with spring flowers and red fall berries. It is one of the best groundcovers for hot, sandy areas.

BEST CLIMATE AND SITE: Zones 2–7, but varies with cultivars. Sandy, dry, acid, poor soil. Full sun.

HEIGHT AND SPREAD: Height 6–12 inches (15–30 cm); spread to 12 feet (3.6 m).

DESCRIPTION: Bearberry forms creeping mats of woody stems clothed in shiny green leaves that turn bronze in winter. The stems are tipped with tiny, waxy, bell-shaped, white to light pink flowers in spring and bright red berries in fall.

GROWING GUIDELINES: Set plants out about 1 foot (30 cm) apart. They can be slow to establish, so be prepared to weed between plants until they fill in. They're difficult to propagate, but you could try layering (covering parts of the creeping stems with soil until roots form); it's best to use nursery-grown transplants.

LANDSCAPE USES: Bearberry is ideal for erosion control on well-drained slopes; it looks particularly nice with rocks. Try it in seaside gardens, too; it thrives in sandy soil.

CULTIVARS: Since the many cultivars are adapted to different areas of North America, check catalog descriptions or plant labels to find types that are hardy to your zone. 'Alaska' is a low-growing, drought-tolerant, very attractive cultivar with dark green leaves. 'Massachusetts' is an East Coast cultivar, somewhat more adapted to damp weather than most, with dark green leaves and small red berries.

Arenaria montana   Caryophyllaceae   *Artemisia stelleriana*   Compositae

MOUNTAIN SANDWORT

BEACH WORMWOOD

Mountain sandwort forms a carpet of narrow, green leaves. The shallow-rooted plants will grow best if you provide some extra water during dry spells.

Beach wormwood looks great combined with small spring bulbs, such as crocuses. Its bushy growth will fill the space when the bulbs go dormant in early summer.

BEST CLIMATE AND SITE: Zones 4–8. Prefers well-drained, sandy, somewhat acid soil; tolerates almost any soil with good drainage. Full sun in the North; partial shade in the South.

HEIGHT AND SPREAD: Height 2–4 inches (5–10 cm); spread to 1 foot (30 cm) or more.

DESCRIPTION: These easy-to-grow, creeping plants form dense mats of grass-like, shiny, gray-green, 1-inch (2.5 cm) foliage. Many five-petaled, 1-inch (2.5 cm) wide flowers bloom just above the foliage in late spring or early summer. The flowers are white with a yellow eye.

GROWING GUIDELINES: Set plants about 1 foot (30 cm) apart in spring or fall. They need little care; just water during dry spells. Propagate by seed or division in spring or fall, or take cuttings of non-flowering shoots in summer.

LANDSCAPE USES: Since mountain sandwort can tolerate some traffic, it's a good choice for planting in crevices between stones in pathways. It's also attractive in rock gardens and for trailing over walls.

OTHER SPECIES:

A. verna, moss sandwort, grows 1–2 inches (2.5–5 cm) tall and spreads rapidly. It has star-like flowers in spring and mossy, evergreen leaves that stand up well in pathways. 'Aurea', golden moss sandwort, has yellowish foliage. Zones 3–8.

BEST CLIMATE AND SITE: Zones 3–8. Grows poorly in hot, humid areas. Well-drained, sandy, dry, poor soil. Full sun.

HEIGHT AND SPREAD: Height to 2 feet (60 cm); spread to 3 feet (90 cm) or more.

DESCRIPTION: Beach wormwood forms low, spreading mounds of deeply lobed, silvery gray, woolly leaves that have a felt-like texture. Clusters of not especially showy, tiny, yellow flowers appear atop gray stems in late summer.

GROWING GUIDELINES: Set plants 2 feet (60 cm) apart in spring or fall. Shear the stems back by half in midsummer to discourage flowering and to promote dense growth. Propagate by division in spring or fall or by cuttings in summer.

LANDSCAPE USES: Beach wormwood is ideal for seaside plantings. Try it in rock gardens or as edgings. The silvery foliage is also useful for separating strong colors in perennial borders.

CULTIVARS: 'Silver Brocade' grows 6–12 inches (15–30 cm) tall and spreads slowly.

OTHER SPECIES:

A. absinthium, common wormwood, is a woody-stemmed perennial with silvery white foliage. It grows 3–4 feet (90–120 cm) tall and spreads several feet. It has naturalized widely in North America. Zones 2–8.

| *Asarum europaeum* | Aristolochiaceae | *Astilbe chinensis* var. *pumila* | Saxifragaceae |

EUROPEAN WILD GINGER

DWARF CHINESE ASTILBE

European wild ginger is one of the best evergreen groundcovers for partial shade. The glossy, leathery leaves and thick, creeping roots are aromatic when crushed.

BEST CLIMATE AND SITE: Zones 4–8. Moisture-retentive, humus-rich, somewhat acid soil. Partial shade.

HEIGHT AND SPREAD: Height 5–7 inches (12.5–17.5 cm); spread to 1 foot (30 cm).

DESCRIPTION: European wild ginger forms spreading colonies of kidney-shaped, evergreen leaves that are up to 3 inches (7.5 cm) wide. In late spring, small, purplish brown flowers bloom beneath the foliage.

GROWING GUIDELINES: Set plants 8–12 inches (20–30 cm) apart in early spring. Don't plant too deep; set the crowns (where the leaves meet the roots) just at the soil surface. Keep them evenly moist the first season after planting; water established plantings in dry weather. Fertilize lightly in early spring with a light topdressing of compost or leaf mold. To propagate, divide in spring.

LANDSCAPE USES: European wild ginger grows quickly into a weed-suppressing clump. Combine it with ferns and shade-loving perennials, such as hostas and crested iris (*Iris cristata*).

OTHER SPECIES:

    A. canadense, Canada wild ginger, grows 6–8 inches (15–20 cm) tall and has large, heart-shaped, deciduous leaves. It tends to spread faster than *A. europaeum* but doesn't offer any winter interest. Handling the leaves can cause dermatitis on susceptible people. Zones 3–8.

The ferny leaves of dwarf Chinese astilbe form in elegant, spreading clumps that are attractive from spring through fall. The pink summer flower plumes are an added bonus.

BEST CLIMATE AND SITE: Zones 5–8. Moist, humus-rich soil. Partial shade; grows in full sun in cool-summer climates.

HEIGHT AND SPREAD: Height of foliage 8–12 inches (20–30 cm); spread 1–2 feet (30–60 cm). Flower stalks to 18 inches (45 cm) tall.

DESCRIPTION: This dwarf astilbe spreads slowly but steadily with attractive, fern-like, shiny leaves. Plumes of flowers—rosy pink with a hint of blue—grow on spikes above the foliage in mid- to late-summer.

GROWING GUIDELINES: Set plants 1–2 feet (30–60 cm) apart during the growing season. Work plenty of compost or other organic matter into the soil before planting to hold moisture and add nutrients. Slugs and snails may be a problem; trap pests under cabbage leaves (destroy trapped slugs daily) or in pans of beer set flush with the soil surface. Propagate by division in spring or fall.

LANDSCAPE USES: Grow dwarf Chinese astilbe at the front of borders, in rock gardens, and as edgings alongside paths or walls. It's a great companion for spring bulbs, since its foliage will expand to cover the ripening bulb leaves and fill the space when the bulbs go dormant. Astilbe flowers dry well and are good for winter arrangements.

| *Bergenia cordifolia* | Saxifragaceae | *Calluna vulgaris* | Ericaceae |

HEART-LEAVED BERGENIA

Sometimes called elephant's ears or heartleaf, this evergreen native of Siberia is grown for its thick, handsome leaves. The flower buds may be killed by very cold winters.

BEST CLIMATE AND SITE: Zones 3–8. Humus-rich, well-drained, moist, slightly alkaline soil; but will grow anywhere if kept watered. Partial shade.

HEIGHT AND SPREAD: Height of foliage to 1 foot (30 cm); spread to 2 feet (60 cm). Flower stems to 18 inches (45 cm) tall.

DESCRIPTION: The heart-shaped, evergreen foliage turns shades of red-bronze in fall and holds the color well into winter. Clusters of tiny, rose-pink flowers hang on stems that emerge from the base of the plant in mid- to late-spring.

GROWING GUIDELINES: Set plants 2 feet (60 cm) apart in spring or fall. It's best to choose a location sheltered from wind so the leaves won't get tattered. Mulch lightly before winter, especially in the coldest parts of its range. Use a loose mulch like coarse leaves, and remove it in early spring so the flower stems can emerge. Cut off old, damaged leaves as needed. Trap slugs under cabbage leaves (remove pests daily) or in pans of beer set flush with the soil surface. Propagate by division in spring, or sow fresh seed in late summer.

LANDSCAPE USES: Leafy clumps of heart-leaved bergenia are dramatic along paths, under shrubs or trees, in large rock gardens, near ponds, and in containers. They combine well with spring bulbs and fine-textured plants like ferns and bleeding hearts (*Dicentra* spp.).

HEATHER

Heather thrives in full sun and infertile, acid soil. In cold climates, protect plants from winter winds by covering them with a light mulch or evergreen branches.

BEST CLIMATE AND SITE: Zones 5–7. Acid, well-drained, poor soil; grows poorly in alkaline or fertile conditions. Full sun necessary to produce flowers, though it will grow in partial shade.

HEIGHT AND SPREAD: Height to 2 feet (60 cm) but varies according to cultivar; spread 2–4 feet (60–120 cm).

DESCRIPTION: The spreading, evergreen mounds of this excellent groundcovering shrub have tiny, scale-like, overlapping leaves covering the branches. Some plants turn red in fall. Tiny, pinkish, bell-shaped flowers bloom along the shoot tips from late summer to fall.

GROWING GUIDELINES: Set plants 12–18 inches (30–45 cm) apart in spring or early fall. Prune off shoots of the previous season in early spring to encourage tight, compact growth. Propagate by seed anytime, by cuttings in early summer, or by layering in spring (cover part of a low-growing stem with soil until new roots form; then separate it from the parent plant).

LANDSCAPE USES: Heather looks great with other shrubs or in masses of several different cultivars. It is excellent for dried arrangements.

CULTIVARS: Numerous cultivars are available in a wide variety of foliage and flower colors. The foliage of 'Robert Chapman' is golden in spring, orange in summer, and reddish over winter.

Campanula portenschlagiana   Campanulaceae

DALMATIAN BELLFLOWER

The trailing stems of Dalmatian bellflower creep over the ground or sprawl over stone walls. This pretty plant is also attractive along the front of flower borders or in pots.

BEST CLIMATE AND SITE: Zones 4–8. Well-drained, sandy soil. Full sun; light shade in hot climates.

HEIGHT AND SPREAD: Height 6–8 inches (15–20 cm); spread to 2 feet (60 cm).

DESCRIPTION: This low-growing campanula has heart-shaped, toothed leaves. It is covered with large numbers of bell-shaped, lavender-blue, 1-inch (2.5 cm) flowers from late spring to midsummer.

GROWING GUIDELINES: Set plants 12–18 inches (30–45 cm) apart in spring. Plants are easy to grow and need no special care. Propagate by division in early spring.

LANDSCAPE USES: Dalmatian bellflower is ideal as a groundcover in rock gardens, on rocky slopes, and in nooks and crannies in stone walls.

CULTIVARS: 'Resholt' has deep violet flowers that are larger than the species. It thrives in partial shade as well as in sunny conditions.

OTHER SPECIES: Certain campanulas are invasive and difficult to control, including *C. rapunculoides,* creeping bellflower, and *C. poscharskyana,* Serbian bellflower. Below are a few better-behaved types. *C. carpatica,* Carpathian harebell, has upward-facing, purple to white flowers. Height 6–12 inches (15–30 cm). Zones 3–8.
C. garganica, Gargano bellflower, forms mats with light blue, star-shaped flowers in early summer. Height 6–10 inches (15–25 cm). Zones 6–8.

Cephalotaxus harringtonia 'Prostrata' Cephalotaxaceae

JAPANESE PLUM YEW

Try Japanese plum yew where you need a large, shrubby groundcover. It's one of the few needle-leaved evergreens that grows well in shady spots.

BEST CLIMATE AND SITE: Zones 6–9. Average, well-drained soil. Partial shade.

HEIGHT AND SPREAD: Height to 3 feet (90 cm); spread to 12 feet (3.6 m) or more.

DESCRIPTION: This shrubby, shade-tolerant evergreen resembles true yews (*Taxus* spp.) but has larger, flat needles. The dark green color is best in shade—too much sun may cause the needles to turn yellowish. The insignificant flowers bear only the male parts, so the plant does not set seed. Japanese plum yew seems to be deer-resistant.

GROWING GUIDELINES: Set plants 3 feet (90 cm) or more apart in spring. Japanese plum yew needs practically no maintenance. Propagate by layering branches (covering them with soil where they touch the ground to encourage rooting).

LANDSCAPE USES: Japanese plum yew is an excellent evergreen groundcover for shady sites. It's a good substitute for yews where deer are a problem.

| *Cerastium tomentosum* | Caryophyllaceae | *Ceratostigma plumbaginoides* | Plumbaginaceae |

SNOW-IN-SUMMER

LEADWORT

Snow-in summer carpets the ground with mats of woolly gray leaves. It can become invasive in spots it likes, so plant it where it can spread, or surround it with a barrier strip.

BEST CLIMATE AND SITE: Zones 2–10. Dry, well-drained, poor soil—even sand. Full sun.

HEIGHT AND SPREAD: Height 6–10 inches (15–25 cm); spread to 3 feet (90 cm) or more.

DESCRIPTION: This fast-growing evergreen with light gray, woolly foliage forms large mats with its creeping stems. Abundant white flowers with star-shaped petals cover the foliage for several weeks in late spring.

GROWING GUIDELINES: Set plants 12–18 inches (30–45 cm) apart in spring. Once they are established, cut the stems back after flowering to prevent seeding. Snow-in-summer can become invasive; divide plants every few years as they get out of bounds, or cut them back hard in early spring to control the spread. Propagate by division or seed in spring or fall, or take cuttings in early summer.

LANDSCAPE USES: Snow-in-summer forms a good groundcover for dry, sunny spots, especially in difficult spots like dry, rocky slopes. Plant it where the spread won't be a problem, or surround the planting with an edging strip.

Leadwort is a wonderful groundcover that adapts to a range of conditions. It is slow to emerge in spring but eventually forms mats of shiny, green leaves that turn reddish in fall.

BEST CLIMATE AND SITE: Zones 5–9. Fertile, well-drained soil is best; tolerates poor, dry soil. Full sun to partial shade.

HEIGHT AND SPREAD: Height 8–12 inches (20–30 cm); spread to several feet (1 m).

DESCRIPTION: Leadwort has deciduous foliage that appears only after the soil warms in late spring; then it quickly forms a tufted mat of shiny, green, 3-inch (7.5 cm) long leaves with pointed ends. The $1/2$-inch (12 mm) wide, cobalt blue flowers appear in late summer and often last until frost. The stems and leaves turn reddish bronze in fall.

GROWING GUIDELINES: Set plants 8–12 inches (20–30 cm) apart in spring for a quick groundcover. In Zone 5, a mulch is necessary for winter protection. Propagate by division in spring or take cuttings in summer.

LANDSCAPE USES: Grow leadwort anywhere you want a tough, adaptable, fast-growing groundcover. It looks wonderful with shrubs or cascading over walls. For spring interest, underplant it with small spring bulbs, such as crocus, reticulated iris (*Iris reticulata*), and squills (*Scilla* spp.). The leadwort foliage will cover the yellowing bulb foliage and fill the space left when bulbs go dormant.

Chamaemelum nobile   Compositae

ROMAN CHAMOMILE

Roman chamomile is a delightful, low-growing herb with feathery, green leaves that have a sweet, apple-like scent. The daisy-like flowers can be used to make a soothing tea.

BEST CLIMATE AND SITE: Zones 3–8. Sandy, poor soil; good drainage is a must. Full sun; tolerates partial shade.

HEIGHT AND SPREAD: Height to about 2 inches (5 cm); spread to 3 feet (90 cm). Flower stems 6–12 inches (15–30 cm) tall.

DESCRIPTION: Small, daisy-like, white flowers with yellow centers appear over the spreading mat of foliage in mid- to late-summer. For groundcover use, it's important not to confuse this perennial species with annual German chamomile (*Matricaria recutita*), which is similar in appearance but grows to 2 feet (60 cm) tall.

GROWING GUIDELINES: Set plants 6 inches (15 cm) apart in spring. New plants need regular watering to keep the soil evenly moist; established, vigorous plants survive without much care. They drop seeds readily, so remove the spent flowers to prevent invasive reseeding. Roman chamomile can take occasional foot traffic, so you can mow established plants several times a season to prevent flowering. Propagate by division or seed in spring or by cuttings in summer.

LANDSCAPE USES: When mowed frequently, plants will become compact and form an aromatic, lawn-like groundcover. Roman chamomile is also charming between the stones on pathways.

CULTIVARS: 'Treneague' is a non-flowering form.

Chrysogonum virginianum   Compositae

GREEN AND GOLD

Green and gold is a low-growing native with dark green leaves and bright golden blooms. It's a natural choice for woodland gardens and for growing beneath trees and shrubs.

BEST CLIMATE AND SITE: Zones 5–8. Well-drained, light-textured, moist, slightly acid soil, with a generous amount of humus and nutrients. Partial shade in the North; full shade in the South.

HEIGHT AND SPREAD: Height 8–12 inches (20–30 cm); spread to 1 foot (30 cm).

DESCRIPTION: Native to the woodlands of eastern North America, green and gold forms rosettes of oval, deep green, slightly hairy leaves. The 1–2-inch (2.5–5 cm) wide, five-petaled, golden yellow flowers give the plant another of its common names: golden star. Green and gold blooms generously in spring and intermittently all summer. The flowers are more prolific where the weather is cool. The plant spreads quickly by underground runners and prostrate stems that root where they touch the soil. Green and gold is deciduous in the North and evergreen in the South.

GROWING GUIDELINES: Set plants 12–18 inches (30–45 cm) apart in spring. Do not overfertilize, or plants tend to become floppy and produce fewer blooms. Needs winter protection in Zone 5. Propagate by division in spring or fall.

LANDSCAPE USES: Green and gold is attractive under trees and shrubs and in wild areas or rock gardens. It makes a low-maintenance groundcover at the edge of woodlands or against rocks or stone walls.

Clematis integrifolia Ranunculaceae

SOLITARY CLEMATIS

Unlike most other clematis, which grow as vines, solitary clematis forms a sprawling mound that makes an unusual and attractive flowering groundcover.

BEST CLIMATE AND SITE: Zones 4–9. Light, loamy, alkaline soil. Full sun.

HEIGHT AND SPREAD: Height 2–3 feet (60–90 cm); similar spread.

DESCRIPTION: Solitary clematis forms bushy mounds of egg-shaped, deciduous leaves. Bell-shaped, lavender-blue flowers bloom over a long period in midsummer, followed by charming silvery seed heads.

GROWING GUIDELINES: Set plants out 2–3 feet (60–90 cm) apart in spring or fall. Maintain an organic mulch (such as compost or shredded leaves) to keep the soil cool and moist; otherwise, plants need no special care. Propagate by seed in late summer or cuttings in late spring.

LANDSCAPE USES: Solitary clematis is not especially showy, but the flowers and seed heads can provide several months of subtle interest. It looks best combined with other plants, as part of a border, or as an accent with other low-growing groundcovers.

CULTIVARS: 'Rosea' has pink flowers.

OTHER SPECIES: Most other clematis species are climbing vines.

Convallaria majalis Liliaceae

LILY-OF-THE-VALLEY

Established clumps of lily-of-the-valley compete well with weeds and can thrive in the same spot for decades with little or no care. They spread quickly by creeping roots.

BEST CLIMATE AND SITE: Zones 2–8. Moist, well-drained, fertile soil enriched with organic matter. Partial to full shade.

HEIGHT AND SPREAD: Height of foliage 6–8 inches (15–20 cm); spread unlimited. Flower height 8–10 inches (20–25 cm).

DESCRIPTION: Lily-of-the-valley is beloved for its fragrant, bell-shaped, waxy, white flowers. Each crown (known as a pip) produces two large, oblong, green leaves and one upright flower spike in late spring. The flowers may be followed by glossy, orange-red berries in summer.

GROWING GUIDELINES: Set plants 4–6 inches (10–15 cm) apart in late fall or very early spring. The deciduous leaves turn brown in mid- to late-summer, so place them where the unsightly appearance isn't a problem. If desired, you can cut down the brown leaves to tidy up the planting. Lily-of-the-valley benefits from an application of compost or leaf mold each fall if the area isn't fertile. Thin out crowded plantings if they stop blooming well. Propagate by division after flowering or in fall.

LANDSCAPE USES: Clumps of lily-of-the-valley are ideal groundcovers in shady borders and foundation plantings and under shrubs and deciduous trees. They also naturalize well for an easy-care cover in low-maintenance areas. The flowers make charming, aromatic spring bouquets.

Coronilla varia   Leguminosae

CROWN VETCH

Crown vetch is a pretty but tough groundcover that's ideal for difficult sites, such as steep slopes. It can be invasive, so keep it away from flower gardens.

BEST CLIMATE AND SITE: Zones 3–9. Dry, sandy, well-drained soil. Full sun.

HEIGHT AND SPREAD: Height to 18 inches (45 cm); spread to 4 feet (1.2 m).

DESCRIPTION: Crown vetch produces feathery, deciduous leaflets on sprawling, vine-like stems. Clover-like clusters of pink and white flowers bloom at the top of the stems through the summer. Crown vetch spreads by rhizomes.

GROWING GUIDELINES: Set plants 1–2 feet (30–60 cm) apart in spring. Once plants are established and start to spread, mow the stems each spring to encourage compact growth. Propagate by division or seed in spring.

LANDSCAPE USES: Crown vetch is an excellent groundcover for banks that are difficult to mow. It's also a good choice for erosion control and for stabilizing the soil in large, dry areas. Plants become invasive in conditions they like, so be wary about putting them near flower borders or rock gardens; they can easily overpower less vigorous plants.

CULTIVARS: 'Penngift' tolerates some shade. Flowers appear in early summer and continue until frost.

Cotoneaster horizontalis   Rosaceae

ROCKSPRAY COTONEASTER

The dense branching habit and horizontal growth of rockspray cotoneaster make it an excellent groundcover. It spreads as the branch tips touch the ground and take root.

BEST CLIMATE AND SITE: Zones 5–8. Light, well-drained, neutral to slightly acid, fertile soil containing a generous amount of humus. Full sun is best; can tolerate light shade.

HEIGHT AND SPREAD: Height 2–3 feet (60–90 cm); spread normally to 6 feet (1.8 m) but unlimited where branches can touch the soil and form roots.

DESCRIPTION: This popular low-growing, woody shrub bears round, 1/2-inch (12 mm) wide, shiny, dark green leaves on horizontally spreading branches. The deciduous leaves turn orange-red in fall. Small, pinkish flowers bloom along the stems in spring, followed by ornamental red berries in fall.

GROWING GUIDELINES: Set plants 2–4 feet (60–120 cm) apart in spring or fall. Prune lightly if needed to keep plants in shape. Cotoneaster is susceptible to a bacterial disease called fire blight, which also attacks other rose-family members (including pears and apples). Fire blight causes shoot tips to turn brown and burnt-looking. Avoid heavy pruning and over-fertilizing, which promote succulent growth that is more disease-prone. San Jose scale, borers, and other insects can be a problem in Southern gardens. The tangled, many-branched stems tend to trap leaves, paper, and debris that you'll need to pick out by hand. Propagate by layering (covering parts of low-growing stems with soil to encourage rooting) or cuttings in summer.

ROCKSPRAY COTONEASTER—CONTINUED

HARDY ICEPLANT

Rockspray cotoneaster is popular for its pinkish spring flowers, its red fall berries, and its glossy green leaves that age to red before dropping by early winter.

Long-blooming hardy iceplant offers a colorful show of purple flowers from summer through frost. It looks wonderful cascading down slopes and over stones in rock gardens.

LANDSCAPE USES: Rockspray cotoneaster is an excellent groundcover for mass plantings, borders, foundation plantings, and rock gardens.

CULTIVARS: 'Robusta' has pink flowers in spring and dark green foliage that turns purplish in fall.

OTHER SPECIES:

C. adpressus, creeping cotoneaster, is a deciduous, slow-growing shrub that reaches 1 foot (30 cm) tall. It bears pinkish flowers and red fruits. 'Little Gem' is an especially dense, low-growing cultivar. Zones 5–8.

C. apiculatus, cranberry cotoneaster, grows to 3 feet (90 cm) tall and has small, round, shiny, semi-evergreen leaves. The pink spring flowers are followed by bright red fall fruits. Zones 5–8.

C. dammeri, bearberry cotoneaster, grows 6–24 inches (15–60 cm) tall, depending on the cultivar. Each plant spreads from 4–10 feet (1.2–3 m). Its shiny green, evergreen or semi-evergreen leaves turn purplish in fall. The white spring flowers are followed by a profusion of red berries in fall. 'Coral Beauty' grows with an upright habit to 3 feet (90 cm) tall with white blooms and coral berries. Zones 5–8.

BEST CLIMATE AND SITE: Zones 7–9. Rich, well-drained, dry soil. Full sun.

HEIGHT AND SPREAD: Height 4 inches (10 cm); spread to 12 inches (30 cm).

DESCRIPTION: This low-growing South African succulent is becoming increasingly popular in the United States for its small, rosy purple, daisy-like flowers, which bloom from summer until frost over mats of narrow, curving leaves.

GROWING GUIDELINES: Set plants 12 inches (30 cm) apart in spring. They like dry soil in winter and do best when temperatures don't go below 50°F (10°C). In warm climates, the plants bloom all year but grow mostly in the summer. Established plants need little care. Propagate by seed or cuttings in spring or summer.

LANDSCAPE USES: Hardy iceplant is a tough, beautiful, long-blooming groundcover for rock gardens or sunny banks.

OTHER SPECIES:

D. nubigenum grows to 2 inches (5 cm) tall and 8–10 inches (20–25 cm) wide. This fast-growing, tough plant has bright yellow flowers in late spring and yellow-green leaves that turn red in winter. Zones 5–9.

Deutzia gracilis   Saxifragaceae

SLENDER DEUTZIA

Grow slender deutzia where you need a tall, spreading, shrubby groundcover. Try it in a foundation planting or shrub border or on a slope.

BEST CLIMATE AND SITE: Zones 5–9. Fertile, well-drained soil. Full sun.

HEIGHT AND SPREAD: Height 3–5 feet (90–150 cm); spread to 3 feet (90 cm).

DESCRIPTION: Slender deutzia is a graceful, mounding shrub from Japan with wide-spreading branches. The arching stems are clad in bright green, oblong to lance-shaped, deciduous leaves and covered with clusters of 3/4-inch (18 mm), white flowers in late spring.

GROWING GUIDELINES: Set plants 3–4 feet (90–120 cm) apart in spring in most places (they can take fall planting in Zones 8–9). After flowering, thin out established plants by cutting some of the oldest shoots to the ground. Plants benefit from winter mulch in the coolest parts of their range. Propagate by cuttings any time during the growing season.

LANDSCAPE USES: Slender deutzias are lovely as large-scale groundcovers in foundation plantings and shrub borders. They look especially attractive among rocks; try them on rocky banks, where their trailing stems can cascade down the slope.

CULTIVARS: 'Nikko' is a dwarf selection; it grows only 12–15 inches (30–37.5 cm) tall and has double, white flowers in late spring. The foliage turns burgundy in fall. Zones 6–9.

Dianthus deltoides   Caryophyllaceae

MAIDEN PINK

Cheerful maiden pinks are wonderful as small-scale groundcovers in sunny spots. Snipping off the spent flowers can promote rebloom later in the season.

BEST CLIMATE AND SITE: Zones 3–8; best where summers are cool and winters are not very cold. Well-drained, slightly alkaline soil. Sun; will tolerate partial shade with a half day of sunlight.

HEIGHT AND SPREAD: Height of foliage to 3 inches (7.5 cm); spread to 3 feet (90 cm). Flower height 6–12 inches (15–30 cm).

DESCRIPTION: Maiden pinks form dense mats of grass-like leaves on trailing stems. The flat, pink or red summer flowers are 3/4 inch (18 mm) wide and have bright crimson eyes.

GROWING GUIDELINES: Set plants about 12 inches (30 cm) apart in spring or fall. If you cut the stems down as soon as the flowers fade, the plants may bloom again later in the season. If you allow the flowers to set seed, plants may self-sow. Maiden pinks benefit from a protective light mulch (such as evergreen branches) in cold-winter areas. Propagate by seed in spring or cuttings in summer.

LANDSCAPE USES: Maiden pinks make a good groundcover for small areas. Try them in rock gardens, on sunny slopes, as edgings, and along the front of flower beds and borders.

CULTIVARS: 'Albus' has white flowers on 6-inch (15 cm) stems. 'Brilliant' has bright red flowers. 'Zing Rose' blooms prolifically from late spring throughout the summer with bright rose flowers on 6-inch (15 cm) stems.

Dicentra eximia Fumariaceae	*Epimedium* x *versicolor* Berberidaceae

FRINGED BLEEDING HEART

PERSIAN EPIMEDIUM

Fringed bleeding heart forms rounded mounds of ferny, blue-green leaves. Nodding, pink flowers bloom above the foliage throughout most of the growing season.

Persian epimedium is a good plant for growing along the edge of woods. Established clumps compete well with tree and shrub roots to get the moisture and nutrients they need.

BEST CLIMATE AND SITE: Zones 3–8. Well-drained, fertile, light soil. Partial shade; tolerates full sun as long as it receives plenty of moisture.

HEIGHT AND SPREAD: Height of foliage to about 1 foot (30 cm); spread 12–24 inches (30–60 cm). Flower height 12–18 inches (30–45 cm).

DESCRIPTION: Fringed bleeding heart forms tidy mounds of feathery, fern-like, blue-green leaves. Numerous pink, heart-shaped, ³/₄-inch (18 mm) flowers bloom for several weeks in late spring and intermittently throughout the season.

GROWING GUIDELINES: Set plants 8 inches (20 cm) apart in early spring. Transplant carefully, since the roots are brittle and break easily. Fringed bleeding hearts may need watering in dry weather. Propagate by seed or division in early spring.

LANDSCAPE USES: Fringed bleeding heart is an excellent flowering groundcover for a shady border, particularly when interplanted with small spring bulbs and other shade-loving plants, such as hostas. It also thrives in a sunny perennial border where shaded by larger plants.

CULTIVARS: 'Alba' produces white flowers beginning in early summer. 'Boothman's Variety' has light pink, heart-shaped flowers and bluish leaves. 'Luxuriant' has deep reddish pink blooms and grows to 15 inches (30 cm) tall. 'Snowdrift' bears white flowers. 'Zestful' has pale pink flowers.

BEST CLIMATE AND SITE: Zones 5–8. Humus-rich, moist, somewhat acid soil. Light to heavy shade; plants tolerate some sun if they receive enough moisture.

HEIGHT AND SPREAD: Height to 1 foot (30 cm); spread 9–12 inches (22.5–30 cm).

DESCRIPTION: Striking, heart-shaped, leathery leaves on wiry stems are purple-red or mottled in early spring and later become green. Clusters of distinctive, hooded, waxy, red-and-yellow flowers that resemble columbines bloom on wiry stems in early- to mid-spring. Persian epimedium is evergreen in the South; leaves in Northern gardens turn brown by midwinter.

GROWING GUIDELINES: Set plants about 12 inches (30 cm) apart in spring. In early spring, cut all of the leaves to the ground to tidy the planting and to make it easier to see the delicate flowers. To propagate, divide after flowering.

LANDSCAPE USES: Use Persian epimedium in shady rock gardens and woodland gardens and as an edging along paths. It is also an excellent foundation plant for the north side of a building.

CULTIVARS: 'Sulphureum' has pale yellow flowers with deep yellow centers in late spring. Its dark green foliage is tinged with bronze in springtime. It is one of the most vigorous, hardy, and fast-spreading cultivars.

Erica carnea   Ericaceae

SPRING HEATH

Spring heath grows in low, spreading clumps with evergreen, needle-like leaves and bell-shaped spring flowers. It prefers a sunny site with moist but well-drained, acid soil.

BEST CLIMATE AND SITE: Zones 5–7. Well-drained, sandy, acid soil with plenty of moisture. Full sun.

HEIGHT AND SPREAD: Height to 18 inches (45 cm); spread to 3 feet (90 cm).

DESCRIPTION: This small, evergreen shrub forms clumps or woody stems with narrow, needle-like, dark green foliage. Clusters of bell-shaped, red flowers bloom along shoot tips over a long period in early spring.

GROWING GUIDELINES: Set plants 3 feet (90 cm) or more apart in spring or early fall. Keep the soil mulched, and water as necessary to keep it evenly moist. Clip plants back after blooming to promote compact growth. Propagate by softwood cuttings in early summer, by division in early spring, or layering (covering parts of low-growing stems with soil to promote rooting) anytime.

LANDSCAPE USES: Spring heath forms an excellent cover for slopes and rock gardens.

CULTIVARS: 'Springwood Pink' has clear pink flowers and bronze foliage in spring. 'Springwood White' has creamy white flowers.

OTHER SPECIES:

E. x *darleyensis* (Darleyensis hybrids), winter heath, remains in bloom throughout the winter months in spreading mounds. 'Mediterranean Pink' and 'Mediterranean White' are among the many cultivars. Zones 6–9.

Euonymus fortunei   Celastraceae

WINTERCREEPER

This evergreen produces long vining stems that take root as they travel over the earth. The clinging stems will also climb up trees, walls, and buildings.

BEST CLIMATE AND SITE: Zones 5–9. Well-drained, slightly acid, fertile, humus-rich soil. Sun to partial shade.

HEIGHT AND SPREAD: Height 1–2 feet (30–60 cm); stems spread to 30 feet (9 m).

DESCRIPTION: The oval, waxy, green, 2-inch (5 cm) leaves become deep red in fall when grown in full sun. Inconspicuous white flowers bloom on mature stems in summer, followed by pink fruits in fall.

GROWING GUIDELINES: Set plants 1 foot (30 cm) or more apart in spring or fall. Trim and shape established plants as needed in early spring. Plants may be susceptible to euonymus scale, especially in warm areas. Spray with organic insecticide such as insecticidal soap, if necessary. Propagate by cuttings in early summer or by layering anytime.

LANDSCAPE USES: Wintercreeper is useful as a low-growing evergreen for erosion control on banks. It grows relatively slowly in shade, but it is one of the best groundcovers for dry, shady spots.

CULTIVARS: 'Colorata', purple-leaved wintercreeper, grows 12–15 inches (30–37 cm) tall and is a dense, spreading groundcover with leaves that turn purple for fall and winter. 'Harlequin' has small green-and-white leaves. 'Kewensis' has very small leaves and a low, 3–4-inch (7.5–10 cm), prostrate growth habit, making it a good choice for small spaces.

| *Galium odoratum* | Rubiaceae | *Gaultheria procumbens* | Ericaceae |

SWEET WOODRUFF

WINTERGREEN

Delicate-looking sweet woodruff is a fast-spreading ground-cover for shady gardens. It can crowd out less vigorous plants but combines well with shrubs and trees.

BEST CLIMATE AND SITE: Zones 3–8. Well-drained, moist, humus-rich, somewhat acid soil. Partial to full shade.

HEIGHT AND SPREAD: Height 6–12 inches (15–30 cm); spread to 2 feet (60 cm).

DESCRIPTION: Sweet woodruff forms carpets of deciduous, 1-inch (2.5 cm) leaves in whorls on square stems. The leaves have a sweet fragrance when dried. In early spring, loose clusters of small, star-shaped, white flowers appear just above the leaves. Sweet woodruff is also commonly called bedstraw and was formerly known as *Asperula odorata.*

GROWING GUIDELINES: Set plants 8 inches (20 cm) apart in spring. Trim back established plants in spring to prevent leggy growth, but always leave the foliage closest to the ground intact. Propagate by division in spring or fall.

LANDSCAPE USES: Sweet woodruff is a charming groundcover for woodland gardens. It is also useful under shrubs, such as rhododendrons. The dried leaves are used in sachets.

Wintergreen spreads slowly to form handsome carpets of glossy evergreen leaves in spots with moist, humus-rich, acid soil. The leaves are accented by bright red fall fruit.

BEST CLIMATE AND SITE: Zones 3–8. Acid, humus-rich, evenly moist soil. Plant in light shade or in sunny spots that get midday shade.

HEIGHT AND SPREAD: Height 3–4 inches (7.5–10 cm); spread to 1 foot (30 cm).

DESCRIPTION: This evergreen native of eastern North America has shiny, oval, 2-inch (5 cm), leathery leaves that become reddish in fall. The leaves are fragrant when crushed. Small, solitary, nodding, urn-shaped, white flowers dangle under the leaves in early summer, and edible, bright red fruits appear in fall. Wintergreen spreads slowly by creeping underground roots.

GROWING GUIDELINES: Set plants about 1 foot (30 cm) apart in spring. Mulch is beneficial in hot climates to keep the roots cool and moist. Propagate by division in spring or fall or by cuttings in summer.

LANDSCAPE USES: Wintergreen makes a nice year-round cover in naturalized woodland plantings, under trees, and in shady rock gardens.

Geranium macrorrhizum   Geraniaceae

BIGROOT CRANESBILL

Bigroot cranesbill grows in spreading clumps to form lush mats of aromatic, lobed, green leaves. The foliage turns reddish in fall and may hold its color into early winter.

BEST CLIMATE AND SITE: Zones 3–8. Well-drained, fairly rich, moist soil; tolerates dry soil once established. Sun or light shade. (Plants prefer not to be in hot sunlight all day, particularly in the South.)

HEIGHT AND SPREAD: Height 12–18 inches (30–45 cm); spread 2–3 feet (60–90 cm).

DESCRIPTION: This slow-spreading, mound-forming perennial is one of many delightful and versatile species of hardy geranium (*Geranium* spp.)—not to be confused with *Pelargonium* spp., the common houseplant geranium. Bigroot cranesbill bears 1-inch (2.5 cm), pink or reddish purple flowers in early summer. The spreading clumps of aromatic, lobed, green leaves stay attractive throughout the season and turn reddish in fall.

GROWING GUIDELINES: Set plants about 2 feet (60 cm) apart in early spring. They need little maintenance, but divide them whenever they become too large and stop blooming well. Propagate by division in spring or fall.

LANDSCAPE USES: Grow bigroot cranesbill in border plantings, rock gardens, and wild gardens and on slopes. It can even take dry shade.

CULTIVARS: 'Ingwersen's Variety' has pale pink flowers in spring and reblooms in summer. *G.* x *cantabrigiense* 'Biokovo', a hybrid of *G. macrorrhizum* and *G. dalmaticum,* is a vigorous grower and has white flowers tinged with pink over fragrant foliage.

Geranium sanguineum   Geraniaceae

BLOOD-RED CRANESBILL

Blood-red cranesbill is an adaptable, easy-care perennial that looks equally wonderful alone in beds and borders and in masses as a flowering groundcover.

BEST CLIMATE AND SITE: Zones 3–8. Prefers well-drained, rich, moist soil; will adapt to most soil types. Sun to light shade.

HEIGHT AND SPREAD: Height 9–18 inches (22.5–45 cm); spread 2–3 feet (60–90 cm).

DESCRIPTION: Blood-red cranesbill forms mounds of deep green, deeply lobed leaves that turn reddish in fall. Five-petaled, 1-inch (2.5 cm), pink to magenta blossoms cover the plant from late spring into summer.

GROWING GUIDELINES: Set plants about 2 feet (60 cm) apart in spring or fall. This adaptable, dependable perennial needs virtually no care. Propagate by division in spring or fall.

LANDSCAPE USES: Blood-red cranesbill is a fine specimen plant in the landscape, perennial border, rock garden, or woodland planting. It is also spectacular in masses, alone or combined with other *Geranium* species.

CULTIVARS: 'Album' has pure white flowers. 'Cedric Morris' is similar to the species but has larger flowers with petals that overlap; it flowers intermittently throughout the summer and early fall. 'Lancastriense', Lancaster geranium, grows only 6–12 inches (15–30 cm) tall and has red-veined pink flowers.

Gypsophila repens   Caryophyllaceae

CREEPING BABY'S-BREATH

Try creeping baby's-breath as a small-scale groundcover for sunny slopes and rock gardens. Cut plants back after flowering to promote compact growth and possible rebloom.

BEST CLIMATE AND SITE: Zones 3–8. Well-drained, not-too-fertile soil. Full sun.

HEIGHT AND SPREAD: Height 6–10 inches (15–25 cm); spread to 2 feet (60 cm).

DESCRIPTION: In late spring, cloud-like masses of tiny, 1/4-inch (6 mm), white flowers cover trailing stems clad in narrow, smooth, gray-green leaves.

GROWING GUIDELINES: Set plants about 16 inches (40 cm) apart in spring. To stimulate new growth and rebloom, cut established plants back by about half immediately after flowering. Creeping baby's-breath doesn't transplant easily, so divide in spring only if absolutely necessary. Propagate by stem cuttings in early summer, or sow seed of the species in spring or fall.

LANDSCAPE USES: Creeping baby's-breath is beautiful when cascading over rocks in rock gardens or trailing over slopes. It is also good for edging perennial borders or walkways.

CULTIVARS: 'Alba' has pure white blooms. 'Bodgeri' has double, pink blooms. 'Rosea' has light pink flower clusters in summer over silver-gray foliage.

Hedera helix   Araliaceae

ENGLISH IVY

English ivy is available in a range of leaf colors and patterns. The plain green ivies tend to be most cold-tolerant, but many of the variegated ones are surprisingly hardy.

BEST CLIMATE AND SITE: Zones 5–9. Prefers moist, well-drained, rich soil; tolerates poor, dry soil. Partial to full shade.

HEIGHT AND SPREAD: Height to 6 inches (15 cm); forms a mat that spreads limitlessly.

DESCRIPTION: This handsome evergreen vine has lobed, green leaves that are 2–5 inches (5–12.5 cm) long on woody stems. The stems creep over the ground, sending down roots as they travel. When they meet an upright surface, they climb with clinging rootlets. These upright stems mature to produce unlobed leaves, green flowers, and black berries.

GROWING GUIDELINES: Set plants about 2 feet (60 cm) apart in spring or fall. Prune as needed to control and direct the growth. Propagate by cuttings in early spring to early summer and by layering (covering parts of the creeping stems to promote rooting) anytime.

LANDSCAPE USES: English ivy is a dependable, fast-spreading groundcover. Use it on slopes for erosion control. It's also attractive as a groundcover beneath deciduous trees. English ivy can quickly become invasive in spots it enjoys, creating a maintenance nightmare when it creeps into lawns and flower borders. Grow it where the spread isn't a problem, or surround it with an edging strip and be ruthless about trimming back any shoots that try to escape.

SUN ROSE

Sun rose, also called rock rose, is a low-growing shrub with small green or gray-green leaves. It blooms for many weeks, although each flower only lasts one day.

BEST CLIMATE AND SITE: Zones 6–8. Well-drained, sandy, neutral to slightly alkaline soil. Full sun.

HEIGHT AND SPREAD: Height 8–18 inches (20–45 cm); spread to 3 feet (90 cm).

DESCRIPTION: This low-growing woody shrub forms spreading mounds of narrow, hairy, evergreen leaves. Clusters of yellow, pink, or white blooms that resemble single roses begin blooming just above the foliage in late spring or early summer.

GROWING GUIDELINES: Set plants 2 feet (60 cm) apart in spring or fall. This shrub needs little or no care. Prune back by one-third to one-half after flowering stops if you wish to stimulate a second bloom. Protect plants with a light winter mulch in the coldest parts of their range; you may also need to trim them back in early spring to remove winter-damaged tips. Propagate by cuttings in summer.

LANDSCAPE USES: Sun rose is a good choice as a drought-tolerant cover for dry, hot, troublesome areas. It is also a fine addition to rock gardens and borders.

CULTIVARS: 'Dazzler' has dazzling magenta flowers. 'Goldilocks', as the name implies, is covered with golden yellow blooms. 'Henfield Brilliant' has bright terra-cotta blooms. 'Rose Glory' has rose-pink flowers. 'Wisley Pink' has delicate pink blooms over silvery foliage.

LENTEN ROSE

Lenten rose is a slow-spreading groundcover with dark green evergreen leaves. Grow it in woodland gardens with ferns, primroses, hostas, and other shade-loving plants.

BEST CLIMATE AND SITE: Zones 4–9. Well-drained, moist, cool, humus-rich soil; will tolerate dry soil once established. Partial to full shade.

HEIGHT AND SPREAD: Height of foliage to about 1 foot (30 cm); spread to 2 feet (60 cm). Flower stems to 18 inches (45 cm) tall.

DESCRIPTION: The large leaves are divided into seven to nine segments. Flowering stems rise from the center of the clump in late winter or in early spring in cold climates. The 3–4-inch (7.5–10 cm) wide flowers range in color from creamy white to deep rose shades, sometimes with reddish spots. All parts of the plant contain the poison helleborin, so they are very poisonous if eaten. Brushing against the foliage can also cause dermatitis in some people.

GROWING GUIDELINES: Set plants about 2 feet (60 cm) apart in spring or fall. They will take several seasons to become well established, so you may want to combine them with another low groundcover to fill the space. Top-dress plantings with aged compost, old manure, or leaf mold to add fertility. Propagate by sowing fresh seed in summer or by division, preferably in late summer. Or dig up and move small self-sown seedlings.

LANDSCAPE USES: Lenten roses form an elegant evergreen groundcover beneath deciduous trees, in shrub borders, and in shady rock gardens.

| *Hemerocallis fulva* | Liliaceae | *Herniaria glabra* | Caryophyllaceae |

TAWNY DAYLILY

RUPTUREWORT

Tawny daylilies are a common sight along roadsides in summer. These tough plants are superb for erosion control on slopes and in hillside plantings.

Rupturewort forms mossy mats of dainty green leaves. It spreads slowly, so save it for small areas or interplant it with another slow-growing groundcover.

BEST CLIMATE AND SITE: Zones 2–9. Adapts to nearly any soil that isn't waterlogged. Sun to partial shade.

HEIGHT AND SPREAD: Height of foliage 2–3 feet (60–90 cm); spread unlimited. Flowering stems grow to 4 feet (1.2 m) tall.

DESCRIPTION: The orange-red, lily-shaped, 3–4-inch (7.5–10 cm) flowers bloom above clumps of arching, grass-like, 2-foot (60 cm) long leaves. Each flower lasts only one day, but plants form many buds to bloom over several weeks. Tawny daylily spreads by thick, tuberous roots. Don't confuse it with lilies of the genus *Lilium,* which are bulbs.

GROWING GUIDELINES: Set plants 1½–3 feet (45–90 cm) apart, depending on how soon you need cover. You can plant anytime, although spring and fall are best. Mulch is beneficial, since plants need plenty of water. Tawny daylilies are very pest-resistant. Divide clumps in late summer when they become overcrowded or when you want more plants.

LANDSCAPE USES: Grow tawny daylilies under deciduous trees, in wild gardens, and along paths, driveways, and roadsides. Their foliage can look tattered by midsummer; plant them where you won't see them close up, or cut back the leaves to get a new flush of growth. Combine daylilies with daffodils for spring interest; the daylily foliage will cover the yellowing daffodil leaves.

BEST CLIMATE AND SITE: Zones 4–9. Light-textured, well-drained, fertile, humus-rich soil, with a pH that's neutral to slightly acid. Full sun to light shade.

HEIGHT AND SPREAD: Height 1–3 inches (2.5–7.5 cm); spreads slowly to cover a wide area.

DESCRIPTION: Rupturewort is a slow-creeping, mat-forming herb with tiny, smooth, moss-like, green leaves. The foliage turns coppery red in winter in warm climates, where it is evergreen (Zones 8–9). Plants are deciduous in cooler zones and may be short-lived in some locations. Flowers are inconspicuous.

GROWING GUIDELINES: Set plants 6–12 inches (15–30 cm) apart, depending on how fast you want to cover the area. Rupturewort spreads slowly, so you'll need many plants to form a quick groundcover. Propagate by division or seed in spring.

LANDSCAPE USES: Rupturewort is lovely cascading over rocks in rock gardens. It's also ideal between stepping stones on paths, although it can't take heavy foot traffic. The mossy mat makes a fine carpet for small spring bulbs, such as crocuses and squills (*Scilla* spp.).

Hosta spp. Liliaceae

HOSTAS

Versatile, easy-to-grow hostas form attractive rounded or arching clumps of foliage in many shades of solid green, blue-green, and yellow as well as variegations.

BEST CLIMATE AND SITE: Zones 3–8. Rich, well-drained, moist soil is best; plants can adapt to most soil types. Partial to full shade.

HEIGHT AND SPREAD: Height of foliage 6–24 inches (15–60 cm) or more; spread 6–48 inches (15–120 cm). Flower stalks can be 6 inches (15 cm) to 5 feet (1.5 m) or more.

DESCRIPTION: The rounded or lance-shaped leaves vary in size from a few inches to several feet long. Spikes of trumpet-shaped flowers in lavender, blue, or white appear on stalks in early-, mid-, or late-summer, depending on the species or cultivar.

GROWING GUIDELINES: Set plants 1–3 feet (30–90 cm) or more apart (depending on their ultimate size) in spring or fall. Divide in spring or fall if you want more plants or if the clumps become too overgrown to bloom; otherwise, they can stay in place for many years. Slugs and snails may be a problem; trap them under cabbage leaves (destroy pests daily) or in pans of beer set flush with the soil surface. Some cultivars, especially those with blue leaves, are less prone to slug damage.

LANDSCAPE USES: Hostas are excellent for shady borders, rock gardens, north- and east-facing foundation plantings, woodland plantings, and slopes. They are ideal under deciduous trees. Hostas combine well with spring bulbs; the expanding hosta leaves will cover the dying bulb foliage.

Houttuynia cordata 'Variegata' Saururaceae

VARIEGATED HOUTTUYNIA

Variegated houttuynia is a fast-spreading groundcover that thrives in moist soil. The showy green, red, and yellow leaves are accented by white flowers in summer.

BEST CLIMATE AND SITE: Zones 5–9. Damp, rich soil; will grow in standing water. Partial to full shade.

HEIGHT AND SPREAD: Height 15–18 inches (37.5–45 cm); spread 18 inches (45 cm).

DESCRIPTION: Variegated houttuynia forms creeping clumps of 2–3-inch (5–7.5 cm) long, green leaves variegated with reds and yellows; the leaves turn purplish in fall. Some people describe the crushed leaves as citrus-scented; others call them foul-smelling. Small white flowers surrounded with white, petal-like bracts in summer resemble tiny dogwood blossoms. Plants are deciduous in cold climates and evergreen in warm areas. The species was named after Dutch horticulturist Martin Houttuyn; the name is pronounced "how-tyne-nia." The cultivar 'Variegata' is also sold as 'Chameleon'.

GROWING GUIDELINES: Set plants 12 inches (30 cm) apart in spring. In ideal (boggy) areas, houttuynia can become invasive. Pull out unwanted plants, or surround the planting with an edging strip that extends several inches into the soil. Propagate by division in spring or fall or take cuttings in summer.

LANDSCAPE USES: Variegated houttuynia is useful for stabilizing banks along ponds and streams. Or try it as a groundcover for moist woodlands. Just make sure you're prepared to deal with the spread; established plantings are tough to eradicate!

St.-John's-wort

One of the easiest groundcovers to grow, St.-John's-wort needs little care. Its bright yellow flowers bloom throughout the summer over the blue-green leaves.

BEST CLIMATE AND SITE: Zones 6–8. Prefers moist, well-drained soil; tolerates dry soil. Sun to partial shade.

HEIGHT AND SPREAD: Height 12–18 inches (30–45 cm); spread to 2 feet (60 cm).

DESCRIPTION: St.-John's-wort is a vigorous, fast-spreading, shrubby perennial. Its trailing stems are clad in shiny, 4-inch (10 cm), blue-green leaves that are evergreen in warm climates. Bright yellow, 2–3-inch (5–7.5 cm) wide flowers with showy stamens bloom throughout the summer. The stems root as they rest on the soil.

GROWING GUIDELINES: Set plants about 2 feet (60 cm) apart in spring or fall. Prune the stems back in early spring to within a few inches of the ground to keep plants compact. Propagate by cuttings after flowering or by seed or division in spring or fall.

LANDSCAPE USES: St.-John's-wort is an excellent groundcover for sun or shade, especially on the West Coast. Try it for erosion control for sandy slopes. Plants can be invasive in spots they like, so grow them where the spread won't be a problem or surround the planting with an edging strip.

CULTIVARS: 'Hidcote' is a popular shrub with large, golden flowers in early summer. Height 3–4 feet (90–120 cm) and spread 4–5 feet (1.2–1.5 m). Zones 6–8.

Perennial candytuft

Perennial candytuft is a dependable, easy-care groundcover that offers evergreen leaves and white spring flowers. It looks especially good combined with small bulbs.

BEST CLIMATE AND SITE: Zones 3–9. Average, well-drained soil. Full sun; tolerates partial shade.

HEIGHT AND SPREAD: Height to 1 foot (30 cm); spread 2–3 feet (60–90 cm).

DESCRIPTION: Perennial candytuft forms neat, compact mounds of somewhat woody stems covered with narrow, 1½-inch (3.7 cm) long, evergreen leaves. The mounds are covered with clusters of flat, white, four-petaled flowers in late spring.

GROWING GUIDELINES: Set plants 12 inches (30 cm) apart in spring or fall. Trim back partway with hedge clippers after flowering to keep plants neat and compact. A layer of organic mulch and watering during dry spells will promote good flowering. In cold climates where you can't depend on winter snow cover, protect plants with evergreen boughs to prevent browning. Propagate by cuttings in summer or seed in spring or fall.

LANDSCAPE USES: Perennial candytuft is a natural choice for rock gardens and rocky slopes. It also makes an excellent four-season edging for borders and paths. Plant with deep purple grape hyacinths (*Muscari* spp.) for a colorful spring combination.

CULTIVARS: 'Autumn Snow' often reblooms at the end of the season; height to 8 inches (20 cm). 'Little Gem' is a dwarf; height to 6 inches (15 cm). 'Snowflake' has more numerous flowers than the species; height to 8 inches (20 cm).

Iris cristata Iridaceae

CRESTED IRIS

Crested iris forms spreading clumps of spiky leaves and delicate spring flowers. Grow it with foamflowers (Tiarella spp.) and other shade-loving wildflowers.

BEST CLIMATE AND SITE: Zones 3–8. Well-drained, moist, fertile, acid, humus-rich soil. Partial shade; will thrive in full sun if soil is moist.

HEIGHT AND SPREAD: Height 6–8 inches (15–20 cm); spread unlimited.

DESCRIPTION: This native American iris has slightly fragrant, flat, deep lavender flowers with yellow, toothed crests on the falls (three outer sepals). The midspring blooms nearly hide the broad, dagger-shaped, 6-inch (15 cm), green leaves that carpet the ground. Each bloom is short-lived, but the foliage remains attractive until dormancy in late summer. Crested iris spreads by rhizomes that creep near the surface of the soil.

GROWING GUIDELINES: Set plants 12 inches (30 cm) apart. Barely cover the roots with soil. Each spring, top-dress plantings with 1 inch (2.5 cm) or so of compost. Slugs may attack crested iris, since they enjoy the same moist conditions. Trap slugs under cabbage leaves (remove pests daily) or in pans of beer set flush with the soil surface. Crested irises don't need frequent division, but you can divide crowded clumps directly after blooming. This is also the best method of propagation.

LANDSCAPE USES: Crested iris adds a nice splash of spring color to rock gardens, woodland gardens, shady borders, and gardens near pools and streams.

CULTIVARS: 'Alba' has white flowers.

Juniperus horizontalis Cupressaceae

CREEPING JUNIPER

Plant creeping junipers for erosion control on slopes or for an evergreen accent in rock gardens and foundation plantings. They prefer full sun and well-drained soil.

BEST CLIMATE AND SITE: Zones 3–9. Prefers well-drained, sandy soil, but tolerates any soil, even clay. Full sun.

HEIGHT AND SPREAD: Height varies with cultivar, from 6–18 inches (15–45 cm); spread also variable to 8 feet (2.4 m).

DESCRIPTION: Creeping junipers are low-growing, evergreen shrubs with spreading branches carrying scaly or needle-like, blue-green leaves. Dark-colored fruits form on short stems in late summer.

GROWING GUIDELINES: Spacing varies according to size; check the ultimate spread in the catalog description or on the plant label before planting. Set out bareroot plants in spring and potted or balled-and-burlapped plants any time during the growing season. Prune in summer only to control size. Don't just shear off shoot tips; cut unwanted stems back to another stem or to the ground. Phomopsis twig blight may be a problem in wet springs, causing browned shoot tips; remove and destroy diseased branches. If bagworms attack, pick off and destroy the larvae. Spray with pyrethrin for spider mites. Propagate by cuttings or seed in summer.

LANDSCAPE USES: Junipers are among the most widely planted evergreen groundcovers. They are ideal for covering slopes, including steep slopes where other plants won't thrive.

CREEPING JUNIPER—CONTINUED

YELLOW ARCHANGEL

*Common juniper (*J. communis*) is available in many colors, sizes, and growing habits. Its foliage often turns brownish in cold-winter areas.*

CULTIVARS: 'Bar Harbor' has blue foliage; height to 1 foot (30 cm). 'Nana' is a dwarf cultivar; height 6–18 inches (15–45 cm). 'Plumosa', Andorra juniper, has light green foliage; height to 18 inches (45 cm). 'Wiltonii', blue rug juniper, has blue-green foliage; height to 6 inches (15 cm).

OTHER SPECIES:

J. chinensis 'Sargentii', Sargent juniper, forms mounds of green, needle-like foliage with white undersides. Height 18–24 inches (45–60 cm); spread to 10 feet (3 m). Zones 4–9.

J. communis, common juniper, comes in many shapes and sizes. 'Depressa', the prostrate juniper, is often seen spreading widely in open fields of poor soil in eastern North America. Zones 2–9.

J. conferta, shore juniper, has pale green, evergreen needles that age to blue-green. Height to 18 inches (45 cm); spread to 8 feet (2.4 m). Tolerates seaside conditions well. 'Emerald Sea' is a popular cultivar. Zones 6–9.

J. procumbens, Japanese garden juniper, has blue-green needles. Height to 5 feet (1.5 m); spread to 15 feet (4.5 m) or more. Zones 4–9.

Yellow archangel is fast-spreading, with long surface runners that take root as they creep over the soil. It can cover dry, shady areas where few other plants grow.

BEST CLIMATE AND SITE: Zones 4–9. Prefers moist, fertile soil; tolerates other soil types. Partial to full shade.

HEIGHT AND SPREAD: Height 12–18 inches (30–45 cm); spreads quickly to cover large areas.

DESCRIPTION: The silvery green, heart-shaped or oval, toothed, 3-inch (7.5 cm) long leaves produce a strong odor when bruised. Dense clusters of small, yellow, hooded flowers bloom in whorls along the stems in late spring. The foliage is evergreen in warm climates but deciduous in cold climates. This species looks similar to dead nettles (*Lamium* spp.) and is sometimes sold as *Lamium galeobdolon.*

GROWING GUIDELINES: Set plants 14 inches (35.5 cm) apart in spring. Because yellow archangel spreads so rapidly and can quickly overpower other plants, surround plantings with an edging strip and ruthlessly remove any shoots that try to sneak out. Propagate by division in spring or fall or by stem cuttings in summer.

LANDSCAPE USES: Naturalize yellow archangel in a woodland garden or other shady area where invasiveness isn't a problem.

CULTIVARS: 'Herman's Pride' forms neat mounds of small, silver-variegated leaves and has yellow spring blooms. It is not invasive like the species. 'Variegatum' has green foliage with silver variegations.

Lamium maculatum   Labiatae

SPOTTED LAMIUM

Spotted lamium, also known as spotted dead nettle, is a vigorous groundcover for shady gardens. It is a good choice for growing under trees and shrubs.

BEST CLIMATE AND SITE: Zones 3–8. Prefers moist, rich soil; tolerates dry shade. Partial to deep shade.

HEIGHT AND SPREAD: Height 12–14 inches (30–35.5 cm); spread to 2 feet (60 cm) or more.

DESCRIPTION: This vigorous plant grows quickly to form a dense cover of dark green, oval or heart-shaped leaves with a distinctive silvery white midrib. Lavender-pink, hooded, 1-inch (2.5 cm) flowers bloom in clusters throughout the summer. Spotted lamium is less invasive than its relative yellow archangel (*Lamiastrum galeobdolon*), but it is still a fast grower.

GROWING GUIDELINES: Set plants 12–14 inches (30–35 cm) apart in spring or fall. Cut plants back by about half in midsummer to promote a new flush of leaves. Plants often self-sow. Propagate by division in spring or fall or by cuttings in summer.

LANDSCAPE USES: Spotted lamium is handsome in wild areas, woodland gardens, and shady rock gardens.

CULTIVARS: 'Alba', white lamium, has white flowers and green leaves with silver centers. 'Aureum' has yellow leaves with a creamy white stripe and pink flowers. 'Beacon Silver' has silvery leaves and pink flowers. 'Shell Pink' has silvery striped leaves and clear pink flowers. 'White Nancy' has silver leaves with green margins and white flowers.

Leucothoe fontanesiana   Ericaceae

DROOPING LEUCOTHOE

Drooping leucothoe forms clumps of arching stems clad in evergreen leaves. Formerly listed as L. catesbaei, *this native shrub is also known as hobblebush and fetterbush.*

BEST CLIMATE AND SITE: Zones 5–9. Moist, fertile, acid soil. Light to heavy shade.

HEIGHT AND SPREAD: Height to 6 feet (1.8 m); spread to 10 feet (3 m) or more.

DESCRIPTION: Drooping leucothoe forms broad colonies of graceful, arching branches with broad, dark purplish green, leathery leaves up to 7 inches (17.5 cm) long that turn bronze in fall. Small, nodding, waxy, bell-shaped flowers with an unpleasant odor bloom along the stems in spring.

GROWING GUIDELINES: Set plants 2 feet (60 cm) or more apart in spring or fall. For best appearance, keep them pruned to about 3 feet (90 cm) by cutting off old stems to ground level after flowering. Propagate by digging up and transplanting rooted stems in spring or fall, by seed in spring, or by cuttings in early summer.

LANDSCAPE USES: Grow drooping leucothoe as a large-scale groundcover under trees or tall shrubs in the same spots rhododendrons would enjoy.

CULTIVARS: 'Girard's Rainbow' has leaves that turn many colors during the growing season, from red to pink to green, yellow, and bronze. 'Nana', a dwarf form, reaches 18–24 inches (45–60 cm) tall and spreads 6 feet (1.8 m) wide.

| *Liriope spicata* | Liliaceae | *Lysimachia nummularia* | Primulaceae |

CREEPING LILYTURF

CREEPING JENNY

Creeping lilyturf spreads by underground runners and can be extremely invasive, so plant it where it can creep freely or contain it with an edging strip.

Creeping Jenny is an attractive groundcover for moist-soil areas where its spread isn't a problem, The yellow-leaved cultivar 'Aurea' is less invasive than the species.

BEST CLIMATE AND SITE: Zones 5–10. Well-drained, moist, fertile, acid soil; tolerates drought. Full sun to deep shade.

HEIGHT AND SPREAD: Height of foliage to 10 inches (25 cm); spread to 18 inches (45 cm). Flower spikes grow 16–18 inches (40–45 cm) tall.

DESCRIPTION: The thick, long, narrow, grass-like leaves have tiny teeth on their margins. The foliage is evergreen in warm climates; it often becomes yellow and unsightly during Northern winters. Spikes of light lavender to whitish, $^{1}/_{4}$-inch (6 mm) flowers bloom above the foliage in mid- to late-summer, followed by black berries.

GROWING GUIDELINES: Set plants 1 foot (30 cm) apart in spring. Mow down the foliage of established plants in early spring to encourage new growth. Propagate by division in spring or fall.

LANDSCAPE USES: Creeping lilyturf forms a durable groundcover for difficult locations such as slopes or under trees and shrubs. It can also tolerate salt spray in seaside plantings.

OTHER SPECIES:

L. muscari, big blue lilyturf, is a fine, sturdy groundcover that forms clumps 12–18 inches (30–45 cm) tall. Pale lavender blooms resembling those of grape hyacinths flower in late summer, followed by black berries. Big blue lilyturf will self-sow, but it isn't as invasive as *L. spicata.* Zones 6–10.

BEST CLIMATE AND SITE: Zones 3–8. Moist, fertile soil. Full sun (in cool climates) to full shade (in warm climates).

HEIGHT AND SPREAD: Height 4–8 inches (10–20 cm); spread to 3 feet (90 cm).

DESCRIPTION: This creeping perennial, also known as moneywort, has shiny, round, $^{3}/_{4}$-inch (18 mm) leaves that resemble coins. The trailing stems bear bright, 1-inch (2.5 cm), yellow flowers throughout the summer. The stems root rapidly as they creep over the soil.

GROWING GUIDELINES: Set plants 8 inches (20 cm) apart in spring or fall. Creeping Jenny can be very invasive, and it rapidly becomes a weed problem when it spreads into lawn areas. Propagate by division in spring or fall.

LANDSCAPE USES: Creeping Jenny is a good groundcover around ponds and streams.

CULTIVARS: 'Aurea', golden creeping Jenny, grows 2 inches (5 cm) tall with golden yellow spring foliage that turns lime green in summer. It is a vigorous mat-forming creeper but not as invasive as the species. Zones 4–8.

OTHER SPECIES:

L. punctata, yellow loosestrife, grows to 3 feet (90 cm) tall with whorls of yellow flowers in early summer. A good naturalizer because it is fast-spreading, but it can be invasive. Zones 3–8.

Mahonia repens Berberidaceae	*Mazus reptans* Scrophulariaceae

CREEPING MAHONIA

MAZUS

If you're looking for an unusual evergreen groundcover for shade, consider creeping mahonia. It offers yellow spring flowers, black fall berries, and blue-green leaves.

Mazus forms ground-hugging mats of small leaves topped with tubular, lipped flowers in spring and early summer. It thrives in moist soil in sun or partial shade.

BEST CLIMATE AND SITE: Zones 6–9. Well-drained, moist, fertile, acid soil. Partial to full shade.

HEIGHT AND SPREAD: Height to 1 foot (30 cm); spread to 6 feet (1.8 m).

DESCRIPTION: Creeping mahonia forms colonies of leathery, blue-green, evergreen leaves that turn purplish bronze in fall. Attractive clusters of fragrant, yellow flowers in spring are followed by small, edible, black, grape-like berries in fall. Plants creep slowly by rhizomes (underground runners). Native to the Pacific Northwest, creeping mahonia is also known as dwarf Oregon grape.

GROWING GUIDELINES: Set plants about 3 feet (90 cm) apart in spring. Plants may need winter protection (like evergreen boughs) in Zone 6. Propagate by division or seed in spring or fall or by cuttings in early summer.

LANDSCAPE USES: Creeping mahonia is an attractive low-growing addition to a shady shrub border or foundation planting.

BEST CLIMATE AND SITE: Zones 5–8. Well-drained, moist, rich soil. Full sun to partial shade.

HEIGHT AND SPREAD: Height 1–2 inches (2.5–5 cm); spread 15–18 inches (37.5–45 cm).

DESCRIPTION: This creeping plant from the Himalayas sends out roots along its stems to form a carpet of bronzy green, toothed, 1-inch (2.5 cm) leaves. Light blue-violet, $^3/_4$-inch (18 mm) flowers have a lower lip spotted in white, greenish yellow, and purple in spring and early summer. Plants are evergreen only in warm climates.

GROWING GUIDELINES: Set plants 12 inches (30 cm) apart in spring. They can be invasive; surround plantings with edging strips if the spread is a problem. Propagate by division in spring or fall or by cuttings in summer.

LANDSCAPE USES: Plant mazus in crevices between flagstones on pathways; it mingles happily with creeping thyme and similar low-growing plants. Grow it in rock gardens as a carpet for small bulbs, like crocuses. Mazus is competitive with grass and will invade lawns.

CULTIVARS: 'Alba' has white flowers.

| *Microbiota decussata* | Cupressaceae | *Mitchella repens* | Rubiaceae |

SIBERIAN CARPET CYPRESS

PARTRIDGEBERRY

Unlike most needle-leaved evergreens, Siberian carpet cypress can grow in shade as well as sun. Its green foliage takes on bronzy tints in fall.

BEST CLIMATE AND SITE: Zones 2–8. Light-textured, well-drained, humus-rich, fertile soil with a pH of 5–7. Sun or shade.

HEIGHT AND SPREAD: Height to 2 feet (60 cm); spread to 5 feet (1.5 m) or more.

DESCRIPTION: This low-growing, spreading shrub from Siberia is an unusual evergreen because it grows well in shade. Its arching, scaly, feathery, green foliage turns bronze in fall. Its tiny cones have scales that cover an oval nut.

GROWING GUIDELINES: Set plants 3 feet (90 cm) or more apart in spring. Once established, Siberian carpet cypress is drought-tolerant and needs little care. Propagate by layering (covering parts of the low-growing stems with soil to promote rooting) or cuttings in early spring.

LANDSCAPE USES: Grow Siberian carpet cypress as a groundcover for slopes and beneath tall shrubs and evergreen trees.

Partridgeberry produces thin, woody, creeping stems with round, evergreen leaves. The white or pink spring flowers are followed by red berries in fall.

BEST CLIMATE AND SITE: Zones 4–9. Prefers cool, moist, humus-rich, acid soil; tolerates dry soil. Partial to full shade.

HEIGHT AND SPREAD: Height 1–2 inches (2.5–5 cm); spread to 2 feet (60 cm).

DESCRIPTION: Partridgeberry is a creeping woody evergreen with tiny, round, deep green leaves, often marked with white veins. White or light pink, trumpet-shaped flowers, $^1/_2$ inch (12 mm) long, bloom in spring in pairs along the stems. Each pair fuses to produce one tiny, $^1/_4$-inch (6 mm), red berry. Partridge and other ground birds enjoy the fruits.

GROWING GUIDELINES: Set plants 18–24 inches (45–60 cm) or more apart in spring. Plants may be slow to start spreading, but established plantings are usually trouble-free. Propagate by division or seed in spring or fall or by cuttings in early summer.

LANDSCAPE USES: Partridgeberry is attractive in shady rock gardens and under trees in woodland plantings. Good companions include ferns, mosses, and other shade-loving plants, such as epimediums (*Epimedium* spp.).

PERSIAN NEPETA

Persian nepeta is an easy-to-grow, old-fashioned, trouble-free garden perennial. Cutting it back after flowering promotes compact growth and encourages rebloom.

BEST CLIMATE AND SITE: Zones 3–8. Light-textured, average, well-drained soil; can tolerate poor (infertile) soil. Full sun.

HEIGHT AND SPREAD: Height of foliage to about 1 foot (30 cm); spread to 20 inches (50 cm). Flowering stems to 18 inches (45 cm) tall.

DESCRIPTION: Persian nepeta grows in mounds of gray-green, aromatic, toothed, evergreen leaves on square stems. Light blue or white, 1/4-inch (6 mm) flowers bloom in early summer. A relative of catnip (*N. cataria*), it too may attract cats.

GROWING GUIDELINES: Set plants 20 inches (50 cm) apart in spring. Trim back halfway after blooming for compact appearance and to encourage reblooming. Plants that are 2 years old or more are not as vigorous as young ones and don't bloom as readily, so you may need to divide or replace them. Propagate by division in spring or by cuttings in summer.

LANDSCAPE USES: Persian nepeta is handsome in rock gardens, in borders, and as edgings.

OTHER SPECIES:

N. x faassenii, catmint, is similar to *N. mussinii* and often sold as that plant. It is a good groundcover with many lavender flowers in early summer. Height to 1 foot (30 cm); spread to 18 inches (45 cm). 'Blue Wonder' has lavender-blue flowers. 'White Wonder' has white blooms. Zones 3–8.

SHOWY SUNDROPS

Showy sundrops spread quickly by underground runners. They bloom in early summer during the day, unlike the many night-blooming species of the Oenothera *genus.*

BEST CLIMATE AND SITE: Zones 3–8. Well-drained, average soil. Full sun to very light shade.

HEIGHT AND SPREAD: Height to 18 inches (45 cm); spread to 2 feet (60 cm) or more.

DESCRIPTION: Showy sundrops produces wiry stems clothed in toothed, green leaves and topped with 2-inch (5 cm), cup-shaped, white flowers that fade to soft pink and turn toward the sun.

GROWING GUIDELINES: Set plants about 2 feet (60 cm) apart in spring or fall. Showy sundrops can be invasive, especially in moist, fertile soil; plant where the spread isn't a problem, or surround the planting with an edging strip that extends a few inches below the ground. Propagate by division or seed in spring or fall.

LANDSCAPE USES: Showy sundrops look wonderful massed in low-maintenance areas, such as dry, sunny slopes.

CULTIVARS: 'Rosea' grows to 15 inches (37.5 cm) with clear pink, 3-inch (7.5 cm) blooms.

OTHER SPECIES:

O. tetragona, common sundrops, grows 1–2 feet (30–60 cm) tall. It forms rosettes of shiny, green, lance-shaped leaves that turn purplish in fall. Bright yellow, cup-shaped, 2-inch (5 cm) flowers bloom on reddish stems in early summer. Spreads quickly. Zones 5–8.

Omphalodes verna   Boraginaceae

BLUE-EYED MARY

Blue-eyed Mary is a charming little groundcover for moist soil in partial shade. Its blue spring flowers closely resemble those of forget-me-nots.

BEST CLIMATE AND SITE: Zones 5–8. Cool, moist, humus-rich soil. Partial shade.

HEIGHT AND SPREAD: Height to 8 inches (20 cm); spread to 2 feet (60 cm).

DESCRIPTION: Blue-eyed Mary is sometimes called creeping forget-me-not because of the resemblance of its loose clusters of lavender-blue, $1/2$-inch (12 mm) flowers that appear in spring. The oval, dark green, textured leaves are evergreen in warm climates. The plant spreads quickly by runners that root as they travel over the soil.

GROWING GUIDELINES: Set these easy-to-grow plants 1 foot (30 cm) apart in spring or fall. Mulch in hot climates to lengthen the bloom period. Propagate by division in spring or by seed in summer.

LANDSCAPE USES: Blue-eyed Mary naturalizes easily on banks or alongside streams. Use it as an underplanting for spring bulbs such as crocuses and dwarf daffodils.

Ophiopogon japonicus   Liliaceae

MONDO GRASS

Mondo grass is an excellent, sod-forming, grass-like perennial from the Orient. It is sometimes confused with lilyturf (Muscari spp.), which it closely resembles.

BEST CLIMATE AND SITE: Zones 7–9. Light-textured, well-drained, humus-rich, fertile soil with a pH of 5–7. Full sun to shade; does not tolerate midday sun in hot climates.

HEIGHT AND SPREAD: Height to 8 inches (20 cm); spread unlimited.

DESCRIPTION: The dark green, coarse-textured leaves are 15 inches (37.5 cm) long and $1/8$ inch (3 mm) wide. Lavender to white, $1/4$-inch (6 mm) flowers bloom in summer in short, loose clusters that are often hidden by the leaves. The flowers are followed by blue, pea-sized fruits. Plants spread by rhizomes (underground runners).

GROWING GUIDELINES: Set plants about 1 foot (30 cm) apart in spring. If the foliage has deteriorated over the winter, you can cut it down in spring. Slugs can be a problem; trap them under cabbage leaves (remove pests daily) or in pans of beer set flush with the soil surface. Propagate by division in spring or early fall.

LANDSCAPE USES: Mondo grass is an excellent groundcover under trees in the South. It is also a fine choice for seaside planting, and it's a good edging for borders.

OTHER SPECIES:

O. planiscapus is similar in growth habit to *O. japonicus,* but its green leaves become purple-black when mature. Zones 6–9.

| *Opuntia humifusa* | Cactaceae | *Pachysandra procumbens* | Buxaceae |

PRICKLY PEAR

ALLEGHENY PACHYSANDRA

Prickly pear is a surprisingly cold-tolerant cactus that makes a unique groundcover for a sunny, dry site. The yellow flowers give way to purplish fruits in fall.

The new spring leaves of Allegheny pachysandra are upright and light green. By winter, they are dark green mottled with silver, and they tend to rest on the ground.

BEST CLIMATE AND SITE: Zones 5–9. Well-drained, dry, sandy soil. Full sun.

HEIGHT AND SPREAD: Height 4–10 inches (10–25 cm); spread unlimited.

DESCRIPTION: This spreading, cold-hardy cactus bears prickly bristles on fleshy, oval pads. Attractive, yellow, cup-shaped, 3–4-inch (7.5–10 cm) flowers with white stamens bloom on short stems in late spring or early summer. Fleshy, purplish, 2-inch (5 cm), pear-shaped fruits form in fall; the fruits are edible but not very tasty. This species is also listed as *O. compressa*.

GROWING GUIDELINES: Set plants at least 18 inches (45 cm) apart in spring. Handle them with leather gloves to avoid the spines. Do not overwater. Prickly pear can become invasive in the South because any portion of stem roots quickly and birds scatter seed; be prepared to remove unwanted plants. Propagate by seed or division in spring.

LANDSCAPE USES: Prickly pear makes an unusual evergreen groundcover for rock gardens, seaside plantings, and other sunny, well-drained locations.

BEST CLIMATE AND SITE: Zones 5–9. Moist, cool, fertile, somewhat acid soil; established plants are drought-tolerant. Partial to full shade.

HEIGHT AND SPREAD: Height 6–10 inches (15–25 cm); spread to 1 foot (30 cm) or more.

DESCRIPTION: A native of the southeastern United States, this species of pachysandra has clumps of whorled, 3-inch (7.5 cm) leaves that are toothed at the ends. The leaves are evergreen in the South but often deciduous in the North. Brush-like spikes of white or purplish flowers spring from the base of the plant in early spring. Allegheny pachysandra spreads by rhizomes (underground runners).

GROWING GUIDELINES: Set plants 6–12 inches (15–30 cm) apart in spring. Mulch with compost or top-dress with aged manure in fall. Mow or cut down all of the leaves in early spring to clean up the planting and make it easier to see the flowers. Propagate by division in early spring or by cuttings in summer.

LANDSCAPE USES: Allegheny pachysandra makes an attractive groundcover on shady slopes, beneath trees, or in woodland plantings. Combine it with spring-blooming bulbs and wildflowers for extra interest.

Pachysandra terminalis	Buxaceae	*Parthenocissus quinquefolia*	Vitaceae

JAPANESE PACHYSANDRA

VIRGINIA CREEPER

Japanese pachysandra is one of the most common evergreen groundcovers for shady spots, especially in the North. Established plantings need little maintenance.

BEST CLIMATE AND SITE: Zones 4–8. Fertile, moist, neutral to slightly acid soil. Partial to deep shade.

HEIGHT AND SPREAD: Height 8–10 inches (20–25 cm); spread unlimited.

DESCRIPTION: Attractive, shiny, dark green, oval leaves, $1\frac{1}{2}$–4 inches (3.7–10 cm) in diameter, grow at the top of upright stems. The leaves are toothed near the ends. In spring, clusters of fragrant, creamy white flowers bloom at the stem tips. On mature plants, the flowers are sometimes followed by white berries in the fall. Japanese pachysandra spreads rapidly by rhizomes (underground runners) but it can be controlled; dense plantings are competitive with weeds.

GROWING GUIDELINES: Set plants 8–12 inches (20–30 cm) apart in spring. The leaves may turn yellow if plants get too much sun or if the soil lacks nutrients. Top-dress plantings yearly with compost or organic fertilizer. Prune back or mow every few years in spring to renew the planting. Euonymus scale can be a problem; cut down and destroy infested plants that have pear-shaped, white-and-gray scales on the leaves. Propagate by division in spring or by cuttings in summer.

LANDSCAPE USES: Japanese pachysandra is a dependable, easy-care groundcover for planting under deciduous or evergreen trees or in any shady area. It forms a good covering for slopes or banks.

Virginia creeper is a native plant that grows as either a groundcover or a clinging vine. The deciduous leaves turn bright red before dropping in fall.

BEST CLIMATE AND SITE: Zones 3–9. Most soil types; salt-tolerant. Sun to partial shade.

HEIGHT AND SPREAD: Height 6–8 inches (15–20 cm); spread unlimited.

DESCRIPTION: This deciduous, woody vine is native to eastern North America. It can either grow along the ground, forming a leafy mat, or it can climb trees, fences, and other upright features by clinging to the support with tendrils. Shiny, green leaves with five leaflets turn shades of brilliant scarlet and red in fall. Birds enjoy the black fruits that come in clusters, like grapes. Virginia creeper is also commonly known as woodbine.

GROWING GUIDELINES: Set plants 2–6 feet (60–180 cm) apart in spring or fall. Prune anytime to control growth. Plantings easily become invasive; grow where the spread isn't a problem, or cut back heavily in late fall if necessary. Propagate by layering (covering parts of the creeping stems with soil to promote rooting) anytime or by hardwood cuttings in early spring.

LANDSCAPE USES: Virginia creeper naturalizes well and is excellent for controlling erosion on steep banks, rocky slopes, and large, open areas. It readily climbs and covers fences, tree trunks, large shrubs, or any rough surface where it can take hold.

CULTIVARS: 'Engelmannii' has smaller leaflets than the species and a more compact growth habit.

PAXISTIMA

Paxistima is an attractive, low-growing, shrub-like evergreen that is native to Virginia. It has many common names, including cliff green, mountain-lover, and rat stripper.

BEST CLIMATE AND SITE: Zones 5–8. Well-drained, sandy, acid soil; can tolerate alkaline conditions. Prefers partial shade but will grow in sun.

HEIGHT AND SPREAD: Height to 1 foot (30 cm); spread to 5 feet (1.5 m).

DESCRIPTION: Shiny, leathery, narrow leaves turn bronze in fall. In late spring, inconspicuous, reddish brown flowers bloom along the stems, followed by small, white fruits. Stems root as they creep along the ground.

GROWING GUIDELINES: Set plants 2 feet (60 cm) apart in spring. Fertilize in early spring with a topdressing of compost or aged manure to encourage faster growth, if desired; otherwise, plants seldom need any attention. Propagate by division in spring or by cuttings in summer.

LANDSCAPE USES: Paxistima is an unusual, shrubby evergreen groundcover for a wild garden, rock garden, or shrub border. It looks great in front of other evergreens in a foundation planting.

OTHER SPECIES:

P. myrsinites, Oregon boxwood, grows to 18 inches (45 cm) tall and spreads to 6 feet (1.8 m). It has a compact growing habit; small, glossy, green leaves; and small, fragrant, purplish flowers. It is an excellent groundcover for the humidity-rich mountains of the Pacific Northwest, where it is native. Zones 5–8.

CREEPING PHLOX

Creeping phlox is available in many colors, making it a versatile plant for mixing with small bulbs and perennials that bloom at the same time.

BEST CLIMATE AND SITE: Zones 2–8. Moist, light, fertile, slightly acid soil. Prefers partial to full shade; will grow in sun.

HEIGHT AND SPREAD: Height of foliage 3–5 inches (7.5–12.5 cm); spread to 18 inches (45 cm). Flower height 6–12 inches (15–30 cm).

DESCRIPTION: Creeping phlox is grown for its masses of delicate lavender, pink, blue, or white, 1-inch (2.5 cm) wide flowers that bloom in late spring. Long, creeping, strawberry-like runners clad in small, oval, evergreen leaves root as they touch the earth to form solid mats. This shade-loving groundcover is native to eastern North America.

GROWING GUIDELINES: Set plants 1–2 feet (30–60 cm) apart in spring. For more compact growth, trim back flowering shoots after blooming. Propagate by division after flowering or by cuttings in late spring to early summer.

LANDSCAPE USES: Creeping phlox is an ideal groundcover for moist woodland plantings, beneath deciduous trees, in front of shady borders, or along the north and east sides of buildings. Try purple cultivars with bright yellow primroses or pink fringed bleeding heart (*Dicentra eximia*), for example.

OTHER SPECIES:

P. divaricata, wild blue phlox or wild sweet William, grows 12–18 inches (30–45 cm) tall. Numerous cultivars of many colors are available. Zones 3–8.

Phlox subulata   Polemoniaceae

MOSS PINK

Moss pink, also commonly called thrift or ground pink, grows best in full sun and well-drained soil. It has bright spring flowers and mossy evergreen foliage.

BEST CLIMATE AND SITE: Zones 2–9. Light-textured, slightly acid, average, well-drained soil. Full sun.

HEIGHT AND SPREAD: Height to 6 inches (15 cm); spread 8–12 inches (20–30 cm).

DESCRIPTION: This popular, low-growing phlox carpets the ground with masses of ³/₄-inch (18 mm), five-petaled flowers in pink, purple, blue, or white for 2–4 weeks in mid- to late-spring. The small, needle-like, evergreen leaves appear mossy.

GROWING GUIDELINES: Set plants 1 foot (30 cm) apart in spring or fall. Water occasionally for best growth, especially when plants are getting established. Mow or prune after flowering for neat, compact plants. Plants may be susceptible to mildew, so place them where they get plenty of air circulation. Propagate by division in fall or by cuttings in spring or early summer.

LANDSCAPE USES: Moss pinks provide a happy spot of springtime color for rock gardens and borders. They are also useful for erosion control on slopes.

CULTIVARS: There are numerous cultivars. 'Blue Emerald' is lavender-blue. 'Blue Hill' has blue flowers with dark blue centers. 'Emerald Pink' is a rich pink. 'Red Wings' has red blooms. 'Tamanomagalei' has white blooms striped with pink. 'White Delight' has white blooms.

Potentilla fruticosa   Rosaceae

SHRUBBY CINQUEFOIL

Shrubby cinquefoil is one of the best low-growing, flowering shrubs for use as a groundcover. It blooms all summer, is cold-hardy, and needs little care.

BEST CLIMATE AND SITE: Zones 2–7. Light-textured, well-drained, humus-rich, fertile soil with a pH of 5–7. Full or nearly full sun.

HEIGHT AND SPREAD: Height 3–5 feet (90–150 cm); spread to 5 feet (1.5 m).

DESCRIPTION: The saucer-shaped flowers are mostly shades of yellow, but some cultivars have white, pink, or orange-red blooms. The deciduous, gray-green leaves turn dark green as the season progresses.

GROWING GUIDELINES: Set plants about 3 feet (90 cm) apart in early spring. Keep plants vigorous and free-blooming by pruning one-third of the oldest stems to the ground each year. If plantings look bedraggled, you can even cut all of the stems back to just above the ground to promote strong, new growth. Propagate by removing rooted suckers in early spring or by cuttings in early summer.

LANDSCAPE USES: Shrubby cinquefoil is perfect for a low hedge or as a colorful, easy-care groundcover in foundation plantings and on slopes.

CULTIVARS: 'Goldfinger' blooms heavily with bright golden flowers all summer and has a compact, upright form. 'Primrose Beauty' is a spreading form with creamy yellow blooms. 'Snowbird' has semidouble, white flowers. 'Tangerine', a spreading form, has yellow blooms with an orange tint. 'Yellow Gem', a very low, spreading plant, has bright yellow, ruffled flowers.

Potentilla tridentata   Rosaceae

THREE-TOOTHED CINQUEFOIL

Three-toothed cinquefoil is an evergreen, mat-forming groundcover with glossy green leaves. It prefers sunny, well-drained sites in cool climates.

BEST CLIMATE AND SITE: Zones 3–7. Well-drained, sandy, slightly acid soil. Full sun.

HEIGHT AND SPREAD: Height to 1 foot (30 cm); spread to 2 feet (60 cm).

DESCRIPTION: Each leaf is divided into three leaflets that are three- to five-toothed at their tips. The leaves turn wine red in fall, giving the plant another common name: wine-leaved cinquefoil. Clusters of tiny, ¼-inch (6 mm), white flowers bloom in early summer and intermittently the rest of the season.

GROWING GUIDELINES: Set plants 1–2 feet (30–60 cm) apart in early spring. Three-toothed cinquefoil spreads fairly rapidly and needs little care. Propagate by removing rooted suckers in early spring or by cuttings in early summer.

LANDSCAPE USES: Three-toothed cinquefoil is a natural choice for covering dry, rocky slopes.

CULTIVARS: 'Minima' is low-growing, reaching only to 3 inches (7.5 cm) tall.

OTHER SPECIES:

P. tabernaemontani, spring cinquefoil, is another groundcovering species. It has five-toothed, evergreen, green leaves and ½-inch (12 mm), bright yellow flowers in late spring. Height to 4 inches (10 cm); spread to 2 feet (60 cm). Zones 4–7.

Primula japonica   Primulaceae

JAPANESE PRIMROSE

Japanese primrose is a tough, hardy, easy-to-grow plant in the right conditions. It thrives in light shade in very moist soil that's rich in organic matter.

BEST CLIMATE AND SITE: Zones 4–8. Well-drained, very moist, fertile garden soil. Light shade.

HEIGHT AND SPREAD: Height of foliage to 1 foot (30 cm); spread to 18 inches (45 cm). Flower stalks grow 18–24 inches (45–60 cm) tall.

DESCRIPTION: Japanese primroses are grown mainly for their late-spring and early-summer blooms. The flowers are up to 1 inch (2.5 cm) wide, and they bloom one tier above the other on strong, upright stems over large clumps of oblong, 10-inch (25 cm) leaves. Cultivars come in many flower colors, including pink, rose, red, purple, and white, with "eyes" of varying shades. Plants self-sow to quickly form large colonies in moist soil. Japanese primrose is also known as candelabra primrose.

GROWING GUIDELINES: Set plants 12–20 inches (30–75 cm) apart in spring in a spot that gets no direct sunlight. Top-dress plantings yearly with leaf mold, aged manure, or compost. Divide clumps when they become overcrowded—usually every 3–5 years—to promote better flowering. Propagate by seed or division in spring.

LANDSCAPE USES: Japanese primroses thrive in moist borders and bog gardens, beside streams and ponds, and in woodland plantings where the cheery flowers brighten up the shade. They are especially attractive when combined with ferns.

| *Pulmonaria saccharata* | Boraginaceae | *Rosa rugosa* | Rosaceae |

BETHLEHEM SAGE

RUGOSA ROSE

The early-spring flowers of Bethlehem sage combine nicely with daffodils and other bulbs. The foliage looks wonderful with hostas, which enjoy the same growing conditions.

BEST CLIMATE AND SITE: Zones 3–8. Moist, well-drained, humus-rich soil. Partial to full shade; tolerates some sun if the soil is moist.

HEIGHT AND SPREAD: Height 8–15 inches (20–37.5 cm); spread 18 inches (45 cm) or more.

DESCRIPTION: These easy-to-grow plants form broad clumps of white-mottled, slightly fuzzy leaves. In early spring, cheery, small, tubular flowers bloom in profusion over mounds of foliage. The pink buds open to pink flowers that age to blue.

GROWING GUIDELINES: Set plants 2 feet (60 cm) apart in spring or fall. Plants may wilt if the soil becomes dry, but they revive quickly when watered; mulch helps to keep the roots moist. Propagate by division after flowering or in fall.

LANDSCAPE USES: The clumps of mottled foliage look nice all summer at the front of the border, under trees, or in a shady rock garden.

CULTIVARS: 'Mrs. Moon' has silver-spotted leaves and pink flowers that mature to blue. 'Sissinghurst White' has pure white flowers and silvery mottled foliage.

OTHER SPECIES:
P. angustifolia, cowslip lungwort, has blue flowers and unspotted green leaves. Zones 2–8.
P. rubra, mountain lungwort, produces coral-red flowers that appear in midspring before the clumps of broad, hairy leaves. Zones 4–8.

Rugosa rose is an upright grower with many arching canes. It forms vigorous colonies, but weeds and grass sometimes invade plantings, so mulch heavily to prevent problems.

BEST CLIMATE AND SITE: Zones 2–9. Well-drained, neutral soil. Full sun.

HEIGHT AND SPREAD: Height to 6 feet (1.8 m); spread unlimited.

DESCRIPTION: This popular shrub rose blooms throughout the summer with either single or semidouble flowers in pink, red, or white. The flowers are followed by bright red ornamental fruits (known as hips) in fall. The hips are rich in vitamin C and can be used to make jelly or tea. The green leaves turn orange in fall.

GROWING GUIDELINES: Set plants 3–5 feet (90–150 cm) apart in the spring or fall. Prune as needed in late winter to remove old stems (cut them to the ground) and to control size. Rugosa roses usually aren't bothered much by pests or diseases. Propagate by transplanting rooted suckers or by hardwood cuttings in early spring or softwood cuttings in early summer.

LANDSCAPE USES: Rugosa rose forms an excellent impenetrable hedge. It's a good choice to plant on banks or slopes where other things won't grow well. Rugosa rose is tolerant of salt spray, so it's ideal for seaside plantings.

CULTIVARS: 'Alba Plena' has double, fragrant, white flowers; it does not produce fruits. 'Belle Poitevine' is rose-pink. 'Chaplain' is bright red. 'F. J. Grootendorst' is red. 'Sir Thomas Lipton' is white.

Rubus calycinoides Rosaceae

BRAMBLE

The fuzzy green leaves of this creeping groundcover turn deep red in fall. Bramble is usually evergreen but may drop its leaves during a very cold winter.

BEST CLIMATE AND SITE: Zones 6–9. Well-drained, humus-rich, fertile soil with a pH of 5–7. Full sun to partial shade.

HEIGHT AND SPREAD: Height 1–2 inches (2.5–5 cm); spread to 2 feet (60 cm).

DESCRIPTION: Bramble is a tough, evergreen groundcover with white flowers and creeping, thornless, woody stems that root as they travel. Popular in the Pacific Northwest, it makes an attractive, dense mat that competes well with other plants. Crinkly, green, lobed leaves turn burgundy red in fall.

GROWING GUIDELINES: Set plants 2 feet (60 cm) apart in spring or fall. Cut out any dead parts in fall or early spring. Propagate in spring or early fall by division (dig the suckers) or by layering (covering parts of the creeping stems with soil to promote rooting).

LANDSCAPE USES: Bramble is an unusual, attractive groundcover wherever you need a tight, evergreen carpet.

OTHER SPECIES:

R. nepalensis is another useful, carpeting groundcover with lobed, crinkled leaves. Height to 2 inches (5 cm); spread to 2 feet (60 cm). Zones 7–8.

Sagina subulata Caryophyllaceae

PEARLWORT

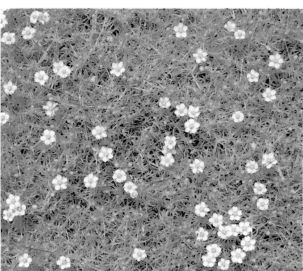

Pearlwort, also known as Irish moss, is a dainty little evergreen for partial shade. It can withstand some foot traffic and looks great growing between stepping stones.

BEST CLIMATE AND SITE: Zones 5–7. Prefers well-drained, moist, fertile soil; tolerates dry, sandy soil. Partial shade.

HEIGHT AND SPREAD: Height of foliage 1–2 inches (2.5–5 cm); spread to 1 foot (30 cm). Flower height to 5 inches (12.5 cm).

DESCRIPTION: This moss-like, perennial, evergreen groundcover forms dense mounds of tiny, 1/4-inch (6 mm) leaves. Numerous small, translucent white flowers bloom in midsummer.

GROWING GUIDELINES: Set plants 1 foot (30 cm) apart in spring. Slugs and snails can be problems; trap them under cabbage leaves (remove pests daily) or in shallow pans of beer set flush with the soil surface. Propagate by division in spring.

LANDSCAPE USES: Grow pearlwort in lightly shaded rock gardens and between flagstones since it tolerates foot traffic.

CULTIVARS: 'Aurea', commonly called Scotch moss, has yellow-green foliage.

LAVENDER COTTON

ROCK SOAPWORT

Lavender cotton is a shrubby, aromatic evergreen that's native to areas of the Mediterranean. The dried leaves and stems were once used indoors to repel moths.

BEST CLIMATE AND SITE: Zones 5–9. Dry, poor, well-drained soil, including sand and gravel. Full sun.

HEIGHT AND SPREAD: Height 18–24 inches (45–60 cm); spread to 3 feet (90 cm).

DESCRIPTION: Lavender cotton forms bushy clumps of many branches with fine, needle-like, aromatic, silvery gray leaves. Bright gold, $^3/_4$-inch (18 mm) flowers bloom in profusion in midsummer. Lavender cotton tolerates both heat and drought.

GROWING GUIDELINES: Set plants 2–3 feet (60–90 cm) apart in spring. Cut stems back by half after blooming each year (or before blooming, if you don't like the flowers) to encourage compact growth. Propagate by cuttings in early summer or by division in early spring.

LANDSCAPE USES: Lavender cotton is ideal for a low-growing hedge or edging and for shrub borders. The gray shade combines well with lavender and low-growing ornamental grasses.

CULTIVARS: 'Nana' is a dwarf form. 'Plumosus' has lacy, silvery gray foliage.

OTHER SPECIES:

S. virens, green lavender cotton, has dark green, fine, needle-like leaves and light yellow flowers in summer. Height to 18 inches (45 cm); spread to 30 inches (75 cm). Zones 7–8.

Rock soapwort produces many bright pink flowers in summer. Cut the stems back by half after flowering to keep plants compact and to promote possible rebloom.

BEST CLIMATE AND SITE: Zones 4–10. Light-textured, average, well-drained soil. Full sun.

HEIGHT AND SPREAD: Height 5–8 inches (12.5–20 cm); spread to 2 feet (60 cm).

DESCRIPTION: Rock soapwort is a trailing, mat-forming plant with semi-evergreen leaves less than 1 inch (2.5 cm) long. Its star feature is the clusters of phlox-like, bright pink, five-petaled, $^1/_2$-inch (12 mm) flowers in early- to mid-summer.

GROWING GUIDELINES: Set plants about 20 inches (50 cm) apart in spring. Propagate by seed in spring, by division in spring or fall, or by cuttings in early summer.

LANDSCAPE USES: Rock soapwort trails beautifully over walls, raised beds, and terraces. It's a good groundcover for sunny slopes.

CULTIVARS: 'Alba' has white flowers that are somewhat smaller than the species. 'Rubra Compacta' forms compact mounds of deep pink to red flowers. 'Splendens' has rose-pink flowers.

OTHER SPECIES:

S. officinalis, bouncing bet, grows to 2 feet (60 cm) tall. Its pale pink flowers bloom over a long period in mid- to late-summer. This invasive, rhizomatous, European import has become naturalized in North America and should be confined to areas far from gardens and lawns. Juice from its roots was once used as a soap substitute. Zones 2–7.

Sarcococca hookerana var. *humilis*   Buxaceae

SWEET BOX

Sweet box is a compact evergreen groundcover for a spot with well-drained, acid soil in partial to full shade. Its small but very fragrant flowers bloom in spring.

BEST CLIMATE AND SITE: Zones 6–8. Well-drained, moist, fertile, acid soil. Partial to full shade; leaves may turn brown if exposed to bright sunlight.

HEIGHT AND SPREAD: Height 1–2 feet (30–60 cm); spread 6–8 feet (1.8–2.4 m).

DESCRIPTION: This evergreen, suckering, woody shrub forms colonies of green stems clad in shiny, leathery, dark green, 2–3-inch (5–7.5 cm) leaves. Inconspicuous, fragrant, white flowers bloom along the stems in early spring. Small, dark red to purple berries may appear in fall.

GROWING GUIDELINES: Set plants about 3 feet (90 cm) apart in spring. Propagate by division or seed in spring or by softwood cuttings in early summer.

LANDSCAPE USES: Sweet box forms an attractive, evergreen groundcover under trees and shrubs and in woodland plantings.

Saxifraga stolonifera   Saxifragaceae

STRAWBERRY GERANIUM

Strawberry geranium is commonly sold as a houseplant, but its rounded, silver-marked, green leaves also make a handsome groundcover in Southern gardens.

BEST CLIMATE AND SITE: Zones 6–9. Moist, well-drained, slightly acid soil. Partial shade; thrives in morning sun and afternoon shade.

HEIGHT AND SPREAD: Height of foliage to 6 inches (15 cm); spread to 18 inches (45 cm). Flower stalks to 1 foot (30 cm).

DESCRIPTION: Strawberry geranium is an excellent evergreen groundcover for the South. It is also called strawberry begonia and mother-of-thousands, as it spreads by runners (like strawberries). The hairy, rounded, dark green leaves are 4 inches (10 cm) wide, have scalloped edges, and are beautifully veined with silver. White flowers bloom on spikes in early summer. This species is also listed as *S. sarmentosa.*

GROWING GUIDELINES: Plant 12–18 inches (30–45 cm) apart in early spring. To propagate, dig up the small plantlets that form on runners and transplant in spring.

LANDSCAPE USES: Strawberry geranium is a handsome and unusual groundcover for shady rock gardens or borders. Grow it under trees and shrubs as well.

OTHER SPECIES:

S. x *urbium,* London pride, grows 6 inches (15 cm) tall with rosettes of rounded $2^{1}/_{2}$-inch (6 cm) leaves. Tiny pink or white flowers bloom 10 inches (25 cm) above the foliage in spring or early summer. Prefers same conditions as *S. stolonifera.* Zones 5–9.

Sedum spurium   Crassulaceae

TWO-ROW STONECROP

Two-row stonecrop is a tough, durable spreader for dry soil. Its mats of fleshy green leaves are topped with clusters of pink flowers in midsummer.

Kamschatka sedum is another species that makes a useful groundcover. It spreads quickly, but it's easy to pull out the shallow-rooted plants if they creep out of bounds.

BEST CLIMATE AND SITE: Zones 3–8. Well-drained, sandy, average to poor soil. Light to partial shade.

HEIGHT AND SPREAD: Height of foliage to 6 inches (15 cm); spread to 2 feet (60 cm). Flower height to 10 inches (25 cm).

DESCRIPTION: This semi-evergreen, creeping succulent quickly forms a carpeting groundcover with dark green, 1-inch (2.5 cm) long leaves that turn reddish in late fall. Flat, 2-inch (5 cm) clusters of pink flowers appear in midsummer. Stems stay reddish throughout the winter.

GROWING GUIDELINES: Set plants 10 inches (25 cm) apart in spring. After blooming, cut off the spent blooms with shears or a string trimmer. Although it spreads quickly, two-row stonecrop is easy to control because it has shallow roots. Propagate by seed or division in early spring or by cuttings in early summer.

LANDSCAPE USES: Try two-row stonecrop as a groundcover on dry, lightly shaded, rocky slopes, alone or mixed with other *Sedum* species.

CULTIVARS: 'Album Superbum' is a vigorous, white-flowered cultivar; Zones 6–10. 'Dragon's Blood' has bronze foliage when mature and deep red blooms. 'Fuldaglut' has reddish pink blooms and bronze foliage that turns burgundy in fall; Zones 5–9. 'Red Carpet' is only 4 inches (10 cm) tall, with small, reddish leaves.

OTHER SPECIES: Many of the 300 or so sedums are fine groundcovers, and the following are especially noteworthy.

S. acre, goldmoss stonecrop, grows to 2 inches (5 cm) tall. It is a vigorous, creeping, evergreen sedum with tiny, slightly succulent, light green leaves. It is a fine background plant for spring bulbs and ideal between stepping stones, but it can be invasive in gardens. Goldmoss stonecrop bears 1/2-inch (12 mm), yellow flowers in late spring. Zones 3–8.

S. kamtschaticum, Kamschatka sedum, grows 6–8 inches (15–20 cm) tall. Small, dark green leaves with scalloped edges grow in attractive, semi-evergreen, succulent whorls around the stem. Plants bear tiny, yellow-orange, star-like flowers in early summer. 'Variegatum' grows 5 inches (12.5 cm) tall with orange-yellow flowers and pale green leaves variegated with pink and white. Zones 3–9.

S. ternatum, crowsfoot sedum, grows to 6 inches (15 cm) and has succulent, blue-green, disc-shaped leaves. Star-shaped, white flowers with purple-red stamens bloom in spring. Plants spread by creeping stems that root where they touch the soil. Zones 4–8.

Sempervivum tectorum   Crassulaceae

HENS-AND-CHICKENS

The round, fleshy rosettes of hens-and-chickens make an eye-catching groundcover in a small area. They are available in a range of sizes and colors.

BEST CLIMATE AND SITE: Zones 5–9; grows well down to Zone 3 as long as there is good snow cover in winter. Prefers well-drained, fertile soil; tolerates rocky, sandy soil and hot, dry spots. Full sun.

HEIGHT AND SPREAD: Height of foliage to 6 inches (15 cm); spread to 8 inches (20 cm) or more. Flower stalks 8–18 inches (20–45 cm).

DESCRIPTION: This evergreen succulent has pointed leaves in flat, open rosettes that are 3–4 inches (7.5–10 cm) wide. New plants form in dense masses around the base of old plants, hence the common name. Small, purple-red, aster-like flowers to 1 inch (2.5 cm) wide bloom in summer. Hens-and-chickens is also commonly called houseleek.

GROWING GUIDELINES: Set plants 18 inches (45 cm) or more apart any time during the growing season. Plants are usually free of pests and diseases, although crown rot and rust sometimes affect them; dust with sulfur if rust becomes a problem. Propagate by splitting off offsets or by seed in spring.

LANDSCAPE USES: In medieval times, hens-and-chickens were believed to ward off lightning and were planted on the roofs of homes, giving the species the name *tectorum*, Latin for "of the roof." These days, hens-and-chickens are more commonly planted in rock gardens, on stone walls, or as small-scale groundcovers.

Stachys byzantina   Labiatae

LAMB'S-EARS

Lamb's-ears has fuzzy leaves that may rot in humid conditions. Plants usually recover and produce new growth when cool weather returns; in the meantime, remove damaged leaves.

BEST CLIMATE AND SITE: Zones 4–8; thrives in Zone 3 with snow cover. Average, well-drained soil; plants tolerate drought once established. Prefers full, hot sun; tolerates light shade.

HEIGHT AND SPREAD: Height of foliage to 8 inches (20 cm); spread to 3 feet (90 cm). Flower stems to 18 inches (45 cm).

DESCRIPTION: This charming groundcover is grown mostly for its woolly, soft, silvery white, 4-inch (10 cm) leaves. Fuzzy, square flowering stems bearing lavender flowers bloom in early- to mid-summer. This species is also listed as *S. lanata* or *S. olympica*.

GROWING GUIDELINES: Set plants 12–16 inches (30–40 cm) apart in spring. Cut back any damaged leaves in spring. Remove flower stems before they bloom, if desired, to keep plantings tidy. Propagate by division any time during the growing season or by seed in spring.

LANDSCAPE USES: The gray foliage of lamb's-ears is an excellent foil for brightly colored flowers in beds and borders. The leafy clumps form an attractive edging for garden paths.

CULTIVARS: 'Helen von Stein', an import from Germany, has large, 4-inch (10 cm) leaves and is not as susceptible to rot as the species. 'Primrose Heron' has woolly foliage tinted yellow to light green. 'Silver Carpet' has no flower spikes, for those who want only a dense carpet of foliage.

Stephanandra incisa Rosaceae	*Symphytum grandiflorum* Boraginaceae

LACE SHRUB

YELLOW COMFREY

If you need a flowering shrub to fill a large area, consider planting lace shrub. Its arching stems bear greenish white flowers in late spring.

BEST CLIMATE AND SITE: Zones 5–9. Well-drained, humus-rich, fertile soil. Full sun.

HEIGHT AND SPREAD: Height 4–7 feet (1.2–2.1 m); spread to 3 feet (90 cm) or more where the lower branches take root.

DESCRIPTION: This deciduous shrub has graceful, arching stems and small, finely cut leaves that give a lacy appearance. Clusters of tiny, greenish white flowers appear in late spring. The leaves turn orange-red in fall. Lace shrub is also known as cut-leaved stephanandra.

GROWING GUIDELINES: Set plants about 3 feet (90 cm) apart in spring. If shaping is needed, trim in early spring. Stems may become winter-damaged, but new spring growth will cover them. Branches sometimes root where they touch moist soil. Propagate by transplanting rooted stem tips, by division in spring, or by cuttings in summer.

LANDSCAPE USES: Lace shrub is a great large-scale groundcover for slopes and shrub borders.

CULTIVARS: 'Crispa' grows only 18–36 inches (45–90 cm) tall. It has a naturally dense growth habit and needs little or no pruning.

Yellow comfrey is an excellent, easy-care groundcover for dry, shady spots. It produces dense, spreading clumps that tend to crowd out most weeds.

BEST CLIMATE AND SITE: Zones 3–8. Light-textured, well-drained soil; tolerates dry, poor soil. Sun or partial shade.

HEIGHT AND SPREAD: Height of foliage to 1 foot (30 cm); spread to 2 feet (60 cm). Flower height to 18 inches (45 cm).

DESCRIPTION: Yellow comfrey forms spreading clumps of oblong, hairy, dark green, deciduous leaves. Clusters of creamy yellow, $^3/_4$-inch (18 mm), tubular flowers rise above the foliage in spring. Yellow comfrey resembles lungwort and is sometimes listed as *Pulmonaria lutea*.

GROWING GUIDELINES: Set plants 18–24 inches (45–60 cm) apart in spring or fall. Established plantings need virtually no care. Propagate by division in spring or fall.

LANDSCAPE USES: Yellow comfrey is an excellent, easy-care, weed-suppressing groundcover for dry, shaded spots.

CULTIVARS: 'Variegatum' has green leaves variegated with yellow and cream.

| *Tellima grandiflora* | Saxifragaceae | *Thymus serpyllum* | Labiatae |

FRINGE CUPS

Fringe cups are ideal for lightly shaded gardens. Their clumps spread slowly but steadily, and they may self-sow in ideal growing conditions.

BEST CLIMATE AND SITE: Zones 5–8. Fertile, well-drained, slightly acid, cool soil. Light shade.

HEIGHT AND SPREAD: Height of foliage to 1 foot (30 cm); spread to 20 inches (50 cm). Flower stems to 2 feet (60 cm) tall.

DESCRIPTION: Fringe cups form tidy clumps of heart-shaped, scalloped, hairy, cupped leaves that are 4 inches (10 cm) wide. The green leaves turn reddish in fall. Loose clusters of small, bell-shaped, nodding flowers with fringed petals are greenish white when they open in spring and turn reddish. Plants are evergreen in warm climates and deciduous in cool zones.

GROWING GUIDELINES: Set plants 18–24 inches (45–60 cm) apart in spring. Divide when plants become crowded. Propagate by division in spring.

LANDSCAPE USES: This slow spreader makes an attractive, dense cover for the rock garden or woodland garden.

CULTIVARS: 'Rubra' has maroon leaves.

MOTHER-OF-THYME

Mother-of-thyme tolerates light foot traffic, making it ideal for a small-scale lawn substitute. Underplant it with small bulbs, such as crocuses, for spring interest.

BEST CLIMATE AND SITE: Zones 4–7; grows well in Zone 3 with snow cover. Well-drained, dry soil that is not too fertile. Full sun.

HEIGHT AND SPREAD: Height of foliage to 2 inches (5 cm); spread unlimited. Flower height 3–4 inches (7.5–10 cm).

DESCRIPTION: Mother-of-thyme is an aromatic, creeping, mat-forming evergreen with tiny, green, $1/4$-inch (6 mm) leaves. Small, $1/2$-inch (12 mm), rose-purple flowers bloom in clusters atop 4-inch (10 cm) stems in summer.

GROWING GUIDELINES: Set plants about 8 inches (20 cm) apart in spring. As long as they grow in full sun, they are remarkably free of pests and diseases. Propagate by division or seed in spring or by cuttings in early summer.

LANDSCAPE USES: The creeping habit of this plant makes it a natural for climbing over rocks in a rock garden or for filling spaces between rocks in a terrace or pathway.

CULTIVARS: 'Album' has white flowers in early summer. 'Coccineum' has reddish purple flowers in early summer over dense mats of green leaves that turn bronze in fall. Zones 3–9.

OTHER SPECIES:
T. pseudolanuginosus, woolly thyme, grows to 1 inch (2.5 cm) with hairy, gray leaves and pink flowers in summer. Zones 4–7.

Tiarella cordifolia Saxifragaceae	*Tolmiea menziesii* Saxifragaceae

ALLEGHENY FOAMFLOWER

PIGGYBACK PLANT

Allegheny foamflower tolerates deep shade and dry conditions once established. It looks great as a groundcover beneath deciduous and evergreen trees.

BEST CLIMATE AND SITE: Zones 3–8. Well-drained, moist, fertile, slightly acid soil. Light shade.

HEIGHT AND SPREAD: Height of foliage to 6 inches (15 cm); spread to 2 feet (60 cm). Flower stems 9–12 inches (22.5–30 cm) tall.

DESCRIPTION: This evergreen native of eastern North American forests forms clumps of heart-shaped, lobed and toothed green leaves. The leaves are up to 4 inches (10 cm) wide and turn bronze to burgundy in fall; they are evergreen in the South. Feathery bottlebrush-like spikes of tiny white flowers bloom in midspring.

GROWING GUIDELINES: Set plants 2 feet (60 cm) apart in spring. Removing spent flower spikes may extend the blooming season. Propagate by division in spring or fall or sow seed in spring.

LANDSCAPE USES: Foamflowers are ideal for massed woodland plantings, shady rock gardens, borders, and edgings.

CULTIVARS: 'George Shenk Pink' has foamy, pink flowers in spring. 'Oakleaf' has deeply lobed leaves and airy, deep pink blooms that last for several weeks.

OTHER SPECIES:
   T. wherryi, Wherry's foamflower, is also listed as *T. cordifolia* var. *collina.* This plant forms nonrunning clumps of light green foliage and pink flowers. Zones 3–8.

Piggyback plant is usually grown indoors, but it also makes a unique groundcover for warm-climate gardens. The cultivar 'Taff's Gold' has yellow-speckled green leaves.

BEST CLIMATE AND SITE: Zones 7–9. Well-drained, fertile, acid soil. Partial to full shade.

HEIGHT AND SPREAD: Height to 10 inches (25 cm); spread to 18 inches (45 cm) or more.

DESCRIPTION: This groundcover is grown for its attractive mounds of 4-inch (10 cm) wide, lobed, toothed, hairy, heart-shaped leaves. New plantlets form at the base of each leaf, hence the name piggyback plant. Inconspicuous spikes of greenish white or brown flowers bloom in late spring or early summer.

GROWING GUIDELINES: Set plants 2 feet (60 cm) apart in spring or fall. Mulch around plants to keep the soil moist. To propagate, divide in spring or dig up rooted plantlets.

LANDSCAPE USES: Grow piggyback plant as a unique groundcover in a shady rock garden or shrub border.

| *Vancouveria hexandra* | Berberidaceae | *Veronica prostrata* | Scrophulariaceae |

AMERICAN BARRENWORT

ROCK SPEEDWELL

American barrenwort may look delicate, but it's a tough, vigorous perennial that spreads by underground stems. It prefers moist soil but can adapt to dry conditions.

BEST CLIMATE AND SITE: Zones 5–8. Moist, well-drained, fertile soil, rich in leaf mold. Prefers partial shade but will tolerate full shade.

HEIGHT AND SPREAD: Height to 1 foot (30 cm); spread to 2 feet (60 cm) or more.

DESCRIPTION: Spreading clumps of wiry stems are topped with thin, heart-shaped, three-lobed, deciduous, green leaves to $1^{1}/_{2}$ inches (3.7 cm) wide. In late spring or early summer, tiny, $^{1}/_{2}$-inch (12 mm), white flowers bloom in drooping clusters just above the leaves.

GROWING GUIDELINES: Set plants 18–24 inches (45–60 cm) apart in spring. They may be slow getting started but will begin to spread by the second growing season. Mulch to keep plants moist and cool in summer. If the soil is sandy, feed plants once a year with compost or leaf mold. To propagate, divide in spring.

LANDSCAPE USES: American barrenwort makes an attractive groundcover beneath trees, in shady rock gardens, and in wild gardens. It's also a nice edging for shady beds of hostas.

OTHER SPECIES:

V. planipetala, inside-out flower, grows 12–18 inches (30–45 cm) tall. Clusters of tiny, white or lavender-tinged flowers bloom in spring. The leaves are normally evergreen, though they may drop in very cold winters. Zones 6–8.

The spreading foliage mats of rock speedwell are accented by spikes of blue flowers in late spring. This plant is a perfect choice for sunny slopes and rock gardens.

BEST CLIMATE AND SITE: Zones 4–8. Well-drained, moist, average garden soil. Prefers full sun; tolerates partial shade.

HEIGHT AND SPREAD: Height 8–10 inches (20–25 cm); spread to 18 inches (45 cm) or more.

DESCRIPTION: Spikes of deep blue flowers bloom on upright stems in late spring above creeping mats of $1^{1}/_{2}$-inch (3.7 cm) green leaves. Rock speedwell is also known as Hungarian speedwell or harebell speedwell.

GROWING GUIDELINES: Set plants at least 2 feet (60 cm) apart in spring or fall. If needed, surround plantings with an edging strip to keep them in bounds. Propagate by division in spring or fall, by stem cuttings in summer, or by seed in spring.

LANDSCAPE USES: Rock speedwell is a charming groundcover in rock gardens and on rocky slopes.

CULTIVARS: 'Alba' has white flowers that bloom over a long season. 'Mrs. Holt' has rose-pink flowers.

OTHER SPECIES:

V. incana, woolly speedwell, has blue flowers to 18 inches (45 cm) above mats of 6-inch (15 cm) gray foliage. Zones 3–8.

V. repens, creeping speedwell, grows to 4 inches (10 cm) and spreads rapidly, with pale lavender flowers in early summer. Nice groundcover for bulbs and in crevices of flagstone paths, but it can become invasive. Zones 3–8.

| *Vinca minor* | Apocynaceae | *Viola odorata* | Violaceae |

COMMON PERIWINKLE

SWEET VIOLET

Common periwinkle spreads quickly once established. Plant it where the spread won't be a problem, or surround it with an edging and cut off shoots that try to escape.

BEST CLIMATE AND SITE: Zones 3–9. Well-drained, average to rich soil. Light to moderately heavy shade; can take sun in cool climates.

HEIGHT AND SPREAD: Height 6–10 inches (15–25 cm); spread unlimited.

DESCRIPTION: This spreading, evergreen vine, also known as creeping myrtle, has glossy, dark green, pointed leaves that are 1–2 inches (2.5–5 cm) long. It forms an attractive carpet in shady spots by creeping over the ground and rooting along its stems. Large numbers of $^3/_4$-inch (18 mm), lavender-blue flowers appear in early spring; plants rebloom sparsely in summer and fall.

GROWING GUIDELINES: Set plants about 2 feet (60 cm) apart in spring or early fall. Shearing in early summer will stimulate thicker growth. Propagate by division anytime or by cuttings in summer.

LANDSCAPE USES: Common periwinkle is an excellent groundcover for erosion control on slopes and steep, shady banks. It is also ideal beneath trees, in woods, and other shady spots. For extra interest, underplant it with daffodils and other vigorous spring bulbs.

OTHER SPECIES:
V. major, big periwinkle, has bright blue, 1–2-inch (2.5–5 cm) flowers in spring. 'Variegata' has leaves edged with creamy white. Zones 7–9.

Sweet violet, also called English violet, is the common violet used by florists. It spreads by runners that take root and produce new plants.

BEST CLIMATE AND SITE: Zones 6–8. Well-drained, moist, fertile, cool soil. Full sun to partial shade; tolerates full shade in hot climates.

HEIGHT AND SPREAD: Height 5–8 inches (12.5–20 cm); spread to 2 feet (60 cm).

DESCRIPTION: Fragrant, five-petaled, deep violet blooms come up in early spring from clumps of heart-shaped leaves that are 3 inches (7.5 cm) long.

GROWING GUIDELINES: Set plants 12 inches (30 cm) apart in spring. Start a new patch when older plants become overgrown and weak. Spider mites may be a problem, causing yellowed or browned leaves; spray cold water over the plants, or use a slurry made from buttermilk, wheat flour, and water.

LANDSCAPE USES: Sweet violet makes a fragrant groundcover in wild gardens and rock gardens and under trees and shrubs.

CULTIVARS: 'Royal Robe' has purple flowers with a white eye on long, 8-inch (20 cm) stems. 'White Czar' has white flowers veined with deep purple on 6-inch (15 cm) stems. Other cultivars come in many shades of blue, pink, purple, and white.

OTHER SPECIES:
V. cornuta, horned violet or viola, grows 6–12 inches (15–30 cm) tall with $1^1/_2$-inch (3.7 cm), fragrant, pansy-like flowers in late spring. Numerous cultivars in many colors are available. Spreads by self-sown seed. Zones 5–9.

| *Waldsteinia fragarioides* | Rosaceae | *Xanthorhiza simplicissima* | Ranunculaceae |

BARREN STRAWBERRY

YELLOWROOT

Barren strawberry has shiny, evergreen leaves that take on a purplish color in cold weather. It grows well in partial shade but will take sun if the soil is moist.

Yellowroot is a low-growing native shrub that makes an unusual and attractive groundcover. The green leaves turn bright colors before dropping in fall.

BEST CLIMATE AND SITE: Zones 5–8. Well-drained, fertile soil. Prefers partial shade; will tolerate sunny spots if kept moist.

HEIGHT AND SPREAD: Height to 6 inches (15 cm); spread unlimited.

DESCRIPTION: This evergreen plant is native to eastern North America. It spreads by creeping roots to form a thick, flat carpet of shiny, strawberry-like foliage that turns purplish in fall. Clusters of five-petaled, 1/2-inch (12 mm) wide, yellow flowers appear on 6–8-inch (15–20 cm) stems in late spring, followed by inedible, dry, hairy fruits.

GROWING GUIDELINES: Set plants about 2 feet (60 cm) apart in spring. Keep watered in dry periods and divide when overcrowded. Propagate by division in early spring or fall or by seed in spring.

LANDSCAPE USES: Grow barren strawberry in rock gardens, on banks and rocky ledges, or cascading over walls.

OTHER SPECIES:

W. ternata grows 6–8 inches (15–20 cm) tall with glossy, green, evergreen leaves and clusters of yellow, strawberry-like flowers in spring. Zones 4–9.

BEST CLIMATE AND SITE: Zones 5–9. Thrives in moist to wet soil; tolerates average conditions. Sun or shade.

HEIGHT AND SPREAD: Height to 2 feet (60 cm); similar spread.

DESCRIPTION: This neat, deciduous shrub, native to the eastern United States, gets its common name from the roots and bark, which are yellow when broken. Whorls of green, fern-like leaves at the ends of the stems turn orange-yellow in fall, forming nice clumps of fall color. In spring, drooping clusters of inconspicuous, tiny, purplish, star-shaped flowers appear before the foliage. Yellowroot spreads by underground roots.

GROWING GUIDELINES: Set plants 2 feet (60 cm) apart in early spring. They need little care and apparently are not bothered by pests. Propagate by division in early spring before plants begin to grow.

LANDSCAPE USES: Yellowroot is an ideal groundcover for damp, shaded areas. It also makes a fine underplanting in a shrub border for fall color.

USDA
PLANT HARDINESS ZONE MAP

The map that follows shows the United States and Canada divided into 10 zones. Each zone is based on a 10°F (5.6°C) difference in average annual minimum temperature. Some areas are considered too high in elevation for plant cultivation and so are not assigned to any zone. There are also island zones that are warmer or cooler than surrounding areas because of differences in elevation; they have been given a zone different from the surrounding areas. Many large urban areas are in a warmer zone than the surrounding land.

Plants grow best within an optimum range of temperatures. The range may be wide for some species and narrow for others. Plants also differ in their ability to survive frost and in their sun or shade requirements.

The zone ratings indicate conditions where designated plants will grow well and not merely survive. Refer to the map to find out which zone you are in. In the plant by plant guides, you'll find recommendations for the plants that grow best in your zone.

Many plants may survive in zones warmer or colder than their recommended zone range. Remember that other factors, including wind, soil type, soil moisture and drainage capability, humidity, snow, and winter sunshine, may have a great effect on growth.

Average annual minimum temperature (°F/°C)

Zone 1	Below -50°F/-45°C	
Zone 2	-40° to -50°F/-40° to -45°C	
Zone 3	-30° to -40°F/-34° to -40°C	
Zone 4	-20° to -30°F/-29° to -34°C	
Zone 5	-10° to -20°F/-23° to -29°C	
Zone 6	0° to -10°F/-18° to -23°C	
Zone 7	10° to 0°F/-12° to -18°C	
Zone 8	20° to 10°F/-7° to -12°C	
Zone 9	30° to 20°F/-1° to -7°C	
Zone 10	40° to 30°F/4° to -1°C	

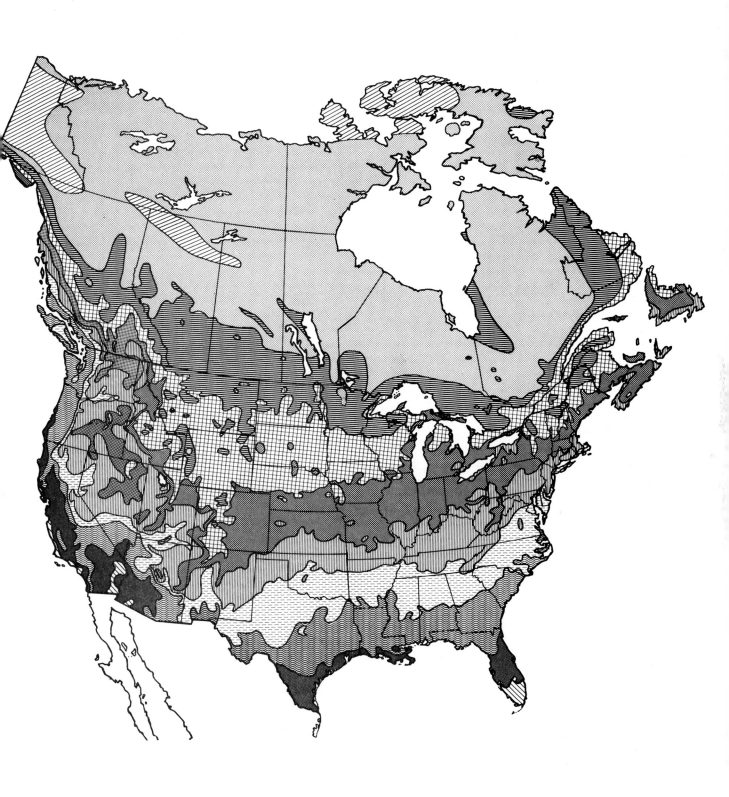

INDEX

The numbers in bold indicate main entries, and the numbers in italic indicate illustrations.

ACKNOWLEDGMENTS

Photo Credits

Addington Turf & Horticultural Consultants: photographer Kenneth R. Smith: pages 31, 33 (right), and 34 (left).

Heather Angel: page 68.

A-Z Botanical: photographer Derek Gould: page 148 (left); photographer Malcolm Richards: page 133 (right); photographer Bjorn Svensson: page 138 (right).

Gillian Beckett: pages 77 (left), 79 (left and right), 84 (left), 108 (right), 109 (left), 110 (right), 112 (right), 116 (right), 118 (right), 119 (right), 121 (left), 122 (right), 124 (left), 128 (right), 130 (right), 131 (left), 134 (left), 135 (left), 141 (left), 148 (right), 149 (left), 150 (left), 151 (left), and 153 (left).

Bluemount Nurseries: photographer Richard Simon: page 81 (left).

Bruce Coleman Ltd: photographer Eric Crichton: pages 28 (right), 44 (top), 47 (bottom), and 64 (top); photographer Geoff Dore: contents page (top left); photographer Michael Freeman: page 26; photographer Andrew J. Purcell: page 49 (bottom left); photographer John Shaw: page 129 (left); photographers Sullivan & Rogers: page 72 (left).

Thomas Eltzroth: pages 11 (left), 17 (left), 27 (left and right), 29 (left), 30 (left), 32 (left and right), 33 (left), 34 (right), 35 (left), 58 (bottom left), 59 (top right), 60 (left), 61, 72 (right), 73 (left), 74 (right), 76 (left and right), 80 (left), 84 (right), 86 (left), 97 (top left), 100 (bottom), 106, 107 (right), 110 (left), 114 (left), 117 (left), 120 (right), 121 (right), 122 (left), 123 (right), 124 (right), 125 (left and right), 126 (right), 127 (left and right), 128 (left), 132 (left), 135 (right), 136 (right), 138 (left), 140 (left), 144 (right), 146 (right), 147 (right), and 152 (right).

Derek Fell: pages 16 (left and right), 28 (left), 29 (right), 30 (right), 35 (right), 36, 58 (top), 67 (bottom), 69 (left), 71 (right), 74 (left), 75 (left), 78 (left and right), 82 (left), 83 (left), 85 (left), 87 (left and right), 88 (right), 89 (left), 94 (bottom), 97 (top right), 111 (left), 126 (left), 131 (right), and 137 (left).

Garden Picture Library: photographer Lynne Brotchie: page 24 (bottom); photographer Linda Burgess: page 38 (bottom); photographer Brian Carter: pages 69 (right) and 153 (right); photographer John Glover: pages 22 (bottom), 39 (top), 54, and 65 (top right); photographer Michael Howes: page 53 (bottom); photographer Lamontagne: pages 43 (bottom) and 58 (bottom right); photographer Jane Legate: pages 23 (right), 39 (bottom), 45 (top), and 46 (bottom); photographer Jerry Pavia: page 60 (right); photographer Joanne Pavia: back cover (top) and page 41 (top); photographer Gary Rogers: page 57 (bottom); photographer Brigitte Thomas: pages 14 (left and right), 25 (top left), and 50; photographer Didier Willery: pages 56 (left), 92, and 96 (top); photographer Steven Wooster: back cover (center), pages 47 (top), and 57 (top).

Holt Studios International: photographer Nigel Cattlin: pages 48, 51 (bottom), 52 (bottom left), 108 (left), 112 (left), 132 (right), and 152 (left); photographer Rosemary Mayer: pages 20 (bottom), 42 (right), and 49 (top); photographer Primrose Peacock: page 147 (left).

Andrew Lawson: opposite title page, opposite contents page, pages 8, 23 (left), 42 (left), 59 (top left), 66 (top), 94 (top), 99 (bottom), and 104.

S & O Mathews: pages 53 (top), 59 (bottom), 65 (bottom), and 103 (top).

Clive Nichols: endpapers, half title page, title page, copyright page, pages 12, 15 (top), 17 (right), 19, 20 (top), 22 (top), 24 (top), 38 (top), 40 (top), 43 (top), 46 (top), 51 (top), 65 (top left), 67 (top), 90, 95 (top and bottom), 96 (bottom), 97 (bottom), 98, 99 (top), 102 (top and bottom), 103 (bottom), 105 (top), 117 (right), 141 (right), and 150 (right).

Nancy J. Ondra: pages 134 (right), 139 (left), and 143 (left).

Jerry Pavia: pages 11 (right), 15 (bottom), 62 (left), 115 (right), and 140 (right).

Joanne Pavia: page 86 (right).

Photos Horticultural: back cover (bottom), pages 18, 21, 25 (bottom left and right), 41 (bottom), 44 (bottom), 45 (bottom), 49 (bottom right), 52 (top and bottom right), 56 (right), 62 (right), 63, 64 (bottom), 66 (bottom), 73 (right), 77 (right), 82 (right), 83 (right), 88 (left), 93, 100 (top), 101, 105 (bottom), and 133 (left).

Rodale Stock Images: photographer John P. Hamel: front cover.

Harry Smith Collection: pages 70, 71 (left), 75 (right), 80 (right), 81 (right), 85 (right), 89 (right), 107 (left), 109 (right), 111 (right), 113 (left and right), 114 (right), 115 (left), 116 (left), 118 (left), 119 (left), 120 (left), 123 (left), 129 (right), 130 (left), 136 (left), 137 (right), 139 (right), 142 (left and right), 143 (right), 144 (left), 145 (left and right), 146 (left), 149 (right), and 151 (right).

Weldon Russell: contents page (bottom left and right) and 40 (bottom).